Challenging the Modern World

RELIGION, POLITICS, AND SOCIETY IN THE NEW MILLENNIUM

Series Editors: Michael Novak, American Enterprise Institute, and Brian C. Anderson, Manhattan Institute

For nearly five centuries, it was widely believed that moral questions could be resolved through reason. The Enlightenment once gave us answers to these perennial questions, but the answers no longer seem adequate. It has become apparent that reason alone is not enough to answer the questions that define and shape our existence. Many now believe that we have come to the edge of the Enlightenment and are stepping forth into a new era, one that may be the most religious we have experienced in five hundred years. This series of books will explore this new historical condition, publishing important works of scholarship in various disciplines that help us to understand the trends in thought and belief we have come from and to define the ones toward which we are heading.

Political Memoirs
    by Aurel Kolnai, edited by Francesca Murphy

Challenging the Modern World: Karol Wojtyła/John Paul II and the Development of Catholic Social Teaching
    by Samuel Gregg

An Uncommon Pontificate
    by Macej Zieba (forthcoming)

Society as a Department Store
    by Ryszard Legutko (forthcoming)

The Scepter Shall Not Depart from Judah: Perspectives on the Persistence of the Political in Judaism
    by Alan L. Mittleman (forthcoming)

Challenging the Modern World

*Karol Wojtyła/John Paul II
and the Development of Catholic
Social Teaching*

Samuel Gregg

LEXINGTON BOOKS
Lanham • Boulder • New York • Oxford

LEXINGTON BOOKS

Published in the United States of America
by Lexington Books
4720 Boston Way, Lanham, Maryland 20706

P.O. Box 317
Oxford OX2 9RU, UK

British Library Cataloguing in Publication Information Available

The hardcover edition of this book was previously catalogued by the Library of Congress
as follows:
Gregg, Samuel, 1969–
    Challenging the modern world : Karol Wojtyla/John Paul II and the development of
Catholic social teaching / Samuel Gregg.
        p.   cm. — (Religion, politics, and society in the new millennium)
    Includes bibliographical references and index.
        1. John Paul II, Pope, 1920–   —Contributions in Christian sociology.
2. Sociology, Christian (Catholic)—History—20th century. 3. Catholic Church—
Doctrines—History—20th century. I. Title. II. Series.
BX1753.G68   1999
261.8'088'22—dc21   99-38145
                                                                             CIP

ISBN 0-7391-0475-6 (pbk : alk. paper)

Printed in the United States of America

♾™ The paper used in this publication meets the minimum requirements of American
National Standard for Information Sciences—Permanence of Paper for Printed Library
Materials, ANSI/NISO Z39.48–1992.

CONTENTS

Omnia ad maiorem Dei gloriam

ABBREVIATIONS

Texts By Karol Wojtyła

AP   *The Acting Person*, 1969.
LR   *Love and Responsibility*, 1962.
MSE   *On the Possibility of Constructing a Christian Ethic on the Basis of the System of Max Scheler*, 1959.
SC   *Sign of Contradiction*, 1976.
SR   *Sources of Renewal*, 1972.[1]

Main Official Texts Considered

CA   Encyclical Letter *Centesimus Annus*, 15 May 1991.[2]
GS   Pastoral Constitution on the Church in the Modern World *Gaudium et Spes*, 7 December 1965.
LE   Encyclical Letter *Laborem Exercens*, 14 September 1981.
OA   Apostolic Letter *Octogesima Adveniens*, 14 May 1971.
PP   Encyclical Letter *Populorum Progressio*, 26 March 1967.
SRS   Encyclical Letter *Sollicitudo Rei Socialis*, 30 December 1987.

Other Documents

AAS   *Acta Apostolicae Sedis* [Acts of the Holy See]. The Vatican gazette published a varying number of times each year. It carries the original text (mostly Latin) of the more important Vatican documents. Number refers to volume.
ASCV *Acta Synodalia Sacrosancti Concilii Oecumenici Vaticani II* [Acts of the Second Vatican Council]. The record of the Council's

---

1. Number following AP, LR, MSE, SC, and SR refers to page number.
2. Number following CA, GS, LE, OA, PP, and SRS refers to paragraph number.

proceedings. The books are arranged first by session of the Council, then the volume of that session: e.g., II-2, means "second session, volume 2." The year in brackets is the date of the volume's publication.

CCC   *Catechism of the Catholic Church*, 11 October 1992.

DH   Declaration on Religious Liberty *Dignitatis Humanae*, 7 December 1965.

DS   Denzinger-Schönmetzer collection of Church documents.

DV   Dogmatic Constitution on Divine Revelation *Dei Verbum*, 18 November 1965.

EN   Apostolic Exhortation *Evangelii Nuntiandi*, 8 December 1975.

ES   Encyclical Letter *Ecclesiam Suam*, 6 August 1964.

LC   Instruction on Christian Freedom and Liberation *Libertatis Conscientia*, 22 March 1986.

LG   Dogmatic Constitution on the Church *Lumen Gentium*, 21 November 1964.

LN   Instruction on Certain Aspects of the "Theology of Liberation" *Libertatis Nuntius*, 6 August 1984.

MM   Encyclical Letter *Mater et Magistra*, 15 May 1961.

PT   Encyclical Letter *Pacem in Terris*, 11 April 1963.

QA   Encyclical Letter *Quadragesimo Anno*, 15 May 1931.

RH   Encyclical Letter *Redemptor Hominis*, 4 March 1979.

RN   Encyclical Letter *Rerum Novarum*, 15 May 1891.

ST   St. Thomas Aquinas, *Summa Theologiae*, Question (q. 64), and Article (a.1); (a.1c = body of the reply, in a.1; ad 4. = reply to fourth objection in relevant article).

VS   Encyclical Letter *Veritatis Splendor*, 6 August 1993.[3]

---

3. Number following CCC, DH, DS, DV, EN, ES, LC, LG, LN, MM, PT, QA, RH, RN, ST, and VS refers to paragraph number.

ACKNOWLEDGMENTS

The support of many people made this study possible. It is based upon the doctoral dissertation that I completed at the University of Oxford in 1998. For this reason, I wish to thank Professor John Finnis of University College, Oxford, for his rigorous supervision and demanding standards of scholarship, as well as Dr. Zbigniew Pelczynski of Pembroke College, Oxford, for his comments and invaluable assistance.

Thanks must also be extended to Michael Novak of the American Enterprise Institute, Dr. Brian Anderson of the Manhattan Institute, Fr. Rodger Charles, S.J., of Campion Hall, Oxford, and Fr. Francis McHugh of St. Edmund's College, Cambridge, for urging me to produce this book. Here I should also single out Fr. Peter L'Estrange, S.J., rector of Newman College, University of Melbourne, for encouraging me to pursue doctoral studies at Oxford. In addition, I am grateful for the support extended by friends at St. Antony's College, Oxford, particularly Dr. John Nagl, Susi Varga, and Dr. Zach Shore. Thanks are also owed to Greg Lindsay, executive director, the Centre for Independent Studies, and Marshal MacMahon, rector of St. John's College, University of Sydney, for their warm welcome to Sydney where most of the final revisions to this text were made. Teresa MacMahon is also thanked for her help in final checks of translations. My editors at Lexington Books, Serena Leigh and Stephen Driver, are thanked for their patience and help.

For their love, I thank my mother, Jeannette Gregg, and my sisters, Sarah and Susannah Gregg, as well as Min.

Finally, readers of this book should observe the following caveat: whatever truth it contains is His. The errors are mine.

1
INTRODUCTION

Amid discord God strikes
At a bell immense,
For the Slavic Pope,
Open is the Throne.
This Pope will not—Italian-like—take fright
At saber-thrust
But brave as God Himself stand and give fight.
For him, the world is dust . . .
Love he dispenses as great powers today
Distribute arms.
With sacramental power, his sole array,
The world he charms.
So behold, here comes the Slavic Pope,
A brother of the people.

(Juliusz Słowacki, 1849).

1.1   A Century of Catholic Social Teaching

When the exiled Polish poet Juliusz Słowacki penned these words in Paris in 1849, he was reflecting upon Pius IX's flight to Gaeta from revolutionaries in Rome. Yet intransigent is not too strong a word for Pius's religious and political stances following his return to Rome in 1850. In 1864, Pius gathered together eighty condemnations drawn from thirty-two of his public documents in his famous *Syllabus Errorum*. Here he denounced the view that the Roman pontiff "can and should reconcile himself to, or join up with, progress, liberalism, and modern civilization."[1] Pius IX (who came to the papacy as a "liberal") gave no quarter to his opponents and received none in return. After his death, as his body was being shifted to a new resting place in 1881, a Roman mob impeded the procession and attempted to throw the corpse into the Tiber.

Pius IX was also the last pope to reign as sovereign ruler over the Papal States which were annexed by the Kingdom of Italy in 1870. In retrospect, the House of Savoy's act of dispossession provided an opportunity for the papacy to elevate itself above secular rulers by focusing attention upon the unique moral authority that it claimed to wield. Pius's successor, Cardinal Gioacchinno Pecci (better known as Leo XIII), certainly achieved this, not least by facilitating a Catholic intellectual revival by commending the study of St. Thomas Aquinas's work in his 1879 encyclical, *Aeterni Patris*.

Pecci's election as pope in 1878 is described by Archbishop George Pell as "a vote for explicit, but moderate change from the policies of Pius IX."[2] This was nowhere more evident than in the Church's social teaching. As well as defending private property, Leo XIII's famous 1891 encyclical, *Rerum Novarum*, focussed upon the condition of new societies which had emerged in the wake of the industrial revolution. It also proposed remedies "for the misery and wretchedness pressing so unjustly at this moment on the majority of the working classes" (RN 3).

The Catholic Church has always outlined principles regarding human behavior in social, economic, and political life.[3] Within nineteenth-century European Catholic communities, however, the belief grew that the Church needed to address modern social problems more explicitly.[4] In certain respects, *Rerum Novarum* represented papal endorsement of this viewpoint. It also introduced a new genre into what is known as "Catholic

---

1. DS 2901–2980, quoting proposition 80 (1861). Note that this statement was taken from Pius IX's Allocution *Iamdudum cernimus* of 18 March 1861, which responded to the extension of Piedmont's anti-clerical laws and prohibitions upon Catholic publications to the rest of Italy. See *Acta Pii IX*, Bk. 1, Vol. III (Graz: Piper, 1971), 220–230. If this were modernity, no pope would welcome it.
2. G. Pell, "*Rerum Novarum*: One Hundred Years Later," *The Boston Conversazioni* (1991), 5.
3. See J. González, *Faith and Wealth: A History of Early Christian Ideas on the Origin, Significance and Use of Money* (New York: Harper and Row, 1990).
4. For a detailed history, see P. Misner, *Social Catholicism in Europe* (London: Darton, Longman and Todd, 1991).

social thought," that of Roman magisterial teaching about "the social question." This book attempts to ascertain the general nature of John Paul II's development of this teaching, and the extent to which such development has been influenced by ideas and emphases expressed in writings composed by Karol Wojtyła prior to his election as pope in October 1978.

1.2   Conceptual Clarification

Before, however, further outlining the aims of this book, certain matters require brief elucidation. Not least among these is the meaning of Roman magisterial social teaching.

What is Roman Magisterial Social Teaching?

In answering this question, one may begin by way of contrast. John Armstrong correctly states:

> Protestantism has no equivalent for the papal encyclicals of the Roman Catholic Church. . . . Its self-understanding and ecclesiology do not permit it to impose a particular point of view on its constituencies. On the other hand, Roman Catholicism, with its papal encyclicals, offers a binding, authoritative body of social teaching that is unique in the religious world.[5]

This is not to say that Protestant and Orthodox Churches avoid contemplating social matters. The World Council of Churches, for example, has produced a large corpus of economic thought. Rather, the difference lies in the Catholic Church's claim to speak *authoritatively* about such issues insofar as they relate to questions of faith and morals. To this extent, the social teaching is binding upon Catholics precisely because it is articulated by the Catholic Church's teaching authority: its *magisterium*.[6]

---

5. J. Armstrong, "One Protestant Looks at *Centesimus Annus*," *Journal of Business Ethics* 12, no. 12 (1993): 933.
6. For the magisterium's role in the Catholic Church, see R. Gaillardetz, *Teaching with Authority: A Theology of the Magisterium in the Church* (Collegeville: Liturgical Press, 1997), esp. chps. 6 and 7. Cf. the critical review by Avery Dulles, S.J., in "The Pope and Bishops: Who Leads and How?," *The Tablet*, 28 June 1997: 836–837.

Here, we will only be considering one articulation of modern Catholic social teaching, that of the Roman magisterium: the teaching authority of the pope, or the pope and bishops in council. The phrase, *Roman magisterial social teaching*, then, refers to the mostly twentieth-century effort by the popes and the Second Vatican Council to articulate a social doctrine relating the inspiration of the Catholic faith to the twentieth century's specific conditions. This being the case, it does not include the social teaching of the Synod of Bishops,[7] bishops' conferences,[8] or the ideas of those writing about social, political or economic issues from a Catholic perspective. All of these, including Roman magisterial teaching (hereafter "Catholic social teaching," "the social teaching" or "the teaching"), may be grouped together under the heading, "Catholic social thinking." The Roman magisterium's social teaching is, however, the focus of this study.

The Sources and Ends of the Teaching

Whence, then, is Catholic social teaching derived, and what is its purpose? In 1986, the Congregation for the Doctrine of the Faith stated:

> The Church's social teaching is born of the encounter of the Gospel message and of its demands summarized in the supreme commandment of love of God and neighbor in justice with the problems emanating from the life of society. (LC 72)

The demands of the gospel message are, of course, profoundly moral in nature. The extract above, however, suggests that the social teaching reflects the fact that the Christian life is not limited to the proper ordering of personal moral life. It also has a social dimension, not least because social life presents man with dilemmas to which he must respond by acting in ways which, like all freely willed acts, meet the gospel's demands. In this sense, Catholic social teaching is directed to guiding man's moral formation and, by virtue of this, to affecting the life of society.

But where does the Church turn when seeking to show man what is

---

7. See, for example, 1971 Synod of Bishops, *Iustitia in Mundo*, AAS 63 (1971): 923–942.
8. See, for example, Catholic Bishops' Conference of England and Wales, *The Common Good* (London: Catholic Truth Society, 1996).

demanded of him when he encounters social issues? The Second Vatican Council (1962–1965) provides an answer to this question in its Pastoral Constitution on the Church in the Modern World *Gaudium et Spes* (1965). This states:

> the Church in the course of centuries has worked out in the light of the Gospel principles of justice and equity demanded by right reason for individual and social life and also for international relations. (GS 63)

These words suggest that the teaching proceeds from the Church's statement of claims throughout history about the ordering of human affairs according to objective principles derived from the natural law ("right reason") and reflection upon Divine Revelation ("the light of the Gospel"). It is best described, then, as a form of *moral theology*. John Paul affirmed this interpretation in his social encyclical, *Sollicitudo Rei Socialis* (1987). The Church's social teaching, he stated, seeks "*to guide* Christian behavior. It therefore belongs to the field, not of *ideology*, but of *theology* and particularly of moral theology" (SRS 41). This is defined in John Paul's encyclical on the Church's moral teaching, *Veritatis Splendor* (1993), as "a science which accepts and examines Divine Revelation while at the same time responding to the demands of human reason" (VS 29).

In light of the magisterial statements outlined above, Germain Grisez appears to be correct in saying that the Church's social teaching essentially concerns the exposition of relevant moral norms which Catholics should use to judge the social situation confronting them, and then, on the basis of that judgment, do what they can to change the situation for the better.[9] To this end, as the 1992 *Catechism of the Catholic Church* states, the social teaching "proposes principles for reflection; it provides criteria for judgement; it gives guidelines for action" (CCC 2423).

Of course, the distinctiveness of the Church's social teaching lies in its close attention to man's life in society. This, however, also provides the teaching with another basis for reflection. In a 1957 article on Pius XII's social teaching, Archbishop Giovanni Montini noted that the term "pastoral teaching" featured in this pope's social documents. Montini then explained: "By pastoral is meant that the teaching is suggested not only by the intrinsic requirements of doctrine but also by the extrinsic needs of

---

9. G. Grisez, *The Way of the Lord Jesus*, Vol. 2, *Living a Christian Life* (Quincy: Franciscan Press, 1993), 262.

people."[10] In effect, the future Paul VI was indicating that the teaching is not only conscious of man's requirements and what is happening in society, but that such factors influence the teaching.

The Council used similar language when it stressed that the Church had a responsibility to discern the "signs of the times" (GS 3–4). According to Grisez, "[t]hese indicate God's presence and purpose in the happenings, needs, and desires of contemporary humankind." Significantly, however, Grisez adds that "the true meaning of situational factors can be discerned only in the light of all the general principles of Christian doctrine and morality."[11] The viewpoint of the political philosopher, James Schall, S.J., is similar: "To read the 'signs of the times' is to interpret personal and historical events, events of the orders of action and making in Aristotle's sense, in the light of some more stable and intelligible, usually divine, order."[12] An analogous process may be said to characterize the magisterium's social teaching. While it is attentive to, and shaped by, the experiences, ideas, discoveries, and events which constitute human history, these are deciphered in light of what has already been "revealed" to the Church. The *Catechism* concisely summarizes this in the following manner:

> The Church's social teaching comprises a body of doctrine which is articulated as the Church interprets events in the course of history, with the assistance of the Holy Spirit, in the light of the whole of what has been revealed by Jesus Christ. (CCC 2422)

1.3   Key Questions

The issues surrounding a pope's personal influence upon developments in Catholic social teaching underlie the questions posed in this book. To this end, it compares the treatment of industrial relations, capitalism, and relations between developed and developing countries in John Paul's three social encyclicals with the handling of these three topics in the teachings of the Council and Paul VI. Two questions are addressed, one of which is broad in nature, the other quite specific.

---

10. G. Montini, "Le Magistère pastoral de S.S. Pie XII," *La Documentation Catholique* 57 (1957): 1147.

11. Grisez, *Living*, 59.

12. J. Schall, S.J., "The Teaching of *Centesimus Annus*," *Gregorianum* 74, no.1 (1993): 17.

- What does this comparative investigation reveal about the character of development in Catholic social teaching during this pontificate?

- To what extent has such development been influenced by thoughts expressed in Karol Wojtyła's published pre-papal writings?

1.4   Main Contentions

Our primary contention is that a *critical engagement* on John Paul's part with the modern world has had a significant effect on development. Like his predecessors, John Paul has reflected upon the significance of particular transformations. Some are portrayed as positive, others negative. These assessments have contributed to developments in social teaching about how people should act in a variety of situations.

There is also strong reason to believe that, in certain instances, John Paul's development of teaching proceeds from an apparent desire to address quite specific audiences and questions. Other developments owe something to John Paul's incorporation of certain "modern" concepts— suitably modified—into the teaching. He has done so in order to deepen aspects of the social teaching whilst simultaneously seeking to facilitate communication between church and world.

In addition, this study demonstrates that John Paul's development of Catholic social teaching is generally characterized by a deepening of its *moral-anthropological* dimension. The result is an increased focus upon man as a *free and creative subject capable of self-realization as that which he ought to be*, and how social life may be ordered so that this truth about man is given its fullest expression. This allows John Paul to articulate a fresh critique of certain ideas, actions and arrangements which, according to the magisterium, contribute to disorder in the social sphere—disorder being understood as those attitudes, activities and structures which hamper man's self-realization of moral good and true freedom.

Whilst this development of Catholic social teaching owes much to John Paul's reflection upon *Gaudium et Spes*, it soon becomes apparent that distinctively "Wojtyłan" ideas, concerns, language and emphases have influenced its character—sometimes quite profoundly, sometimes in relation to very specific matters. Certainly, as Cardinal Henri de Lubac,

S.J., put it, John Paul is "a man of *Gaudium et Spes*."[13] But while Wojtyła's *post*-conciliar writings drew much inspiration from this document, they continued to explore ideas expressed in his *pre*-conciliar publications. The results of this synthesis have shaped many of the developments found in John Paul's social teachings.

A possible objection to our line of inquiry might be that over a period of time a person's ideas will change considerably, thereby making assessment of the impact of thoughts expressed in one set of writings upon another body of texts more difficult. It is, however, as possible in principle that someone may maintain a consistency of approach and a confidence in certain ideas over a long period of time, as it is that his thoughts will radically alter. Indeed, even if a person's ideas change fundamentally, it is likely that significant continuities will remain.

In Karol Wojtyła/John Paul II's case, there prevails a remarkable harmony in the moral-anthropological themes pursued in his pre-pontifical works and many teachings developed in his encyclicals. Though Wojtyła's writings did not focus on Catholic social teaching per se, they did provide a basis upon which he could develop magisterial social teaching in particular directions. In the words of one Polish commentator:

> Karol Wojtyła did not concern himself, at least in his main works . . . with social problems in a systematic manner. Wojtyła was not a theorist . . . of the Catholic social science, but in his works, both books and articles, we can find many opinions in the realm of social theology and philosophy, social ethics as well as social axiology.[14]

Wojtyła's interest first in ethics and then philosophical anthropology led him to make the "sovereignty of the acting person-subject" the primary theme of his thought. This lead him to certain conclusions, many of which have influenced John Paul's social teaching.

• Wojtyła explored the nature of the human act as a holistic event for man as a person. He refused to absolutize some dimensions of that event and reduce or reify others. As Anselm Min states, Wojtyła

---

13. Cited in J.B. Hehir, "John Paul II: Continuity and Change in the Social Teaching of the Church," in *Co-Creation and Capitalism*, J. Houck and O. Williams, C.S.C., eds. (Lanham: University Press of America, 1983), 131.

14. M. Nowaczyk, "Karol Wojtyła's Social Thought," *Dialectics and Humanism* 6, no. 4 (1979): 79.

studied the human act so as "to grasp the pre-analytic wholeness of concrete human existence and to make this philosophically intelligible without, in the process of theorizing, again reducing it to abstraction."[15] Identifiably Aristotelian-Thomistic concepts were used in this process, and were reflected in the resulting picture of man as a free self-determining subject. This view of man and the process by which he actualizes his own fulfillment significantly shaped John Paul's teaching on human work in his 1981 social encyclical, *Laborem Exercens*. Because this encyclical placed Catholic teaching about work at the heart of the social question, these Wojtyłan ideas proceeded to influence teaching about each of the three subject areas considered in this book.

- Having underlined action's significance for man's self-realization, Wojtyła considered the reality that action often involves "inter-action." This led Wojtyła to articulate ideas about the nature of opposition to others, solidarity with others, and alienation from oneself and others. Aspects of these propositions have influenced various developments of teaching contained in John Paul's encyclicals.

- Wojtyła viewed the acting person as ultimately a God-centered creature. He consequently viewed man's intellect, will, and human acts as orientated towards truth and the acquisition of moral good. This is, of course, an orthodox Catholic position.[16] From this basis, however, Wojtyła critiqued alternative propositions about man and the ends of his action. He suggested that by their trivialization of man's spiritual dimension, certain attitudes and actions could only lead to man's degradation. These thoughts are reflected in those developments of teaching which highlight how inversion of the primacy of moral-spiritual growth over other forms of human progress is at the root of much social disorder and alienation in the modern world.

In advancing these propositions, this book offers an alternative to those commentaries on John Paul's social encyclicals which portray them primarily in terms of the Church's teachings moving towards or away

---

15. A. Min, "John Paul II: Anthropology of Concrete Totality," *Proceedings of the American Catholic Philosophical Association* 58 (1986): 120–121.
16. See GS 15–17; VS 39–40.

from certain political positions. Examples of such writing may be found in
the work of two North Americans. In 1982, Gregory Baum argued that
Laborem Exercens had shifted the teaching towards approval of a form of
socialism via a dialogue with Marxism.[17] Conversely, in 1991, Mary
Hobgood contended that magisterial teaching had developed in a three-
fold and essentially contradictory manner. She described the teaching as
oscillating between "organic-social," "liberal," and "radical-liberationist"
economic models.[18]

Whilst such commentaries provide interesting insights, this book
suggests that, insofar as they amount to explanations of the nature of
development in the social teaching, these and similar studies are
inadequate. Certainly, development does reflect the magisterium's
response to political, philosophical and economic propositions made at
different times by Catholics and non-Catholics alike. Nevertheless, the
process by which development occurs is too complex for it to be
understood as resulting largely from, for example, an engagement with
Marxism. By identifying and analyzing the developments in teaching
contained in John Paul's social encyclicals, we discover that development
owes a great deal to a concern with far deeper questions than the relative
merits of various political-economic ideas. Richard Neuhaus's comment
on *Centesimus Annus* is applicable to the whole of development in
Catholic social teaching during this pontificate: "Readers will miss the
gravamen of this encyclical if they do not recognize that it is, first and
foremost, an argument about human nature."[19]

1.5   A Preview

We begin with an examination of certain teachings articulated in *Gaudium
et Spes*, particularly the Council's understanding of how the Church
should engage with the modern world, why it considers the building of a
just social order to be important, and its view of the nature of authentic
human progress. Also briefly examined in chapter 2 is the Pastoral
Constitution's treatment of the relationship between the use and ownership

---

17. See G. Baum, *The Priority of Labor* (New York: Paulist Press, 1982).
18. See M. Hobgood, *Catholic Social Teaching and Economic Theory* (Philadelphia:
Temple University Press, 1991).
19. R. Neuhaus, "An Argument about Human Nature," in *A New Worldly Order*, G. Weigel,
ed. (Washington, D.C.: Ethics and Public Policy Center, 1992), 123–124.

of material goods. A clear understanding of the Council's teaching on these matters is vital to any serious and lengthy study of post-Vatican II Catholic social teaching.

In chapter 3, we trace Karol Wojtyła's intellectual history and outline the primary themes pervading his pre-papal writings. This sets the stage for chapter 4's comparison of the Council's teachings on the nature and ends of human work with those contained in *Laborem Exercens*. Attention at this point is given to the influence of Wojtyłan ideas upon *Laborem Exercens*'s teaching on this matter. It illustrates that this encyclical's developments of teaching about work have been shaped by the integration of aspects of *Gaudium et Spes*'s teaching about human activity, with ideas expressed in Wojtyła's writings about work and the human act.

With the appropriate background established, the next three chapters examine the three cases through which this book's arguments are tested. The concluding chapter summarizes the general character of development, the extent to which it has been influenced by Wojtyłan thought, and some of the implications of our conclusions.

But before proceeding further, there are several matters that must be addressed. The most significant of these involves explaining the meaning of "development" in Catholic social teaching and how this occurs.

1.6   Questions of "Development"

Over the past century there have been many significant transformations in the social, economic and political order upon which the magisterium has reflected. As a consequence of contemplation of changes such as the industrial revolution, the welfare state's emergence and communism's demise, the social teaching has "developed." It does not do so, however, simply because of external phenomena.

According to John Coleman, S.J., John Paul's "earlier writings as Professor Karol Wojtyła of Lublin and cardinal-archbishop of Krakow should have alerted readers to a different voice in Catholic social teaching."[20] Few, however, have given this factor comprehensive consideration when attempting to explain developments in the teaching since 1978.

---

20. J. Coleman, S.J., "The Culture of Death," in *The Logic of Solidarity*, G. Baum and R. Ellsberg, eds. (Maryknoll: Orbis, 1989), 94.

At the beginning of John Paul's pontificate, several commentators hypothesized that developments in the social teaching would be influenced by Wojtyła's philosophical thought. The most extensive speculation was contained in George Huntston Williams's *The Mind of John Paul II* (1981). This text provides an introduction to the different influences upon Wojtyła's pre-pontifical mindset.[21] For our purposes, however, Williams's book is inadequate for the simple reason that John Paul had not yet issued any social encyclicals at the time of its publication.

In 1982, Baum claimed that Wojtyła had been closely involved with Polish Catholic personalists influenced by the ideas of the French Catholic thinker, Emmanuel Mounier, especially his interest in a dialogue with Marxism. This factor, Baum maintained, had contributed to the distinct changes in nuance and terminology occasioned by Pope John Paul's *Laborem Exercens*.[22]

Yet having advanced this contention, Baum did not attempt to prove its validity by examining any of Wojtyła's writings. He simply assumed that as one allegedly sympathetic to "Mounier personalism," Wojtyła was involved in the Polish Catholic-Marxist dialogue, and that many of *Laborem Exercens*'s developments of teaching represented continuation of this exchange. The nature of Wojtyła's "engagement" with Marxism was somewhat more complex than suggested by Baum. It suffices to state at this point that attention to Wojtyła's writings indicates that

> it is wrong to suppose that when he invoked words such as "alienation" . . .
> Wojtyła was simply using "marxist" language. The papal vocabulary of
> moral interrogation and condemnation has its own sources, and if modern
> social theories have adopted or adapted similar language, this does not
> suggest that they mean the same thing.[23]

---

21. See G. H. Williams, *The Mind of John Paul II* (New York: Seabury Press, 1981). More extensive in this regard is Rocco Buttiglione's *Karol Wojtyła: The Thought of the Man Who Became John Paul II* (Cambridge: Eerdmans, 1997); cf. G. Kalinowski, "La réform du thomisme et la phénoménologie chez Karol Wojtyła selon Rocco Buttiglione," *Archives de philosophie* 49, no. 1 (1986): 127–146. See also the essays in *La filosofia di Karol Wojtyła*, R. Buttiglione, ed. (Bologna: CSEO, 1983); *Karol Wojtyła e il pensiero europeo contemperaneo*, C. Esposito, ed. (Bologna: CSEO, 1984); and *The Thought of Pope John Paul II: A Collection of Essays and Studies*, J. McDermott, S.J., ed. (Rome: Editrice Pontificia Gregoriana, 1993).
22. See Baum, *The Priority*, 3–5.
23. T. Judt, "Holy Warrior," *New York Review of Books* 43, no. 17 (1996): 10.

John Finnis's short study of *Laborem Exercens* avoids Baum's error. Finnis examines its teachings in light of *Gaudium et Spes* and Wojtyła's *The Acting Person*. He demonstrates that much of *Laborem Exercens* may be legitimately understood as a commentary on *Gaudium et Spes*'s teachings on human activity. "But so, too," Finnis adds, "is much of Karol Wojtyła's philosophical work on human personality and action."[24] Finnis then illustrates how *The Acting Person*'s ideas about action's "subjective" and "objective" dimensions owe much to reflection upon the Council's statements about human activity. The results, in Finnis's view, are reflected in *Laborem Exercens*, particularly its use of the subjective-objective distinction to explain work's significance for man.

The general failure, however, of many commentators to follow Finnis's example of carefully delineating the linkages between Wojtyłan ideas and John Paul's development of the teaching leaves certain questions unanswered. Precisely what concepts, for example, do Wojtyła's writings build into the word "solidarity"? Which of these have influenced John Paul's encyclicals? In addition, few commentators consider the issue of *how* ideas contained in a pope's pre-papal writings may influence the social teaching. They seem to assume that simply by being pope, an individual can shape the teaching as he wishes.

Such presumptions are very problematic. Michael Walsh correctly states that "[n]o matter how different his approach may be, each pope likes to present his teaching as in direct continuity with that of his predecessors. He cannot challenge earlier teaching, without calling his own authority into question."[25] Put another way, popes are not "absolute monarchs": their exercise of magisterial authority cannot contradict previous teaching. Moreover, there is a methodological issue to be considered. As Rocco Buttiglione notes: "The criteria and the hermeneutical methods of philosophical thought differ from those which can be used to interpret the Pope's teaching, which have as their immediate antecedents not the thinking of the philosopher Wojtyła, but the acts of his predecessors and the entire Magisterium of the Church in its historical development."[26]

In summary, then, we need to clarify two issues:

---

24. J. Finnis, "The Fundamental Themes of *Laborem Exercens*," in *Catholic Social Thought and the Teaching of John Paul II*, P. Williams, ed. (Chicago: Northeast Books, 1982), 21.
25. M. Walsh, Introduction to *Proclaiming Justice and Peace*, M. Walsh and B. Davies, O.P., eds. (London: CAFOD, 1991), xiv.
26. Buttiglione, *Karol Wojtyła*, 306.

- how the social teaching develops; and

- how ideas contained in pre-papal writings may influence the social teaching.

Development in the Teaching

The subject of how the Catholic Church develops its teaching is enormous in breadth, especially since Newman's seminal study of the question.[27] We confine ourselves here to outlining those aspects of the matter relevant for our needs, using recent magisterial texts as the primary reference points.

The Council's Dogmatic Constitution on Divine Revelation *Dei Verbum* (1965) describes the foundation of the Church's teaching as the Word of God, that is, the divine Revelation by which God "communicates both Himself and the eternal decrees of His will concerning the salvation of mankind" (DV 6). This Revelation is transmitted to the Church in two interrelated ways. One is through Scripture, "the speech of God as it is put down in writing" (DV 9). The other is through "Tradition": the apostles handed on to the faithful "by the spoken word of their teaching, by the example they gave, by the institutions they established, what they themselves had received—whether from the lips of Christ, his way of life and his works, or whether they had learned it at the prompting of the Holy Spirit" (DV 7).

Taken together, Scripture and Tradition make up "a single sacred deposit of the Word of God, which is entrusted to the Church" (DV 10). This statement underlines the Church's commitment to what it calls the "deposit of faith" [*depositum fidei*], in the sense of "safe-keeping."[28] It means that magisterial texts are produced by an institution committed to the preservation and proclamation of teachings which the Church considers to be of permanent validity. These documents are therefore intended to communicate not simply with an immediate audience, but with

---

27. See J. Newman, *An Essay on the Development of Christian Doctrine* (Westminster: Christian Classics, 1968). For a summary of theories about development of doctrine with bibliography, see J. Walgrave, "Doctrine, Development of," *New Catholic Encyclopedia*, Vol. IV (New York: McGraw-Hill, 1967), 940–944.
28. See 1 Tim. 6:20; 2 Tim. 1:12–14, 4:8.

the future, distant if need be. Any study of magisterial development must therefore take into account this commitment. To ignore it would be to dismiss as irrelevant the effect of the institution's proclaimed mission upon the documents that it produces.

But while emphasizing the Church's responsibility to protect the *depositum fidei*, the Council states that over time

> there is a growth in insight into the realities and words that are being passed on. This comes about in various ways. It comes through the contemplation and study of believers who ponder these things in their hearts. It comes from the intimate sense of spiritual realities which they express. And it comes from the preaching of those who have received, along with their right of succession in the episcopate, the sure charisma of truth. (DV 8)

Apart from highlighting the role played by study, inner spiritual understanding, and the magisterium in giving Revelation what Joseph Ratzinger calls its "dynamic character,"[29] these words encapsulate the meaning of development. They indicate that development is not about increasing knowledge in the sense that mistakes in observation and errors in reasoning are overcome, as Revelation does not originate in human reasoning. Nor does development involve repudiating what was believed in the past. Rather, it proceeds from the fact that the linguistic formulations used by the Church do not exhaustively encapsulate the revealed truth. Hence, the Church periodically improves upon the language used in its teaching to deepen its knowledge of the truth it possesses.[30]

The Church often does so because it is necessary to expound its teaching in new contexts. John XXIII's opening speech to the Second Vatican Council made this very point:

---

29. J. Ratzinger, "The Transmission of Divine Revelation," in *Commentary on the Documents of Vatican II*, Vol. IV, H. Vorgrimler, ed. (New York: Herder and Herder, 1969), 186.

30. The Catholic understanding of "development" should not therefore be confused with "creationism" (the idea that doctrines are given in some final form at a given moment) or "evolutionism" (the emergence of doctrinal "novelties" with past doctrines becoming extinct once new conditions prevail). See M. Evans, "How 'Catholic' is Liberal Catholicism?" *Priests and People* 3, no. 7 (1989): 50.

This certain and unchanging teaching (i.e., Christian doctrine in its completeness), to which the faithful owe obedience, needs to be more deeply understood and set forth in ways adapted to the needs of our time. Indeed, this deposit of faith, the truths contained in our time-honored teaching [*seu veritates, quae veneranda doctrina nostra continentur*], is one thing; the manner in which these truths are set forth (with their meaning preserved intact [*eodem tamen sensu eademque sententia*]) is something else.[31]

Development, then, involves concordance with stated teaching, but also what Rodger Charles, S.J., aptly calls "non-contradiction."[32] This takes the form of deepening understanding of the teaching and setting it forth in a manner suited to the conditions of the time.

A similar process gives rise to development in the social dimension of the Church's teaching. In *Sollicitudo Rei Socialis*, John Paul states:

following in the footsteps of my esteemed predecessors in the See of Peter [I wish] to reaffirm the *continuity* of the social doctrine as well as its constant *renewal*. . . .

This twofold dimension is typical of her teaching in the social sphere. On the one hand it is *constant*, for it remains identical in its fundamental inspiration, in its "principles of reflection", in its "criteria of judgement", in its basic "directives for action" and above all in its vital link with the Gospel of the Lord. On the other hand, it is ever *new*, because it is subject to the necessary and opportune adaptations suggested by the changes in historical conditions and by the unceasing flow of events which are the setting of the life of people and society. (SRS 3)

The consistency of the social teaching, then, lies in its foundation in the Revelation communicated to the Church and its continued statement of principles for reflection, criteria for judgment, and directives for action. Its "newness"—its development—involves the setting forth of this teaching in a manner appropriate for changing circumstances.

---

31. John XXIII, "Address at the Opening of Vatican II," AAS 54 (1962): 792. On precisely what Pope John said, see letters to the editor by J. Finnis, *The Tablet*, 14 December 1991: 1544–1545; 4 January 1992: 14; 18 January 1992: 70–71; 1 February 1992: 140; 8 February 1992: 170. See also GS 62.
32. See R. Charles, S.J., *The Social Teaching of Vatican II* (Oxford: Plater Press, 1982), 148.

The Influence of "Pre-Papal" Thought

Turning, then, to the second matter requiring clarification, one may suggest that as a pope contemplates how the social teaching might be set forth in ways suitable for new conditions, there may be scope for him to draw upon his pre-papal ideas. It is, however, difficult to prove, definitively, direct causality between ideas in, for example, Wojtyła's texts and magisterial development. This would require presently unavailable access to the drafts of John Paul's encyclicals.

It would, however, be naïve to think that development is not influenced by the different background, ideas, and interests that each pope brings to his exercise of the magisterium. John XXIII insisted that "each pontificate receives its characteristics and its countenance, as it were, from the pontiff who directs it and imparts a particular personality to it."[33] Paul VI's first encyclical, *Ecclesiam Suam*, is described by some as reflecting his long interest in dialogue between the Church and "the world."[34]

Others, however, suggest that much of John Paul II's teaching has been written by the pope himself. In 1990, for example, Williams contended that this pope "is inclined to write greater proportions of his encyclicals and other communications than did his predecessors, who in general indicated the broad lines of what was desired and left it to staffs of specialists to draft the actual document, to be reviewed and modified by the pontiff in question."[35] Indeed, John Paul's alleged practice was criticized by Karl Rahner, S.J., in his discussion of the pope's 1979 encyclical, *Redemptor Hominis*. "The Pope is not writing private documents," he argued, "and should enlist theological help."[36]

At present, there is no direct evidence to prove or disprove Rahner and Williams's claims about the writing of John Paul's encyclicals. Verification would require currently unobtainable access to the drafts of these documents. Nevertheless, we will see that there are good reasons for supposing that those drafting and contributing to these texts will regard a

---

33. John XXIII, "Homily at Solemn Pontifical Mass," AAS 50 (1958): 884.
34. See Y.-M. Congar, O.P., "Moving towards a Pilgrim Church," in *Vatican II: By Those Who Were There*, A. Stacpoole, O.S.B., ed. (London: Geoffrey Chapman, 1986), 142–143.
35. G. H. Williams, "Karol Wojtyła and Marxism," in *Christianity under Stress*, Vol. 2, *Catholicism and Politics in Communist Societies*, P. Ramet, ed. (Durham: Duke University Press, 1990), 374.
36. Cited in G. H. Williams, "The Ecumenical Intentions of John Paul II," *Harvard Theological Review* 75, no. 2 (1982): 143 n.7.

pope's pre-papal writings as an important substantive and literary source for the ideas to be articulated in these documents.

Before becoming pope, Karol Wojtyła was (as well as a pastoral priest, bishop, and cardinal) a respected academic. The holder of the professorial Chair of Ethics at the Catholic University of Lublin, Wojtyła published widely in Western and Polish journals (both secular and religious) on social, philosophical and ethical issues for over twenty-five years. To grasp the seriousness with which Wojtyła was taken as a scholar, it is worth citing the words of Mainz's Johannes Gutenberg University when it awarded him an honorary doctorate in 1977:

> Cardinal Wojtyła has demonstrated new methodological paths for the Christian ethic through a phenomenological foundation and a continuation of Christian personalism . . . he has convincingly portrayed the inviolable dignity of man in an original demonstration of philosophical anthropology, thereby making a very admirable contribution to the present moral-theological discussion on norm theory and basic values and winning great honor for himself.[37]

As one of his critics states, "[this] Pope is a genuine thinker, however one judges the content of his thinking. He has personally thought-out positions on most questions."[38] One is therefore bound to ask how much of this thought has influenced the teachings of the magisterial authority exercised by Wojtyła as John Paul II.

Judging such matters is, however, complicated by the fact that encyclicals are rarely, if ever, composed in their entirety by a pope. Normally other figures, for a variety of reasons (such as economic expertise), will be asked to contribute to the drafting process. Naturally there is much speculation about the influence of particular persons upon individual documents.[39] It is nonetheless hard to substantiate these claims without the named individuals verifying such conjectures. This rarely

---

37. "Doktorat honoris causa księdza kardynała Karola Wojtyły" [Honorary Doctorate for Cardinal Karol Wojtyła], *Notificationes e Curia Metropolitana Cracoviensi* 9/10 (1977): 237–238.

38. P. Hebblethwaite, "Pope John Paul II as Philosopher and Poet," *Heythrop Journal* 21, no. 2 (1980): 132.

39. See, for example, G. Zizola, "Les revirements d'une encyclique," *L'Actualité religieuse dans le monde* 90 (1991): 10–11.

occurs, and never during the pontificate in which an encyclical is written.[40] One should, however, remember that in the end, final authorial responsibility for these documents belongs to the pope: they are truly *his* texts, for without his signature denoting his assent to every word of their content, they lack magisterial authority and are destined to be merely archival curiosities.

Despite the lack of access to drafts, some claims may be made about the preparation of magisterial texts addressing the social question and how pre-papal ideas might influence these texts. Some of these are based upon reasonable assumptions. Others proceed from extrapolations made from knowledge of *Rerum Novarum*'s preparation—the only encyclical whose drafts are in the public domain.

For a start, one may suppose that popes occasionally write significant fragments of these documents themselves.[41] They are, moreover, normally initiated by the pope, and usually because he wants to say something about particular questions. It would be surprising if the ideas that an individual brings to the papacy did not exert some influence at this point. Election to the papacy does not, after all, mean that a person is suddenly disconnected from all that they have previously written.

It is also the case that a pope will probably provide some ideas and even reasonably extensive guidelines for an encyclical which are then fleshed out by committees and individuals. In *Rerum Novarum*'s case, the first draft was composed in Italian by Matteo Liberatore, S.J., a specialist in political economy. His sketch was based upon general propositions outlined by Leo XIII.

A process then follows with the pope and other delegated individuals reading and amending draft texts. The four drafts of *Rerum Novarum*, for example, passed through the hands of not only Liberatore and Leo XIII, but Cardinal Zigliara, and Cardinal Mazzella and Monsignor Boccali. The final Latin translation was made by Alessandro Volpini.[42]

What is known, then, about *Rerum Novarum*'s composition, suggests

---

40. In 1971, Oswald von Nell-Breuning, S.J., claimed that he had been QA's prime drafter. See O. von Nell-Breuning, S.J., "The Drafting of *Quadragesimo Anno*," in *Readings in Moral Theology*, Vol. 5, *Official Catholic Social Teaching*, C. Curran and R. McCormick, S.J., eds. (New York: Paulist Press, 1986), 60–68.

41. Nell-Breuning claims that QA 91–96 came directly from Pius XI's pen. See Nell-Breuning, "The Drafting of *Quadragesimo Anno*," 62.

42. See G. Antonazzi, *L'enciclica 'Rerum Novarum,' testo autentico e redazioni preparatorie dei documenti originali* (Roma: Edizioni di storia e letteratura, 1992).

that several minds contribute to the formulation of magisterial social texts. None of this means, of course, that pre-papal ideas cannot affect ensuing developments in teaching. Whenever a pope contributes to the drafting of a text, there is every possibility that this may occur. Moreover, one may reasonably assume that some of those contributing to the preparation of an encyclical may consult the pope's pre-papal writings at some stage of the drafting process, particularly if the pontiff concerned, like Karol Wojtyła or Giovanni Montini, wrote prolifically before becoming pope. They are, after all, drafting a text for the pope.[43] It is consequently their responsibility to write in a manner consistent with what is known to be his general thinking. To this, there are few better systematic guides than his pre-papal writings.

For all of these reasons, then, it is likely that ideas expressed in Giovanni Montini's writings, for example, will find some expression in Paul VI's magisterial documents. A cautionary note should, however, be added. Even in the unlikely event that a pope wrote a magisterial text completely by himself, one would expect him to avoid overutilizing the theological-philosophical approach that characterized his pre-papal writings. In *Veritatis Splendor*, John Paul stated that "the Church's Magisterium does not intend to impose upon the faithful any particular theological system, still less a philosophical one" (VS 29). In doing so, the pope drew attention to an important feature of the Church's exercise of its magisterium—what might be called a "self-denying ordinance" which restrains a pope (and drafters of magisterial texts) from overorientating magisterial teaching towards any one of a number of alternative but orthodox Catholic theological-philosophical positions. This makes the task of discerning pre-papal influences upon developments in teaching more difficult, but not impossible.

1.6   Issues of Method

How, then, is one to go about studying the texts relevant to our purposes? Michael Schuck stresses that any credible uncovering of patterns in papal thought requires "exhaustively gathering and assembling papal ideas, then

---

43. Thomas Reese, S.J., claims that there is a tradition within the Roman Curia that, over time, officials regularly contributing to papal documents should be "able little by little to enter into the mentality of the pope and become good ghost writers." T. Reese, S.J., *Inside the Vatican* (Cambridge/London: Harvard University Press, 1996), 192.

examining their resemblances and reversals over time."[44] There is, in other words, no shortcut around thorough comparative analysis of the relevant texts when attempting to identify development.

In light of our analysis of how development occurs and how pre-papal ideas may influence development, this study takes the view that textual interpretation involves familiarizing readers with a document's context, and how this might have contributed to development. Like John Coleman, S.J., however, we "do not think that the relativities of history deserve the final say" in the study of development,[45] and that, in any event, one of the ways of contextualizing magisterial documents is to "see any encyclical in continuity with the other writings, allocutions, and actions of the papacy."[46] In this regard, Schuck puts one of *Gaudium et Spes*'s methodological contributions to magisterial development into proper perspective. Though he agrees that the Council's emphasis upon "reading the signs of the times" has influenced post-conciliar social teaching, he maintains that "[w]hatever the popes' new sensitivity to history means, it does not involve commitment to the idea that moral principles and policies are created by ascertaining the numerically predominant will of either the laity or theologians at a given historical moment."[47]

Our focus is therefore upon what Schuck recommends: comparative exegetical analysis of the texts. Ultimately, development is *encapsulated* in magisterial documents and it is in texts that Wojtyła expressed his own ideas. It is to them, then, that we will primarily look to uncover the *internal evidence* which attests both to development and the influence of Wojtyłan ideas and emphases.

Identifying Development

Given that development has been defined on the basis of the Church's understanding of the term, we will discern developments in the social teaching by:

• judging whether, in the process of rearticulating and extending the

---

44. M. Schuck, *That They May Be One* (Washington, D.C.: Georgetown University Press, 1991), xi.
45. J. Coleman, S.J., "Development of Church Social Teaching," in *Official Catholic Social Teaching*, 186.
46. Coleman, "Development of Church Social Teaching," 181.
47. Schuck, *That They May Be One*, 157.

Church's teaching in light of unfolding events, new ideas, and changing conditions, John Paul's encyclicals introduce a new idea into the teaching; and

- determining whether, in the same process, his encyclicals expand upon an element, or reveal a new aspect of, an idea previously articulated by the magisterium.

To make such assessments, we examine the treatment of the relevant subject area by *Gaudium et Spes, Populorum Progressio* and *Octogesima Adveniens*. This is compared to the teaching on the same subject contained in John Paul's encyclicals. The variations highlighted as a result of this comparison are considered in light of the above criteria to see if they indicate that a development in the teaching has occurred.

Ascertaining Contextual Factors

In itself, a comparison of the relevant texts is insufficient for identifying and explaining development. One also needs to ascertain the events and conditions which the magisterium may be reflecting upon. To this end, Coleman offers several guidelines. These include noting the movements and on-going disputes within Catholic social thought to which magisterial documents may be responding. He also suggests that one should be cognizant of which theological viewpoints were regnant at different periods.[48] The magisterium's attention is not, however, confined to changes and occurrences in the Catholic domain. Hence, it is important to surmise the events and broader transformations in the world to which the magisterium may be reacting at different points of history.

Fortunately, the magisterial texts state what some of the "external factors" are, albeit with varying degrees of explicitness. Though we need not accept these declarations at face value, they do provide a starting point for relating the texts to the generalized but distinct circumstances to which the Roman magisterium is responding. This permits the drawing of legitimate interpretative inferences from "environment" to magisterial development.

---

48. Coleman, "Development of Church Social Teaching," 177–178.

Assessing the Wojtyłan Influence

Gauging the influence of Wojtyłan ideas upon development requires a summary of Wojtyła's intellectual history and an introduction to the primary themes pervading his major works. This occurs in chapter 3. It is supplemented by chapter 4's comparison of *Gaudium et Spes*'s statements about human work with *Laborem Exercens*'s teaching on this subject. The identified developments of teaching on this matter are then considered in light of the ideas expressed in Wojtyła's major writings about the nature of human work and actions. John Paul himself identifies work as a key to the social question (LE 3). It is therefore an appropriate point to begin ascertaining the influence of Wojtyłan thought upon John Paul's development of Catholic social teaching.

In each of the ensuing chapters on industrial relations, capitalism, and relations between developed and developing nations, the identified developments of teaching are examined in light of what has been ascertained about Wojtyła's thought. Where appropriate, this is augmented by reference to other Wojtyłan writings which may have contributed to particular developments.

1.7   Source and Case Selection

In answering the questions posed, this study generally confines itself to examining the teachings of *Gaudium et Spes* (1965), *Populorum Progressio* (1967), *Octogesima Adveniens* (1971), *Laborem Exercens* (1981), *Sollicitudo Rei Socialis* (1987), and *Centesimus Annus* (1991). On occasion, these are supplemented by consideration of other authoritative texts which touch upon matters of social teaching, such as the Congregation for the Doctrine of the Faith's 1984 and 1986 Instructions.[49] This occurs when there is evidence to suggest that these documents have significantly contributed to developments in teaching.

The primary Wojtyłan texts considered include *Love and Responsibility* (1960), *The Acting Person* (1969), *Sources of Renewal* (1972), and *Sign of Contradiction* (1977). A number of Wojtyła's articles,

---

49. For the authority of CDF documents, see R. Ombres, O.P., "The Roman Curia Reorganized," *Priests and People* 3, no. 7 (1989): 62; J. Finnis, "Faith and Morals: A Note," *The Month* 21 (1988): 564–566.

poems, and dramatic compositions are also examined.

Whilst the coverage of primary texts is extensive, it should be noted that there are an enormous number of addresses and documents which could be construed as part of John Paul's social teaching. His three social encyclicals, however, are the most authoritative and comprehensive expression of this teaching. The same principle underlies the selection of pre-John Paul magisterial texts.[50] As for Wojtyła's writings, these have been chosen on the basis of their relevance to the issues under discussion.

At this point, one might ask why we do not directly examine pre-conciliar social teaching. Put simply, *Populorum Progressio, Octogesima Adveniens,* but most importantly, *Gaudium et Spes* are more than sufficient for our purposes. To cite Charles on this matter:

> The great advantage of *Gaudium et Spes* is that it sets out the main principles of the social teaching of the Church as it had been evolved in the social encyclicals until the time of the Council, and it does so very coherently, clearly and succinctly. Further, it brings in those questions of ethics of the family and of political ethics which are so much a part of the Church's social teaching, but which we were not used to seeing treated so comprehensively in the social encyclicals. The pre-Vatican II social encyclicals and *Gaudium et Spes* are, of course, not in any way in opposition. Indeed, it was the sophistication and the thoroughness with which those encyclicals had dealt with the political/economic issues in the years since 1891 which enabled the Council to bring together the elements of Catholic teaching on these matters with such effectiveness.[51]

For these reasons, reference is generally made to pre-conciliar teachings only when the Council, Paul VI, or John Paul II evidently expects their reader to do so, or if it is of particular assistance in explaining an aspect of development.

The subjects of industrial relations, capitalism, and relations between developed and developing countries have been chosen as focuses for this study for the following reasons.

---

50. The 1971 Synod document, *Iustitia in Mundo,* will primarily be considered for contextual purposes. Synodal documents, as a *counsel* to the pope, do not enjoy a papal/conciliar type of authority. See J. Finnis, "Catholic Social Teaching since *Populorum Progressio* – 1," *Social Survey* 27, no. 7 (1978): 217.
51. Charles, *The Social Teaching of Vatican II,* 5–6.

- They reflect modern Catholic social teaching's gradual embrace of a multilevel analysis of the social order.

- Each topic is a central focus of at least one of John Paul's social encyclicals.

Given that each of the subjects covered by the three case studies are particularly extensive in themselves, we concentrate upon a number of issues within each case study. These have been chosen with a view to providing a broad indication of the character of developments in teaching on that topic.

There is admittedly a risk that the choice of case studies will skew the emerging picture of overall development. But to focus on one topic and ignore every other unit of analysis would be to neglect the breadth of the teaching and thereby produce misleading conclusions. A judgment based, for example, only on a study of teaching about industrial relations, would dramatically overestimate the Wojtyłan influence upon overall development and attach unwarranted significance to events in Poland in 1981. On the other hand, a book which sought to embrace every single topic considered by the teaching would be unmanageable. Our case selection avoids these problems by combining specificity and breadth of analysis with manageability.

1.8 The Relevance of Catholic Social Teaching

Anyone involved in the study of politics or political thought might ask, what is the significance of Catholic social teaching for these fields of intellectual inquiry? The answer is, in short, manifold. Reflecting upon *Centesimus Annus*, Milton Friedman (a non-Catholic, self-described as a classical liberal) submits that the teaching warrants attention because:

> it comes from the head of a major institution in the modern world, a pre-eminently multinational institution with members in the hundreds of millions throughout the world, an institution that has great influence on the beliefs and day-to-day activities of these hundreds of millions. It deserves attention not because of its philosophical depth or lack thereof, not because of its wisdom or lack thereof, not because of its teachings, however admirable or the reverse, but because it offers evidence of how the present

leadership of that institution is likely to exert its influence in coming years.[52]

Certainly, the Roman magisterium's social teaching represents an exposition of the thinking underlying the papacy's assessment of, and reactions to, particular events and changes throughout history. *Centesimus Annus*, for example, devotes an entire chapter to analyzing communism's collapse in Central-Eastern Europe (CA 22–29). Hence, if one wishes to ascertain the Catholic Church's position on such politically important questions, then these texts are of significance.

Secondly, there is a clear expectation on the Catholic Church's part that in political, social and economic activity, as in any other, Catholics should be guided by a Christian conscience, conformed to God's law and submissive to papal and episcopal teaching insofar as it authoritatively articulates that law in the gospel's light.[53] No other Christian church holds such a position, as they do not accept that the pope and bishops in communion with him still carry out the mandate of Christ given to the successors of Peter and the other apostles to teach in His name. Thus, not only is it conceivable that the magisterium may condemn, for example, an ideology such as Marxism,[54] but for Catholics the condemnation itself automatically raises the serious question of whether or not, for instance, they may support Communist parties. As one commentator states, the teachings "are presented as moral rather than political judgements. But unless they are meaningless statements, designed merely to soothe the conscience of the utterer without changing the situation, they are political through and through."[55]

In this regard, the social teaching sets a significant segment of the parameters for action and thought by those who purport to be contemplating political and economic questions from a Catholic viewpoint. Developments in the teaching may therefore open up new possibilities for political activity and reflection on the part of such people, encourage them to reexamine particular issues, rule out potential endeavors, or even legitimate proposed courses of action. An example of

---

52. M. Friedman, "Goods in Conflict," in *A New Worldly Order*, 75.
53. See LG 24–25; DH 14; GS 43, 50.
54. See, for example, John XXIII, Encyclical Letter *Ad Petri Cathedram*, AAS 51 (1959), 526.
55. P. Hebblethwaite, "The Popes and Politics: Shifting Patterns in Catholic Social Doctrine," *Daedalus* 11, no. 1 (1982): 85.

this last category is the role played by John XXIII's *Mater et Magistra* in assisting Italian Christian Democrats such as Aldo Moro to legitimize their party's alliance with sections of the Italian Left in 1961.[56]

Moreover, Catholic social teaching has been accorded a certain degree of attention in regions with predominantly Catholic populations,[57] and/or in countries where the Catholic Church has played a significant political role.[58] It has also been given considerable regard by those political groupings which, to varying degrees, claim to derive some of their philosophical inspiration from its constituent documents. The pre-war Center party in Germany and Popular party in Italy may be regarded as examples of such movements.[59]

This is not to say, however, that the magisterium's articulation of a formal social teaching since 1891 has not been viewed with misgivings by some Catholic commentators. In 1979, Marie-Dominique Chenu, O.P., claimed that Catholic social teaching was a nineteenth-century "ideological relic." In his view, it reflected "the ideology of the bourgeoisie in the nineteenth century" and therefore could not be described as a doctrine. Leo XIII's defense of private property was, according to Chenu, just what the Catholic middle classes wanted to hear in 1891.[60] But, Chenu argued, "faith is not an ideology—it should not be an unconscious way of legitimizing personal prejudices."[61]

Whatever the merits of Chenu's analysis, the fact that John Paul has issued three social encyclicals since 1978 indicates that the Pope believes that the magisterium should continue to expound a social teaching. In 1982, Peter Hebblethwaite posited that he had done so for two reasons: first, it provided the pope with a platform to criticize liberation theology

---

56. See S. Magister, *La Politica Vaticana e l'Italia, 1943-1978* (Roma: Riuniti, 1979), 116–137.

57. See, for example, A. Kim, "The Vatican, Marxism, and Liberation Theology," *Cross Currents* 34, no. 4 (1984/1985): 439–455.

58. See, for example, G. Weigel, *The Final Revolution* (Oxford: Oxford University Press, 1992), 153–154; A. Rhodes, *The Vatican in the Age of the Dictators, 1922-1945* (London: Hodder and Stoughton, 1973), 127, 146–147.

59. See E. Evans, *The German Center Party, 1870-1933: A Study in Political Catholicism* (Carbondale: Southern Illinois University Press, 1974); J. Molony, *The Emergence of Political Catholicism in Italy: Partito Popolare, 1919-1926* (Totowa: Rowman and Littlefield, 1977).

60. M.-D. Chenu, O.P., *La "doctrine sociale" de l'église comme idéologie* (Paris: Cerf, 1979), 90.

61. Chenu, *La "doctrine sociale,"* 89–90.

whilst presenting an alternative; secondly, it allowed him to comment upon developments in Poland, without appearing to interfere directly in Polish affairs.[62]

This book shows, however, that Hebblethwaite misses the central point. Certainly, Catholic social teaching has provided John Paul with a means for commenting on certain events and changes. But, more importantly:

> this pope has not given up confidence . . . in the capacity of the *Doctor omnium* to compose, on the basis of natural law and revelation, a teaching document on so generic and not so specifically Christian an issue as work, with intended relevance for all parts of the world and for all conditions of men and even for confessions of faith beyond the Christian.[63]

1.8   Conclusion

John Paul II's pontificate has been this century's longest. It may even eclipse that of the inaugurator of "modern" Catholic social teaching, Leo XIII. This opportunity has been used by John Paul to shape the teaching in ways that address what he, as Karol Wojtyła, considered to be man's aspirations and dilemmas in the modern world. According to his spokesman, Joaquín Navarro-Valls, the Pope's goal is nothing less than the establishment of a Christian alternative to "the humanistic philosophies of the 20th century—Marxism, structuralism, the atheistic ideas of the post-Enlightenment. They were simply among the tools of the age. Wojtyła said no, we have something new, we don't have to copy. Let ·· humbly build a new sociology, a new anthropology, that is based on something genuinely Christian." The Pope, says his spokesman, believes that he has at least laid the groundwork for this task.[64] Here we see the extent to which this ambition has been realized in relation to the social teaching, and how much it has been shaped by thoughts formed by Wojtyła before he occupied Peter's Chair.

---

62. Hebblethwaite, "The Popes and Politics," 93, 96.
63. G. H. Williams, "John Paul II's Concepts of Church, State and Society," *Journal of Church and State* 24, no. 3 (1982): 478.
64. J. Navarro-Valls cited in J. Elson, "Lives of the Pope," *Time*, 26 December 1994 – 2 January 1995, 39.

2

THE CHURCH IN THE WORLD

2.1 Introduction

The Second Vatican Council's Pastoral Constitution on the Church in the Modern World, *Gaudium et Spes*, is a unique document. No council had ever before tried to state the Church's relationship to "the world." Many stress that *Gaudium et Spes* balances pre-conciliar Catholic social teaching's reliance upon natural law philosophy with more direct explorations of biblical, patristic, christological, and ecclesiological themes.[1] In this regard, *Gaudium et Spes*, as one commentator states, "did more than simply encapsulate the best of seventy-five years of an evolving Catholic social-economic tradition. It also contained in embryo some of the fundamental ideas that later church documents would adopt and expand."[2]

Here we explore those aspects of *Gaudium et Spes* of particular importance for the post-conciliar social teaching's engagement with the modern world. This involves briefly delineating some of the primary influences upon the Pastoral Constitution's genesis and drafting. These, however, are considered with a view to providing context for an analysis of several specific matters.

---

1. See, for example, F. McHugh, "A Century of Catholic Social Teaching," *Priests and People* 5, no. 5 (1991): 173–177.
2. M. Velásquez, "*Gaudium et Spes* and the Development of Catholic Social-Economic Teaching," in *Questions of Special Urgency*, J. Dwyer, ed. (Washington, D.C.: Georgetown University Press, 1986), 187.

- One is *Gaudium et Spes*'s understanding of how the Church should engage with the modern world.

- Another concerns the Pastoral Constitution's explanation of why the promotion of a just social order in the modern world is not simply desirable, but necessary, as well as its teaching about what constitutes *true* temporal progress.

- The Constitution contains a rather precise statement concerning the use and possession of material goods. As this is an issue central to Catholic social teaching, both before and after the Council, it requires detailed attention.

2.2   A Document *ad extra*

Gaudium et Spes's evolution as a text is well-documented[3] and need not be elaborated upon here. Several points are nonetheless worth highlighting. Perhaps the most striking is that no provision was made for such a document in the preparatory work for the Council. It might not have emerged at all but for the actions of Cardinal Léon-Joseph Suenens. Suenens later claimed that John XXIII asked him in March 1962: "Who is attending to the making of an overall plan for the whole Council?" Suenens replied that, though seventy draft *schemata* were in preparation, no one was thinking on that scale. According to Suenens, Pope John then asked him if he would like to produce such an agenda.[4]

Suenens states that his plan was ready by April 1962, and shown to a meeting of cardinals held at the Belgian College in July that year at which Cardinal Giovanni Montini was present.[5] John XXIII also appears to have assimilated its general thrust. Hints of this may be seen in his radio message of 11 September 1962, which referred to the distinction between the Church *ad intra* and *ad extra* on which Suenens's plan hinged.[6]

In simple terms, Suenens's plan stated that the Council's work fell naturally into two main fields. It had to consider:

---

3. See, for example, P. Delhaye, "Histoire des textes de la Constitution pastorale," in *L'église dans le monde de ce temps*, Vol. I, Y.-M. Congar, O.P., and M. Peuchmaurd, O.P., eds. (Paris: Cerf, 1967), 215–277; C. Moeller, "History of the Constitution," in *Commentary*, Vol. V, 1–76.

4. L.-J. Suenens, "A Plan for the Whole Council," in *Vatican II*, 88.

5. Suenens, "A Plan," 90.

6. See John XXIII, *Radio-Television Message*, AAS 54 (1962), 680.

- the Church *ad intra*—that is, the Church in itself, but with the aim of helping it to respond better to its mission in the world; and

- the Church *ad extra*—that is, the Church as it faces the world of today.[7]

In dealing with the *ad extra* dimension, Suenens proposed that the Council focus on four areas:

- the Church and "family society;"

- the Church and "economic society;"

- the Church and "civil society;" and

- the Church and "international society."[8]

Whilst aspects of these subjects were considered in other conciliar documents,[9] *Gaudium et Spes* embraces them all comprehensively.[10]

An impetus was added to Suenens's plan becoming the Council's dominant motif by a letter written by Cardinal Montini to Cardinal Amleto Cicognani, the Holy See's secretary of state, dated 18 October 1962. Referring to what he considered to be "the lack, or at least the failure to announce the existence of, an organic, thought-out and logical program for the Council,"[11] Montini alluded to the existence of Suenens's plan. Montini added that, in his view, the Council required at least three sessions. The third, he suggested, should be devoted to "the relationship between the Church and the world which surrounds it, which is outside it, and removed from it."[12]

On 4 December 1962, Suenens took the initiative—for which he claims he had Pope John's approval[13]—of effectively proposing his plan as the Council's overall agenda. During a speech to the Council, Suenens stated

---

7. See Suenens, "A Plan," Appendix IV: The Plan Submitted to John XXIII, 97.

8. Suenens, "A Plan," Appendix IV, 101–102.

9. See, for example, DH 13–15 for church and civil society.

10. See GS 47–52 for the family; 63–72 for economic society; 73–76 for civil society; 77–90 for international society.

11. Suenens, "A Plan," Appendix V: Letter from Cardinal Giovanni Montini to Cardinal Amletto Ciciognani, secretary of state. The Vatican, 18 October 1962, 102–103.

12. Suenens, "A Plan," Appendix V, 104.

13. Suenens, "A Plan," 91.

that if the study of the Church was to be considered Vatican II's focal point, then "the Church must be considered not only *ad intra*, as it is in itself, but also *ad extra*, as it relates to the world."[14] The modern world, he added, expected the Church to address certain major questions. What, for example, did the Church have to say about the human person? What did it have to say about social justice? What was the duty of rich nations to third world nations?[15] The next day, Montini endorsed Suenens's approach, submitting that "[t]he Church must knowingly and clearly show forth action proper to itself in these times."[16]

The effect of these interventions became evident during the first meeting of the Council's Coordinating Commission between 21-27 January 1963. The number of draft *schemata* was reduced from seventy to twenty. These were then ordered according to Suenens's *ad intra–ad extra* distinction. According to one Council historian, Suenens submitted that the schema on "The Community of Nations" should be incorporated in a wide-ranging draft dealing with man in society, marriage, culture, the economic order, social justice, the community of nations, and peace.[17] Suenens's proposal was accepted, and the resulting draft text was known as Schema XVII—the forerunner to *Gaudium et Spes*.

How, then, was the Council to reflect upon and address the world? Archbishop Marcos McGrath, C.S.C., states that this issue caused much disagreement in late November 1963, during a plenary session of the "Mixed Commission" responsible for Schema XVII. One Eastern European bishop, for example, considered it unthinkable that a council should consider such "tangential" matters as economics. Rahner, on the other hand, argued that if the Council was to consider such themes, then it should do so theologically; that is, only reaching doctrinal conclusions on the basis of revealed truth. Several bishops, however, maintained that any document seeking to address the modern world had to start from a consideration of the world's problems and speak to mankind on its own terms.[18]

This last approach reflected many influences of which two were particularly important. The first was Pope John's conviction that the Church needed to accord attention to the "signs of the times," a belief first

---

14. ASCV, I–4 (1971), 4 December 1962, 233.
15. ASCV, I–4, 227.
16. ASCV, I–4, 5 December 1962, 292.
17. G. Caprile, S.J., *Il Concilio Vaticano II*, Vol. II, *Primo Periodo* (Roma: Civiltà Cattolica, 1968), 329.
18. See M. McGrath, C.S.C., "Social Teaching since the Council," in *Vatican II*, 328.

given expression in *Humanae Salutis*, the apostolic constitution by which he convoked the Council on 25 December 1961:

> we make ours the recommendation of Jesus that one should know how to discern "the signs of the times," and we seem to see now, in the midst of so much darkness, a few indications which auger well for the fate of the Church and humanity.[19]

To "discern the signs of the times," then, suggests that one should not only pay close attention to what is happening in the world, but also identify where "the finger of God," so to speak, is manifesting itself in the here-and-now. John's secretary, Archbishop Loris Capovilla, expresses a similar view:

> The biblical phrase "signs of the times" (Mt. 16:3) is a clear and concise commitment to the various concerns and anxieties of the modern world, this overriding pastoral concern, based on a view of the *via christiana* operating in the history of the world.[20]

A second major influence upon the Council's approach to the modern world was the focus upon "dialogue" by significant conciliar figures. In his 4 December speech, Suenens used this term to describe the way in which he believed the Church should address the modern world.[21] More importantly, the former Cardinal Montini—as Paul VI—stressed the importance of engaging in "dialogue" with the world in his first encyclical, *Ecclesiam Suam* (1964). In a general audience on the day preceding its appearance, Paul stated that this encyclical presented "dialogue" as "the art or style that must inspire the Church's ministry to the dissonant, voluble, complex concert that is the contemporary world."[22] In the encyclical itself, Paul specified that dialogue involves getting to know the world (ES 69); it "forces us to go more deeply into the subject of our investigations and to find better ways of expressing ourselves. It will be a slow process of thought, but it will result in the discovery of elements of truth in the opinion of others . . . it will make us wise; it will make us teachers" (ES 83).

---

19. John XXIII, Apostolic Constitution *Humanae Salutis*, AAS 54 (1962), 7.
20. L. Capovilla, "Reflections on the Twentieth Anniversary," in *Vatican II*, 118.
21. See ASCV, 4 December 1962, 223.
22. Paul VI, "General Audience," AAS 56 (1964), 606. See also A. Casaroli, "Paolo VI e il dialogo," *Il Regno*, 11 November 1984, 594–595.

The effect of these emphases upon the Schema may be observed in Paul's comments when presented with the final program of the drafting commission's work on 16 February 1965. Paul stressed that one of the Schema's main aims was to break down the view of the Church and the modern world as antagonistic forces.[23] He also insisted that the Schema be designated a "pastoral constitution" as opposed to a "dogmatic constitution" such as *Dei Verbum*—not to lessen its authority but rather to ensure that its manner of addressing the modern world was appropriate.[24]

2.3 A Dialectical Approach

We see, then, that important figures at the Council believed that the Pastoral Constitution should facilitate closer attention on the Church's part to what is happening *in* the modern world as well as a conversation *between* church and world. But looking at the end product, one discovers that *Gaudium et Spes*'s approach is somewhat more complex. Certainly, it devotes much attention to what the Council perceives as the rapid changes characterizing the modern world; the notion that the Church can learn much from the world is also underlined. These emphases, however, are balanced by an affirmation of certain constants, and an insistence that everything must ultimately be assessed in light of Revealed truth.

By way of illustration, one might consider the Council's words about history in paragraphs 5 and 10 of *Gaudium et Spes*. Paragraph 5 states:

> History itself is accelerating [*acceleratur*] on so rapid a course that individuals can scarcely keep pace with it. . . . And so the human race is passing from a relatively static conception of the nature of things to a more dynamic and evolutionary conception. (GS 5)

Rapid change, then, is understood as a new constant. This, however, is balanced by paragraph 10's stress that in the midst of this seemingly perpetual acceleration some things remain fixed and immutable:

> The Church believes that in her Lord and Master are to be found the key, the center and the purpose of the whole history of mankind. And the Church affirms, too, that underlying all that changes there are many things

---

23. See G. Cottier, O.P., "Interventions de Paul VI dans l'élaboration de *Gaudium et Spes*," in *Paolo VI e il rapporto Chiesa-Mondo al Concilio* (Brescia: Instituto Paulo VI, 1991), 25.
24. Cottier, "Interventions," 24.

that do not change, and that have their ultimate foundation in Christ who is the same yesterday, today, and forever. (GS 10)

Thus, while the Council considers the modern age to be characterized by ceaseless transformation, it attests that there are certain fundamentals which *never* change precisely because they are derived from the God–Man Himself who simultaneously pervades and transcends history.

A similar balance permeates *Gaudium et Spes*'s treatment of the theme of dialogue. The first aspect of dialogue considered by the Council concerns "the possibility of expressing the message of Christ in suitable terms" (GS 44). There is nothing especially new about this. The picking out of words from the great babble of human conversation is a risk which Christianity has always, from the very beginning, been willing to run. The Council itself states that, "[t]he Church learned early in its history to express the Christian message in the concepts and languages of different peoples and tried to clarify it in the light of the wisdom of their philosophers" (GS 44). Aquinas's synthesis of Aristotelian philosophy with Christian thought is a prominent example.

The Council expands its understanding of dialogue when it affirms the Church's willingness to profit "from the experience of past ages, from the progress of the sciences, and from the riches hidden in various cultures, through which greater light is thrown on the nature of man and new avenues to truth are opened up" (GS 44). On one level, these words constitute acknowledgment that the Church has no monopoly on discerning the truth.[25] But they also affirm that the Church can *develop* its knowledge of the truth by engaging with others' ideas as they emerge throughout history. As Congar states, dialogue, in the Council's view, "involves reciprocity; the world has something to contribute."[26]

Gaudium et Spes does, however, qualify these statements by indicating that listening to others does not mean uncritically accepting their propositions. Consciousness of, and attention to, truth of Revelation plays a central role in the process of discernment which occurs:

> it is the task of the whole people of God . . . to listen to and distinguish the many voices of our time, *and to interpret them in the light of the divine Word* in order that the revealed truth may be more deeply penetrated, better understood, and more suitably presented. (GS 44) [italics added]

---

25. In Christian thought, this position is expressed as early as Rom. 1:18–2:24.
26. Y.-M. Congar, O.P., "The Role of the Church in the Modern World," in *Commentary*, Vol. V, 220.

Once again, a type of "dialectic" characterizes the Council's position, this time between discoveries which emerge "outside" the Church and the Revelation preached by the Church. The former are deciphered in light of the latter. The resulting "synthesis" serves to deepen the Church's understanding of Revealed truth; it also assists the Church in expressing this truth in ways comprehensible to the world at that moment in time.

The Pastoral Constitution's description of the "signs of the time" method also emphasizes listening *and* discernment.[27] Its opening paragraphs state that "[a]t all times the Church carries the responsibility of reading the signs of the time and interpreting them in light of the Gospel" (GS 4). Later in the text, the Council adds:

> Moved by that faith [the Church] tries to discern in the events, the needs, and the longings which it shares with other men of our time, what may be genuine signs of the presence or of the purpose of God. For faith throws a new light on all things and makes known the full ideal which God has set for man, thus guiding the mind towards solutions which are fully human. (GS 11)

Thus, there is always a two-step process: *identifying* what out of many events and needs of the present time might be "signs" of God's presence or purpose; and then *analyzing* them from the Gospel's viewpoint. Grisez explains this approach in the following way:

> The Council's method proceeds neither solely by deduction from general principles nor solely by induction from experienced situations but by dialectical reflection on data in the light of faith. This process uses both deductive and inductive reasoning to arrive at synthetic insights.[28]

On the basis of the cited extracts, this seems to be an accurate interpretation. One may add that the Council's words indicate that the Church is expected "at all times" to pay attention to what is happening in

---

27. The word "description" is used here because, despite its importance, the Council does not define the phrase, "the signs of the times." GS simply provides a description and outlines some of its consequences for the life of faith. See M.-D. Chenu, O.P., "Les signes des temps: Réflexion théologique," in *L'église dans le monde de ce temps*, Vol.II, 205–225. Moeller suggests that the Council employs the phrase sparingly because it was aware that the term is used in the Bible in reference to something quite different—the eschatological signs of the last days. See C. Moeller, "Preface and Introductory Statement," in *Commentary*, Vol. V, 94.

28. Grisez, *Living*, 59 n.114.

the world. A "fortress church" is therefore not an option. On the other hand, the Church is obliged to be critically reflective, and its reflection is to be informed by Revelation. The true meaning of signs, then, can only be discerned in light of all the general principles contained in the Gospel. It follows that no true discernment of signs can lead to judgments at odds with these principles.

The purpose, however, of developing these synthetic insights goes beyond deepening the Church's knowledge of the truth. As observed, the Council states that they assist in revealing the "full ideal which God has set for man." They help, in short, to uncover that which man is duty-bound to *actualize*: the transformation of himself and his world in ways which anticipate the world that is to come.

2.4 Transforming the Worldly Order

Gaudium et Spes's third chapter focuses upon the meaning of human activity, and forms a crucial basis for John Paul's development of Catholic social teaching. But at present, it is more important to grasp the Pastoral Constitution's understanding of the ultimate significance of human activity. This is contained in paragraphs 38 and 39 of the text, both of which break down false dichotomies between eternal salvation and temporal commitment.

Paragraph 38 begins by stating that Christ "reveals to us that 'God is love' (1 Jn. 4:8) and at the same time teaches that the fundamental law of human perfection, and consequently of the transformation of the world, is the new commandment of love." The view that the world's development is a *consequence* of man's striving for perfection implicitly disputes, of course, the notion that the key to "perfecting" man is to change his world. Though the two are inseparable, the Council maintains a distinct order of precedence. Here one should also note that when it speaks of the world's transformation through love, the Council indicates that it has more than "grand events" in mind. "This love," it states, "is not something reserved for important matters, but must be exercised above all in the ordinary circumstances of daily life" (GS 38).

In the same paragraph, we also find an implicit rebuke of those—like the unnamed East European bishop—who would rigidly separate the Christian concern for the afterlife from consideration of temporal affairs:[29]

---

29. See also A. Aver, "Man's Activity Throughout the World," in *Commentary*, Vol. V, 198–200.

Christ is now at work in the hearts of men by the power of his Spirit; not only does he arouse in them a desire for the world to come but he quickens, purifies, and strengthens the generous aspirations of mankind to make life more humane and conquer the earth for this purpose. (GS 38)

Thus, although man's ultimate destiny is eternal life, he cannot neglect this world. This would be to deny the Spirit which is active in the world by virtue of being operative in men's hearts. To work for a just temporal order—to make life more humane—is therefore in accordance with God's Will.

As one would expect, the Council cautions that man should never equate his ultimate salvation with the establishment of a more humane temporal order: "We have been warned, of course, that it profits man nothing if he gains the whole world and loses or forfeits himself" (GS 39). Instead, the building of a better world is to be understood as *anticipating* the world which is to come:

the expectancy of a new earth should spur us on, for it is here that the body of a new human family grows, foreshadowing in some way the age that is to come. That is why, although we must be careful to distinguish earthly progress clearly from the increase of the kingdom of Christ, such progress is of vital concern to the kingdom of God, insofar as it can contribute to the better ordering of society. (GS 39)

To cite one theologian, these words indicate that

there is a close relationship between temporal progress and the growth of the Kingdom, but these two processes are distinct. Those engaged in the latter not only cannot be indifferent to the former; they must show a genuine interest in and value it. However, the growth of the Kingdom goes beyond temporal progress. In short, there is close relationship, but no identification.[30]

The "New Jerusalem," so to speak, will not be realized in this world. Nevertheless, a careful reading of the Council's words indicates that it believes earthly progress to contain intimations of the future world when it contributes to a more just social order—"the better ordering of society." In some way, then, one may say, as the Council does, that "here on earth, the kingdom is mysteriously present" (GS 39).

---

30. G. Gutiérrez, *A Theology of Liberation* (Maryknoll: Orbis, 1973), 171.

The type of "progress" that the Council has in mind, however, is not primarily material. Above all, it is *moral*. The building up of the world must begin with man "building up" himself. This is apparent from the Council's identification of human progress with the spreading "on earth [of] the fruits of our nature and our enterprise—human dignity, brotherly communion, and freedom" (GS 39).

Of course, these words—freedom, dignity, communion—parallel the French revolutionary slogan of *liberté, égalité, fraternité*. But the Council differs from the men of the Revolution by emphasizing that such goods foreshadow the ultimate happiness to come, rather than a Rousseauian-like earthly bliss.[31] Moreover, by portraying these goods as "the fruits of our nature and enterprise," the Council indicates that they are *integral* to man, but must be realized through his actions and work. This is, of course, the classic natural law proposition expressed in the Aristotelian thought that man must actualize his potential.

Most of the second half of *Gaudium et Spes* is directed to explaining how people should order their actions in a variety of situations—familial, cultural, economic, political—so that these may be transformed in ways which prefigure and build up the Kingdom. Particularly significant in this regard is the Council's teaching about how people should order the relationship between their use and possession of material goods—an issue which has, from the beginning, been central to Catholic social teaching.

2.5 Material Goods

A Neglected Area?

In his commentary on Vatican II, Karl Barth asked why *Gaudium et Spes* set forth so few concrete positions.[32] Precisely what he meant by this is unclear, as the Pastoral Constitution articulates very concise teachings on a variety of subjects. This may have reflected the concern of some figures that the Church had not said enough in the past about certain topics. As part of the *ad extra* deliberations proposed in his plan, for example, Suenens argued that the Church must

---

31. See also P. Ladriere, "La Révolution française dans la doctrine politique des papes de la fin du XVIIIe a la moitie du XXe siècle," *Archives de Sciences Sociales des Religions* 33 (1988): 110–112.

32. See K. Barth, *Ad Limina Apostolorum* (Edinburgh: T. and T. Clark, 1967), 28.

strongly condemn injustices and social inequalities in the distribution of
wealth. In the eyes of the underdeveloped countries, the Church must
appear to be the Church of all and above all of the poor. Moralists have
devoted thousands of volumes to every detail of the sixth commandment:
there is practically nothing written on the obligation to give one's surplus to
others, nor tne social implications of goods created for the use of everyone.
The social and communitarian implications of genuine Christianity must be
vigorously pointed out.[33]

Suenens's comment that Christian "moralists" had said little in the past
about the use of material goods—superfluous to one's needs or
otherwise—was scarcely accurate. One need only refer to Aquinas's
commentaries on the rights and duties of property ownership and the
scores of patristic and scholastic writings on almsgiving.[34] Even prior to
the Council, modern Catholic social teaching dealt extensively with such
topics.[35] Still, it remains that this subject was accorded prominent attention
in Suenens's plan, and, in due course, John XXIII's September 1962 radio
message.[36] In light of these influences, it was likely that questions
surrounding the use and ownership of goods would be considered in at
least one *ad extra* document.

The Council examines material goods in *Gaudium et Spes*'s chapter on
socio-economic life. When the first draft of this chapter was presented to
the Council, only two pages of text were submitted. Refusing to see the
subject given marginal treatment, Cardinal Wyszyński of Warsaw insisted
that the attached fifteen page supplement to the proposed text become part
of the Schema itself.[37] Following revisions by the responsible commission,
the two printed pages of the 1964 text became eight pages in the document
submitted to the Council on 21 September 1965.[38] It was this which, after
minor amendments, received conciliar approval.

The Teaching

The critical words regarding material goods are to be found in the

---

33. Suenens, "A Plan," Appendix IV, 101.
34. See C. Avila, *Ownership: Early Christian Teaching* (Maryknoll: Orbis, 1983).
35. See M. Habiger, O.S.B., *Papal Teaching on Private Property, 1891-1981* (Lanham: University Press of America, 1990).
36. See John XXIII, *Radio-Television Message*, 1962, 682.
37. See ASCV, III–6 (1975), 5 November 1964, 273.
38. See ASCV, IV–1 (1977), 21 September 1965, 491–498.

heavily annotated first six sentences of *Gaudium et Spes*'s 69th paragraph. They outline not only the principles governing the correct use of goods, but also the relationship between use and possession. The first two sentences state:

> [1] God has destined the earth and all it contains for the use of all human individuals and peoples, in such a way that, under the direction of justice accompanied by charity, created goods ought to flow abundantly to everyone on a fair basis [refers to Pius XII and John XXIII]. [2] One must always bear this universal destination of goods in mind, no matter what forms property may take as it is adapted, in accordance with diverse and changeable conditions, to the legitimate institutions of peoples. (GS 69)[39]

These words reiterate the magisterium's position concerning material goods as it stood in the immediate pre-conciliar period. Paragraph 69's first sentence refers to Pius XII's statement that "the goods created by God for all men should in the same way reach all, justice and charity helping."[40] The effect is to underline the primacy of the principle that the earth is to be used by and on behalf of *all* people. This does not mean that in the beginning human persons jointly owned the material world, with each having an equal share. Rather, it means that nothing in "subhuman" creation ever comes with a label saying: "this good is meant for this person but not that one, this group but not that." In the beginning and now, God provides material goods for the use of all.

The second sentence indicates that *how* the earth's resources are to be used for the benefit of all is basically left to people to work out rationally and together. But it also indicates that any appropriation of possession by individuals is to be seen as only a means (and even then only as one means among possible others) of ensuring common use. It follows, then, that property rights are intrinsically limited by their common origin and end: any right of property is not therefore primary and absolute, but only secondary and intermediate.

The next three sentences of paragraph 69 specify the implications of the primacy of common use for the manner in which individuals use their property:

---

39. For ease of reference, the number of each sentence in paragraph 69 has been inserted into the text.
40. The footnote reads: "Cf. Pius XII, Encycl. *Sertum Laetitiae*, AAS 31 (1939), 642." See this reference for the citation.

[3] For this reason, in using those goods, people should consider the exterior things which they legitimately possess not only as their own but as common, in the sense that their possessions should benefit not only themselves but others as well [refers to Aquinas, Leo XIII, and Pius XII]. [4] Therefore every man has the right to possess a sufficient amount of the earth's goods for himself and his family. [5] This has been the opinion of the Fathers and Doctors of the Church, who taught that men are bound to come to the aid of others, and to do so not merely out of their superfluous goods [refers to St. Basil, Lactantius, St. Augustine, St. Gregory the Great, St. Bonaventure, St. Albert the Great, and John XXIII]. (GS 69)

The emphasis that one's goods must be used to benefit others as well as oneself flows naturally from the primacy of the common use principle. Some, however, regard the sentences above as "radicalizing" magisterial teaching on the use and possession of goods. Manuel Velásquez, for example, argues that paragraph 69's fifth sentence "overturns the traditional Thomistic view that owners of private property are obligated to put only their 'superfluous' wealth . . . at the service of the needy."[41]

A closer look at the sentences above and their attached references suggests that a rather different point is being made. The first text referred to by the third sentence is from Aquinas's *Summa Theologiae* (ST, II-II, q.32, a.5, ad 2). Here Aquinas answers the argument that because people have a right to keep what is their own, almsgiving is never a strict duty in justice. Previously in the same article from the *Summa*, Aquinas points out that almsgiving is a matter of precept if two conditions are met: one has more than enough to meet one's own needs and those of one's dependents; and some other person or persons cannot survive unless one makes one's surplus available. In this context, Aquinas's answer to the objection is that any earthly good which God gives people is theirs in the sense that they own it, but not in the sense that they alone may use it; for insofar as they do not need it to satisfy their own needs, others should be able to use it to satisfy theirs.

But before one concludes that this actually proves the correctness of Velásquez's contention (on the grounds that Aquinas apparently limits one's assistance of others to whatever is superfluous to one's needs), the second text referred to by the third sentence should be examined (ST, II-II, q.66, a.2). In this extract, Aquinas gives three reasons why appropriation of property to particular owners is morally licit and even necessary. First, people tend to take better care of what is theirs than of what is common to

41. Velásquez, "*Gaudium et Spes*," 179.

everyone, since individuals tend to shirk a responsibility which is nobody's in particular. Second, if everyone were responsible for everything, the result would be confusion. Third, dividing up things generally produces a more peaceful state of affairs, whilst sharing common things often results in tension. Individual ownership, then— understood as the power to manage and dispose of things—is justified. However, the *use* of things is, according to Aquinas, a different matter. In regard to use, one is not justified in holding things as exclusively one's own (*ut proprias*) but should rather hold them "as common, in the sense that one must be ready to share them with others in need.

So paragraph 69's fifth sentence does *not* represent an "overturning of Thomistic principles" because Aquinas does not limit assistance of others in need to superfluous goods. The principle of common use, in Aquinas's view, means that people should be ready to share their goods with those in need. The status of the goods, as superfluous or not, is irrelevant. To provide a concrete example: a person's use of his house, for example, to shelter someone in need may not actually be a case of assisting with superfluous goods; rather, it is an instance of a person sharing a good which is essential for his own well-being. To share the use of one's goods with others does not therefore necessarily presuppose that the giver discontinues their own use or ownership of that good.

Furthermore, Velásquez's position ignores the Council's teaching precisely about "superfluity" in paragraph 69's fifth and sixth sentences. Here the Council effectively distinguishes between two cases: "need" and "extreme necessity."

The fifth sentence serves two purposes. One is to provide magisterial precedent for the Council's teaching, expressed in the fourth sentence, that each person may possess enough to meet the needs of himself and his family. It also specifies that people are bound to assist others with their superfluous goods. This is reinforced by a long list of attached references.[42] One of these, from St. Basil, specifies that superfluity belongs of right to the needy, even though it is not in fact theirs, because superfluous goods are allowed to people only by way of trust so that they

---

42. The relevant footnote (no.10) is the longest in the Pastoral Constitution. This indicates the Council's awareness of the complexity and importance of the question. It is probable that Aquinas is not cited in this footnote, precisely because, as Marcus Lefébure points out, it is not clear in Aquinas that what counts as superfluous is measured by others' needs. See M. Lefébure, O.P., "Private Property According to St. Thomas and Recent Papal Encyclicals," in *St. Thomas Aquinas, Summa Theologiae*, Vol.38, *Injustice* (Edinburgh: University of Edinburgh Press, 1975), Appendix 2, 277 n.14.

should have the merit of discharging this trust well.[43] The last reference in the relevant footnote is to a radio-television address by John XXIII.[44] This specifies that superfluity must be calculated according to the needs of others.

The fifth sentence, however, needs to be read in light of the sixth. This explains what "not merely out of superfluous goods" means—and fatally undermines Velásquez's argument:

[6] When a person is in extreme necessity he has the right to supply himself with what he needs out of the riches of others. [refers to Aquinas] (GS 69)

Thus, in cases of *extreme necessity*, the question of whether a good is superfluous or not becomes irrelevant. The attached reference makes this explicit: "In this case the old principle holds good: 'In extreme necessity all goods are common, that is, they are to be shared' " (GS 69 n.11). In other words, under the stress of urgent necessity, the secondary differentiation of ownership is resolved back into the primary principle of common use in its primitive form. For determination of what constitutes extreme necessity, the Council's footnote refers to the conditions outlined by Aquinas.[45] The strictness of these conditions[46] indicates that although the Council considers use to be primary, it also views individual possession to be important; hence, there must be very good reasons for usurping it.

---

43. It reads: "Cf. St. Basil, *Hom. in illud Lucae "Destruam horrea mea,"* n.2: *PG* 31, 263." See this reference for Basil's statement.

44. It reads: "As regards the determination of what is superfluous today cf. John XXIII, *Radio-Television Message*, 11 September 1962, AAS 54 (1962), 682: 'It is the duty of every man . . . to calculate what is superfluous by the measure of the needs of others and to see to it that the administration and distribution of created goods be utilized for the advantage of all'."

45. It reads: "On the other hand for the scope, the extension and the way this principle is be applied in the text, besides modern authors, cf. St. Thomas, ST, II-II, q.66, a.7. Clearly, for the correct application of the principle, all the moral conditions required must be fulfilled."

46. The criterion from the reference to Aquinas is: "if the need be so manifest and urgent that it is evident that the present need must be remedied by whatever means be at hand (for instance when a person is in some imminent danger, and there is no other possible remedy), then it is lawful for a man to succor his own need by means of another's property." ST, II-II, q.66, a.7. Elsewhere, Aquinas provides a clearer indication of what constitutes "imminent danger." In discussing almsgiving, he states that "it is not every sort of need that binds us as a matter of strict obligation, but only what is a matter of life and death. This is where Ambrose's dictum applies, 'Feed the man who is dying. Refuse, and you kill him.'" ST, II-II, q.32, a.5. The same dictum is cited by GS 69's seventh sentence.

In any case, we have established that Velásquez's claims about the respective positions of the Council and Aquinas are, at best, misleading. The Council's teaching overturns nothing of Aquinas's thought about the use and ownership of goods. Both hold that people must use goods to benefit others as well as themselves; each considers people duty-bound to assist those in need with their superfluous goods; and, in instances of extreme necessity, both view the question of whether or not a good is superfluous as immaterial.

2.6 Conclusion

When considering developments in Catholic social teaching, it soon becomes apparent that the question of realizing the primacy of common use—and the problems emanating from its non-realization—underlies much magisterial teaching, including that of John Paul II. Moreover, John Paul's development of the teaching also owes something to the Council's understanding of history, its ideas about the nature and realization of true temporal progress, as well as the Council's view of how dialogue and reading the signs of the times can assist the Church in engaging with the modern world.

But perhaps the Pastoral Constitution's most significant impact upon John Paul's teachings was of an indirect nature. For among the bishops who participated in all four Council sessions and the debates surrounding *Gaudium et Spes*'s drafting was Karol Wojtyła. In many respects, the Constitution confirmed for him the importance of ideas pursued in his own writings. Nevertheless, it also contributed to the evolution of Wojtyła's thought, the pre-papal history of which we now consider.

3

A PHILOSOPHER FROM KRAKÓW

3.1 Introduction

On 16 October 1978, thirteen years after the Council's closure, Cardinal Karol Wojtyła was elected pope. Unlike Paul VI, Wojtyła had spent much time in pastoral activity and none in the Roman Curia. Like Paul VI, however, Wojtyła had led an active intellectual life. Having taught in the Jagiellonian University's Theology Faculty, he accepted a lectureship at the Catholic University of Lublin in 1954, and held its Chair of Ethics between 1956 and 1978.

Our purpose here is not to analyze Wojtyła's major works comprehensively. Rather, the intention is to sketch the intellectual influences shaping them and highlight significant continuities and developments in thought. A secondary aim is to clarify Wojtyła's place in the post-war Polish Catholic-Marxist dialogue. The picture that some commentators present of Wojtyła in this discussion is misleading and a source of misapprehension concerning John Paul's social teaching.

Before, however, embarking upon these tasks, an important contextual factor should be noted. Censorship was a fact in Communist Poland and though its intensity varied, this inevitably affected intellectual activity. In Leo Strauss's opinion, censorship "compels all writers who hold heterodox views to develop a peculiar technique of writing, the technique which we have in mind when we speak of reading between the lines."[1]

---

1. L. Strauss, *Persecution and the Art of Writing* (Chicago: University of Chicago Press, 1952), 24.

Gordon Skilling describes how such an atmosphere results in many adopting attitudes of "self-censorship" so as to avoid state restrictions while maintaining their intellectual integrity.[2]

Despite his status as Cardinal-Archbishop of Kraków, Wojtyła was not immune from this atmosphere. One does not, for example, find him critiquing Marxist thought in articles first published in Poland. The closest to which Wojtyła came to this was a polemical 1957 article against "scientific ethics."[3] It focussed, however, upon the regime's promotion of "positivistic culture" rather than Marxism per se. By contrast, Wojtyła was more explicit in disputing fundamental Marxist premises in writings initially published in the West.[4]

But censorship may, paradoxically, have had its benefits. In discussing East German intellectual life, Timothy Garton Ash suggests that censorship indirectly encouraged intellectuals to concentrate on "fundamental" matters instead of dissipating their energies among the many issues clamoring for attention in an open society. Imposed limitations, therefore, may actually have had the artistic advantage of causing writers to plumb the depths of one or two profound questions.[5] Although it is difficult to ascertain if this phenomenon affected Wojtyła, his writings do focus on a limited number of themes. They are devoted, by and large, to providing an ethical-anthropological answer to the question: what is man?

3.2 The Pre-Conciliar Works

Wojtyła's intellectual interests always extended beyond ethics. His pre-war philology studies at the Jagiellonian expressed his abiding interest in literature, poetry, and drama, as did his published poems and plays.

---

2. See H.G. Skilling, *Samizdat and an Independent Society in Central and Eastern Europe* (London: Macmillan, 1989), 225.

3. See "Problem etyki naukowej" [The Problem of a Scientific Ethic], *Tygodnik Powszechny* 11, no. 10 (1957): 3.

4. An example: Wojtyła's 1977 paper—"Il problema del costituirsi della cultura attraverso la 'praxis' umana" [The Problem of the Constitution of Culture through Human "Praxis"], *Rivista de Filosofia Neo-Scolastica* 69, no. 3 (1977): 513–524—was published in an Italian journal in 1977. The same article appears nowhere in Polish journals until late 1989 under the title of "Problem konstytuowania się kultury proprzez ludzką praxis," *Ethos* 2, no. 8 (1989): 39–49. The article's refutation of Marxist conceptions of praxis would not have been viewed favorably by regime censors.

5. See T. Garton Ash, *The Uses of Adversity* (London: Granta, 1991), 14.

None of these compositions will be considered in this chapter. For the present, it is enough to state that they are not complacent compositions. Many are set in very modern surroundings—factories, quarries—and depict outrage and compassion in conflict. In several commentators' views, Wojtyła's plays ask hard questions about how one achieves self-realization and the nature of freedom in the modern world.[6]

Prior to examining Wojtyła's main pre-conciliar writings, mention should be made of his first doctoral thesis, *Faith According to St. John of the Cross*,[7] written in Rome under the supervision of Réginald Garrigou-Lagrange, O.P., in 1948. This five part dissertation describes the soul's ecstatic agony and its nights of despair as it journeys through mysticism to faith. Wojtyła suggests that John of the Cross showed that contemplation as a mystical experience leads to true faith and inner union with God.[8] Wojtyła adds, however, that, according to John, faith alone is not enough to achieve a psychological union of the intellect with God. It must be faith nourished by love and illuminated by gifts of the Holy Spirit, especially of wisdom and reason.[9]

Wojtyła's attention to the place of reason in a mystic's writings may reflect Garrigou-Lagrange's influence. Apart from being a specialist on St. John, Garrigou-Lagrange was a leading authority on Aristotelian-Thomistic metaphysics. The importance of scholasticism in general for Wojtyła's thought cannot be underestimated. For despite his later engagements with phenomenology, Wojtyła's writings "repeatedly declare the value of Thomism and that he is making this system the basis for his own work."[10]

An Encounter with Max Scheler

Wojtyła's first published work was based on the *Habilitationsschrift* he presented to the Jagiellonian's Theology Faculty in 1953. Entitled *Ocena*

---

6. See, for example, A. Marczewski, "Man in the Face of Fundamental Questions: Encounters with Karol Wojtyła's Dramaturgy," *Dialectics and Humanism* 10, no. 1 (1983): 114–118.

7. *Faith According to St. John of the Cross*, tr. J. Aumann, O.P. (San Francisco: Ignatius Press, 1981).

8. *Faith*, 83.

9. *Faith*, 153. See also "O humaniźime św. Jana od Krżyza" [The Humanism of John of the Cross], *Znak* 7, no. 1 (1951): 6–20.

10. J. Gałkowski, O.P., "The Place of Thomism in the Anthropology of Karol Wojtyła," *Angelicum* 65, no. 2 (1988): 82.

możliwości zbudowania etyki chrześcijańskiej przy założeniach systemu Maksa Schelera [On the Possibility of Constructing a Christian Ethic on the Basis of the System of Max Scheler] (1959), it inquires whether Scheler—a sometime-Catholic philosopher formed in Edmund Husserl's phenomenological school[11]—had succeeded in providing a satisfactory basis for Christian ethics. Wojtyła maintains that Scheler fails. Arguing that ethical values are grasped in Scheler through feelings rather than reason, Wojtyła believes that this is far too subjective. To his mind, Christ is more than a "genius of the heart." Christ's ethical teaching leads to the perception of an objective moral order, which man may then realize in his life through free will (MSE 34)—an orthodox Thomist argument. Thus, Wojtyła concludes, "it will always be the task of a theologian-ethician to scrutinize the ethical value of human actions in light of objective principles" (MSE 125).

Despite these criticisms, Wojtyła's analysis of Scheler was of great importance for his later works. Anna-Teresa Tymieniecka claims that it affected Wojtyła's approach to ethical questions.[12] There is some truth to this. Scheler introduced Wojtyła to phenomenological methods of grasping the ethically positive or negative as they are lived through the *experience* of human acts. As Scheler's *Der Formalismus* states, "the person *is* and experiences himself only as a being that *executes acts*."[13] While Wojtyła does not quite go this far, he does maintain that "[c]onsistent phenomenology will reveal to us ethical values as they appear in the person's experience 'on the occasion' of acting" (MSE 125).

The Jesuit historian of philosophy, Frederick Copleston, believes that whilst phenomenological analysis is capable of fruitful application, "the use of the method does not necessarily mean that the user can be called a 'disciple' of Husserl."[14] Wojtyła himself sought to avoid this label. Though claiming that Scheler's approach could assist Catholics in facilitating "an analysis of ethical facts on a phenomenal and experiential plane" (MSE 122), Wojtyła was careful to add that "[a] Christian thinker, and specifically a theologian, although availing himself in his writings of

---

11. For a history of phenomenology, see F. Copleston, S.J., *A History of Philosophy*, Bk. 3, Vol. VII, *Fichte to Nietzsche* (New York: Image Books, 1985), 430–436. For Scheler, see J. Staude, *Max Scheler* (New York: Free Press, 1967).

12. See A.-T. Tymieniecka, "The Origins of the Philosophy of John Paul II," *Proceedings of the American Catholic Philosophical Association*, 53 (1979), 18.

13. M. Scheler, *Formalism in Ethics and Non-Formal Ethics of Values* (Evanston: Northwestern University Press, 1973), 385.

14. Copleston, *Fichte to Nietzsche*, 435.

the phenomenological experience, cannot be a phenomenologist" (MSE 125). Wojtyła's writings would retain a phenomenological stress on what the experience of action reveals about man. Nevertheless, they also insist that beyond human acts, there is an objective moral order, and that man's freedom depends upon these acts conforming with that order.

The Ethics of Love

Wojtyła's next major publication was his work on sexual ethics, *Love and Responsibility* (1960). In his 1994 book, *Crossing the Threshold of Hope*, Pope John Paul stated that *Love and Responsibility* reflected his pastoral involvement with students attempting to resolve problems associated with marriage.[15] Williams suggests that *Love and Responsibility* is best understood in this context.[16]

Wojtyła himself, however, claims that "[t]he book is, by and large, of a philosophical character—for ethics is (and can only be) part of philosophy" (LR 16–17). Certainly, the chapter entitled "First Meaning of the Word Using" makes claims which go beyond the particular questions addressed by the text. The book also reveals much about Wojtyła's intellectual development. It reflects, for instance, Wojtyła's assimilation of phenomenological emphases: "experience of the truth of values," he comments, "is of the utmost importance" (LR 197). This "Schelerian" attention to the experiential is, however, integrated into another framework. As the Pope put it retrospectively:

> it is from a pastoral point of view that, in *Love and Responsibility*, I formulated the concept of a *personalistic principle*. This principle is an attempt to translate the commandment of love into the language of philosophical ethics.[17]

What kind of "personalist" was Wojtyła? In the year following *Love and Responsibility*'s appearance, he published an article entitled "Personalizm tomistyczny" [Thomistic Personalism]. It grounds Aquinas's metaphysics and philosophy of man as a concrete being in an understanding of man as a person with an innate tendency to form inter-

---

15. See John Paul II, *Crossing the Threshold of Hope* (London: Cape, 1994), 200.
16. See Williams, *The Mind*, 151–152.
17. *Crossing*, 200–201.

personal relationships.[18] It also criticizes liberalism and totalitarianism as erroneous modern interpretations of the proper relationship between person and society.[19] In general terms, there seems to be little question that the article reflects the influence of neo-Thomist scholars such as Jacques Maritain in European Catholic intellectual circles of the time. Maritain's critique of liberalism and totalitarianism, for example, closely resembles Wojtyła's position.[20]

Given his Schelerian-like attention to experience, one would hesitate before characterizing Wojtyła as a "Thomist-personalist" per se. Nevertheless, he does essentially conceptualize man in these terms. *Love and Responsibility*, for example, presents man as a person who is love-centered and directed. The term "person," according to Wojtyła, captures man's uniqueness. It embraces his ability to reason, his possession of an inner spiritual life directed to truth and goodness (LR 21–23), and the fact that he possesses the free will which makes man "his own master, *sui juris* as the Latin phrase has it" (LR 24). These comments essentially build Thomist concepts into an anthropology of man as a person.

The book then turns to explaining the basic principles which should order human relationships. In discussing the meaning of the verb "to use," Wojtyła states that on no account should one person be used merely as a means to another's end. This "elementary truth," as Wojtyła calls it, has been recognized by many outside the Catholic tradition. He refers, for example, to Immanuel Kant's moral imperative that one should "act always in such a way that the other person is the end and not merely the instrument of your action" (LR 27–28).[21] Wojtyła's fear, it seems, is that if everyone treats each other instrumentally, then everyone will become an object in others' projects, with social life consequently degenerating into a mire of reciprocal instrumentalism.

Wojtyła then argues that relationships based on love avoid such problems. "Loving," he states, begins when two people "seek a common good . . . [this] unites the persons involved internally, and so constitutes

---

18. See "Personalizm tomistyczny" [Thomistic Personalism], *Znak* 13, no. 5 (1961): 671–673.

19. "Thomistic Personalism," 674–675.

20. See, for example, J. Maritain, *The Person and the Common Good* (London: Geoffrey Bles, 1947), 63–73.

21. This is Wojtyła's paraphrase of the version of Kant's Categorical Imperative which reads: "act so to treat humanity, whether in your own person or in that of any other, always at the same time as an end, and never merely as a means." Cited in F. Copleston, S.J., *A History of Philosophy*, Bk. 2, Vol. VI, *Wolf to Kant* (New York: Image Books, 1985), 328.

the essential core around which any love must grow." Loving is, Wojtyła adds, "the only clear alternative to using a person as the means to an end" (LR 28): it "precludes the possibility that one of them might be subordinate to the other" (LR 29).

Having criticized instrumental interpretations of "use," Wojtyła suggests that the verb may also be understood in terms of "to enjoy," in the sense of "experiencing pleasure" (LR 32–34). This leads him into a critique of utilitarianism. The positing of the experience of pleasure as the primary good is understood by Wojtyła as central to utilitarian thought: "the recognition of pleasure in itself as the sole or at any rate the greatest good, to which everything else in the activity of an individual or a society should be subordinated." But, Wojtyła explains, "[q]uite obviously that which is truly good, that which morality and conscience bid me do, often involves some measure of pain and requires the renunciation of some pleasure" (LR 36).

Though Wojtyła associates utilitarianism with Jeremy Bentham and John Stuart Mill, the importance of his remarks, for our purposes, lie in the fact that he describes the "utilitarian attitude" as "characteristic of modern man's mentality and his attitude to life" (LR 35). Rather than devote himself to the pursuit of pleasure, *Love and Responsibility* proposes that man should pursue virtue. It notes, however, Scheler's concern that modern man has become resentful of this task (LR 143). This was a theme to which Wojtyła returned during the Vatican Council.

3.3 The Post-Conciliar Works

Karol Wojtyła attended all four of the Council sessions. He spoke a total of twenty-two times, with six of his speeches being on the draft of the Pastoral Constitution.[22] The first of these objected to the tone of the draft. Wojtyła insisted that it "should speak in such a way that the world sees that we are not so much teaching the world in an authoritarian way, but rather we are seeking the true and just solution of the difficult problems of life together with the world. The fact that the truth is already known to us is not in question, but it is a question of the way in which the world will find it for itself and appropriate it." Wojtyła called this method "heuristic," defined as "allowing the student to find the truth as if from his own

---

22. See ASCV, III–5 (1975): 298–300, 680–683. III–7 (1975), 380–382. IV–2 (1977): 660–663. IV–3 (1977): 242–243, 349–350.

resources" [*permittendo discipulo veritatem quasi ex suis invenire*].[23]

While these words do not quite amount to an affirmation of dialogue as outlined in the preceding chapter, they do suggest that the search for truth provides grounds for collaboration between the Church and those outside it. Nor would it be difficult to move from Wojtyła's position towards stating that the Church may learn from the results of others' investigations. Wojtyła had already proved his own willingness to do so by incorporating Scheler's attention to experience into his own work. Moreover *Love and Responsibility*'s reference to Kant demonstrates that Wojtyła had also acknowledged that people outside the Church were capable of recognizing truth "on their own."

In the same address, however, Wojtyła indicated that he viewed the modern world as ambiguous and even somewhat contradictory:

> The modern world is new in good and new in evil. It contains new values but also new crises. It is a world of new closeness between peoples and nations, but, at the same time, a world that is threatening and dangerous in a new way for each person and entire societies. It is a world of progress and luxury, in which the majority suffers simultaneously from hunger.[24]

Indeed, during the Council's fourth session, Wojtyła suggested that the draft chapter of *Gaudium et Spes* entitled, "The Role of the Church in the Modern World," lacked "a sense of Christian realism." It underestimated, he stated, "the modern world's sinful features." In this regard, Wojtyła singled out what he saw as modern man's disinclination to pursue virtue.[25]

In texts written after the Council, Wojtyła elaborates on what he views as some of the modern world's problems. Broadly speaking, he suggests that in the midst of so much contemporary earthly progress, man is losing a truthful understanding of himself. A desire to counter this trend—to increase "understanding of the human person for the sake of the person himself" (AP 22)—underlies Wojtyła's most important work, *The Acting Person*. Its introduction states:

> Ceaseless speculations about the various trends in the development of mankind—for example, the quantitative aspects of development, the progress of culture and civilization with all the resulting inequalities and dramatic consequences—are a powerful impulse for the philosophy of the

---

23. ASCV, III–5 (1975), 21 October 1964, 299.
24. ASCV, III–5, 300.
25. ASCV, IV–2 (1977): 661–662.

person. . . . Having conquered so many secrets of nature the conqueror himself must have his own mysteries ceaselessly unraveled anew. (AP 21)

Action as the Key to Man

Wojtyła believes that if man is to be good—to be virtuous—he requires greater knowledge of what he is. To unravel this mystery, *The Acting Person* proceeds from the premise that "action *reveals* the person." But immediately one thinks about human actions, Wojtyła says, one sees that their uniqueness is derived from their moral significance: "Morality constitutes their intrinsic feature and what may be viewed as their specific profile, which is not to be found in acting that assumes agents other than a person" (AP 11). The acts of animals, for instance, lack a moral dimension because animals are not persons. Thus if one considers "how man becomes good" in terms of "what is man," one cannot avoid seeing that ethics has an anthropological dimension. Wojtyła himself states:

the history of philosophy is the tale of the age-old encounter of anthropology and ethics. That branch of learning which has as its aim the comprehensive study of moral goodness and evil—and such are the aims of ethics—can never evade the state of affairs that good and evil manifest themselves in actions, and by actions they become a part of man. (AP 11– 12)

For this reason, Wojtyła sets himself against "unanthropological" tendencies in contemporary thought:

in modern philosophy, particularly in contemporary philosophical thought, there is a visible tendency to treat the problem of ethics somewhat apart from anthropology. . . . [But] the total elimination of anthropological conclusions from ethics is not possible. The more a philosophical reflection becomes comprehensive, the more anthropological questions tend . to appear. (AP 12)

Upon what sources, then, does Wojtyła base his ethical-anthropological study of man through action? One foundation, strictly speaking, is not philosophical at all. According to Wojtyła:

While writing the book . . . the author attended the Second Vatican Council and his participation in the proceedings stimulated and inspired his thinking about the person. It suffices to say that . . . *Gaudium et Spes* . . . not only brings to the forefront the person and his calling but also asserts the belief in his transcendent nature. (AP 302 n.9)

Gaudium et Spes provided even more stimulus for *The Acting Person* than Wojtyła acknowledges. For the moment, however, we will focus on identifying other influences upon this text.

Tymieniecka's editorial introduction to *The Acting Person*'s English edition places Wojtyła's book in the context of the reaction of phenomenologists such as Roman Ingarden against the "positivism" which "reduced the human to the empirical." Though conceding that Wojtyła had no contact with Ingarden until after *The Acting Person*'s original publication, Tymieniecka underlines Scheler's phenomenology as critical to this work, and relegates the thought of Aristotle, Aquinas, and Kant to the status of "points of reference."[26]

Wojtyła's draft preface to the English edition, however, has a different emphasis: "The author owes everything to the systems of metaphysics, of anthropology, and of Aristotelian-Thomistic ethics on the one hand, and to

---

26. A.-T. Tymieniecka, "Editorial Introduction," AP xxi. There is considerable disagreement about the accuracy of parts of Tymieniecka's editing of AP's English edition. For Tymieniecka's account, see A.-T. Tymieniecka, "A Page of History or from *Osoba i Czyn* to *The Acting Person*," *Phenomenology Information Bulletin* 3 (1979): 3–52.

Both Jean-Yves Lacoste and Georges Kalinowski regard the result as potentially misleading. See J.-Y. Lacoste, "Vérité et liberté: Sur la philosophie de la personne chez Karol Wojtyła," *Revue Thomiste* 81, no. 3 (1981): 586–614; G. Kalinowski, "Autour de *The Acting Person*," *Revue Thomiste* 82, no. 4 (1982): 626–633. Kenneth Schmitz agrees: "the editor, by differing paraphrases of scholastic Latin terms, has supplanted an older technical language for another more contemporary [phenomenological] one. [This] obscures the continuity of the author's thought with older traditions of thought." K. Schmitz, *At the Center of the Human Drama* (Washington, D.C.: Catholic University of America Press, 1993), 60. An example of the problems associated with the Tymieniecka edition is its statement that "[m]an fulfils himself as a person, as 'somebody' " (AP 153). It excludes the qualification, "in the sense of traditional metaphysics," which appears between the words "person" and "as" in the Polish text.

Nevertheless, there is little question that Wojtyła revised parts of AP throughout the 1970s in anticipation of its English publication. See Williams, *The Mind*, 186; J. Kwitny, *Man of the Century* (London: Little, Brown, and Company, 1997), 245–246, 266, 272, 310. It is, however, unlikely that Wojtyła personally revised AP's final chapter. Indeed, the Tymieniecka edition includes a literal translation of this chapter as an appendix.

Conscious of these problems, the author decided to use the 1981 English edition but had questionable English renderings checked against the Polish edition. Schmitz recommends using the literal translation of AP's final chapter rather than Tymieniecka's edited version. See Schmitz, *At the Center*, 60. With two exceptions, this advice has been followed.

phenomenology, above all in Scheler's interpretation, and through Scheler's critique also to Kant, on the other hand" (AP xiv). Scholastic thought is thus underlined as at least equally significant as phenomenology.

Yet, as Józef Tischner points out, Wojtyła's *actual* preface goes further.[27] It states that, despite phenomenological efforts, modern philosophies have been unable to cognize man as a complete unified being—an evident reference to their separation of ethics from anthropology. By contrast, "in traditional Aristotelian thought," Wojtyła argues, "it was the very conception of the "human act" which was seen as the manifestation of man's unity as well as its source." Hence, Wojtyła claims that "by introducing this approach to man through action we may yield the necessary insights into the unity of the human being" (AP viii). In a later article, Wojtyła is more specific on this matter:

> Although I arrived at the concept of the "human act" within the framework of a phenomenological inquiry of Husserlian orientation it has to be pointed out that it coincides with the notion of *actus humanus* as elaborated by Thomas Aquinas. "*Actus humanus*" follows from the nature of the acting person, from man understood as the subject and author of his action. Indubitably the most valuable element in Thomas' concept of *actus humanus* is that it *expresses the dynamism* of a concrete being – man.[28]

The Acting Person's Thomist orientation is evident from numerous references to Aristotle, Aquinas, Joseph de Finance's act-Thomism, and existential Lublin Thomists like Stanisław Kamiński, Mieczysław Krąpiec, and Jerzy Kalinowski (AP 358–359).[29] At the same time, Wojtyła's attention to action also reflects a certain sympathy for existentialism, partly because it avoids the mistake of positivist "Anglo-Saxon analysts" (AP 12) in whose writings "anthropological questions are almost entirely disregarded or limited to marginal remarks on the freedom of will and determinism" (AP 301 n.3). Though Wojtyła has his disagreements with Jean-Paul Sartre,[30] the latter's *Being and Nothingness*

---

27. See J. Tischner, "L'aspetto metodologico dell'opera *Persona e Atto*," in *La filosofia*, 101.
28. "The Intentional Act and the Human Act, that is, Act and Experience," *Analecta Husserliana* 5 (1976): 279–280 n.2.
29. For Wojtyła's position vis-à-vis these Polish thinkers, see S. Kowalczyk, "Personalisme polonais contemporain," *Divus Thomas* 88, no. 1/3 (1985): 58–76.
30. See M. Jaworski, "Sartre, l'uomo e Papa Wojtyła," *CSEO documentazione* 143 (1979): 2–15.

is commended for its attention to philosophy's anthropological dimension (AP 12).

It remains, however, that Husserl, Scheler and Ingarden are also cited extensively in *The Acting Person*, with the Husserlian slogan "*zurück zum Gegenstand*" [back to the object] being quoted twice (AP xiii–xiv). This constitutes an invitation to look at man in his multidimensional existence and activity. Husserlians usually call this process "reduction." Wojtyła, however, gives it a specific definition: "By phenomenological reduction we mean the moment of the fullest and simultaneously the most essence-centered visualization of a given object" (AP 78). The "moment" which Wojtyła has in mind—the human act—may reflect, alongside Aquinas's tract on this topic,[31] the influence of Scheler's *Der Formalismus* which states that "the *whole person* is contained in *every* fully concrete act— without being exhausted in his being in any of these acts."[32]

It goes without saying that by attempting to comprehend the person through a study of acts, Wojtyła's approach is un-Cartesian. He chooses to begin with the experience of acts, taken in the broad Husserlian sense of "self-givenness" (AP 9).[33] Thus, as Wojtyła explains earlier in the text:

> Our approach runs counter to another trend of modern philosophy. Since Descartes, knowledge about man and his world has been identified with the cognitive function—as if only in cognition and especially through knowledge of himself, could man manifest his nature and his prerogative. And yet, in reality, does man reveal himself in *thinking* or, rather, in the actual enacting of his existence? . . . it is in reversing the post-Cartesian attitude toward man that we undertake our study: by approaching him through action. (AP vii–viii)

However, these words also suggest that Wojtyła's motives for "getting back to the object" have a decidedly *un*-Husserlian objective. Husserl's phenomenology was designed to lead to "the positing of consciousness itself, rather than the human person, as the absolute to which all objects are relative."[34] Husserl himself defined phenomenology as a method of establishing, against irrationalism, a kind of super-rationalism which transcended the inadequate old rationalism and yet vindicated its

---

31. See ST, I-II, q.6-21.
32. Scheler, *Formalism*, 377.
33. See also AP 301 n.1.
34. S. Dinan, "Karol Wojtyła's Phenomenological Anthropology," *New Scholasticism* 55, no. 3 (1981): 319.

innermost objectives. Thus Husserl was actually a thoroughgoing rationalist and idealist for whom the *vision* of the object was basically the *constitution* of the object.[35]

Wojtyła, by contrast, rejects the autonomy of consciousness and posits action as the primary source of moral meaning. *The Acting Person*'s first chapter ascertains what it means to be conscious of oneself acting. In doing so, Wojtyła makes extensive use of Thomistic terminology (*potentia-actus, actus secundus, actus humanus et hominis, agere et pati,* etc). Although he agrees that consciousness [świadomość] is unique to man, Wojtyła holds that it must not be absolutized, for this would reduce "being" to "perception" (AP 33–34), and—though Wojtyła does not state this—lock up man in the inner fortress of idealism.

Yet Wojtyła does not seek to obliterate the idea of consciousness. In a later paper, he suggested that it was important to

realize the specific importance of consciousness for subjectivity. This aspect was not much developed in the scholastic tradition. . . . [However] since the time of Descartes consciousness has been absolutized, as is reflected in our times in phenomenology through Husserl. . . . [But although] [c]onsciousness is not an independent subject, it is central for understanding personal subjectivity. . . . Consciousness interiorizes everything man recognizes, together with what he knows by acts of self-knowledge; it makes all this the content of the subject's experience.[36]

For this reason, *The Acting Person* relativizes consciousness by grounding it within the totality of the person's existence as a being which possesses cognitive, emotional and spiritual capacities, as well as free will and the ability to act (AP 39–59). Upon this basis, Wojtyła is able to reassert a pre-modern understanding of man, suitably modified to encapsulate a non-idealistic and relativized consciousness.

Wojtyła then considers the relationship between existence and acts, and underlines the primacy of the former over the latter, "[f]or it is man, as the dynamic subject, who is their origin" (AP 72). This anti-determinist position is reinforced by Wojtyła's emphasis upon the role of the person's will in realizing objective values, and the part played by reason in guiding

---

35. See Copleston, *Fichte to Nietzsche*, 432–435. For the incompatibility of Husserl's phenomenology and Wojtyła's neo-Thomism, see P. Hebblethwaite, "Husserl, Scheler and Wojtyła: A Tale of Three Philosophers," *Heythrop Journal* 27, no. 4 (1986): 441–445.
36. "The Person: Subject and Community," *Review of Metaphysics* 33, no. 2 (1979): 277–279.

the will: "nothing," claims Wojtyła in a characteristically Thomist expression, "may be the object of will unless it is known" (AP 114).

At the same time, Wojtyła specifies that the person's capacity to recognize values and realize them through freely willed acts does not mean that man is somehow free "from" objective values. Rather, man is free "for" values. Because acts of will involve striving "for" something, they carry within themselves "a form of dependence" on values (AP 132). Nor does choosing simply mean turning towards one value and away from others. It means deciding which of the possible objects presented to the will correspond to *the truth* (AP 137). For this reason, Wojtyła rejects the "logical positivist" argument of A.J. Ayer and others that values are not objects of cognition in the sense that they do not need to be seen as true.[37] The person, Wojtyła insists, has access to the truth through knowledge and, in the wake of knowledge, through freely willed acts (AP 155).

Human freedom is thus understood as more than free choice. It involves man freely acting as he *ought* after ascertaining the truth. Indeed, Wojtyła identifies human happiness ("felicity") "not with the availability of freedom as such but *with the fulfillment of freedom through truth*" (AP 175). Here Wojtyła is at one with *Gaudium et Spes* which, as Ratzinger states, opposes the tendency to confuse freedom with absence of commitment, and underlines man's moral responsibility in opposition to any form of determinism.[38] Freedom, the Council states, is directed to an end: "It is only in freedom that man can turn himself towards what is good." Unfortunately, it adds, "[t]he people of our time often cherish [freedom] improperly, as if it gave them leave to do anything they like." Against such propositions, *Gaudium et Spes* insists that man's dignity involves him "freely attaining his full and blessed perfection" and "freely choosing what is good" (GS 17). In *Dignitatis Humanae*, the Council articulates a similar position, though with a stronger anthropological emphasis: "It is in accordance with their dignity that all men, because they are persons, that is, a being endowed with reason and free will and therefore having personal responsibility, are both impelled by their nature and bound by a moral obligation to seek the truth, especially religious truth" (DH 2). Again, we observe an insistence that reason and free will are, by virtue of what man is, directed towards truth.

Wojtyła proceeds to portray man's capacity to respond freely to moral truth through action as evidence of his spiritual nature. Moral truth,

---

37. See AP 312 n.55.
38. See J. Ratzinger, "The Dignity of the Human Person," in *Commentary*, Vol. V, 139.

Wojtyła says, is "immaterial" in the sense that "it is not flesh" (AP 185). Yet man does "experience" it, most notably through his conscience (AP 154–155). On these grounds, Wojtyła contends that man must have an interior spiritual dimension—something possessed by no other "creature of flesh." Not only does this reveal the person's ultimate anthropological uniqueness (which is, we recall, *The Acting Person*'s aim), but it also underlines, in Wojtyła's view, the indispensability of metaphysics if one wishes to "unravel" man's nature as a being of spirit and flesh (AP 185–186).

The meaning of action is not yet, however, exhaustively discussed. Experience tells us that actions are performed with others. Wojtyła deals with this in *The Acting Person*'s final chapter, entitled "Intersubjectivity and Participation." In Wojtyła's view, "acting together with others" can go wrong. The two extremes to be avoided are "individualism" and "totalism." This echoes the anti-liberal/anti-totalitarian position articulated in "Thomistic Personalism." Lacking a proper concept of the person acting together with others, these systems are portrayed as lacking the correlative concept of "community," a form of social organization in which participation—in the sense that all people are able to "participate" freely in the moral goods available to all—occurs (AP 328–332).

Wojtyła then outlines authentic and non-authentic "attitudes" towards "acting together with others": the former include "solidarity" and "opposition"; the latter embrace "conformism" and "noninvolvement" (AP 341–348). According to Wojtyła, when people act together authentically, they become aware that the "other" is their "neighbor." Here the evangelical commandment of love is evoked, because its structure, Wojtyła maintains, reflects this world of "neighborliness." Wojtyła's *envoi* is the rather un-Marxist suggestion that while alienation may proceed, in part, from man's relationship to the "system of things," it is ultimately derived from man's lack of neighborly love towards others (AP 353–354).

Apart from representing the most systematic expression of Wojtyła's ethical-anthropological ideas, *The Acting Person* provides an insight into his thoughts about much modern philosophical discourse. As well as expressing disapproval of its tendency to neglect the anthropological, Wojtyła insists—in opposition to Ayer and others—that knowledge of truth is critical for man's choice of the good and realization of freedom.

Yet *The Acting Person* also manifests a receptiveness to certain contemporary insights. Alongside using modified phenomenological methods such as "reduction," modern concepts such as "consciousness" and "alienation" are incorporated into the work. *The Acting Person* may thus be said to engage in "dialogue" in the manner envisaged by *Gaudium et Spes*. It acknowledges insights into the truth which emerge outside the Church, and uses language familiar to certain audiences to present arguments about human nature. It may be for this reason that much of *The Acting Person* reads like neo-Thomism couched in Husserlian language. Andrew Wilder, O.P., agrees, suggesting that Wojtyła "is in nearly all of his philosophical efforts continually struggling to express his convictions in concepts and according to divisions which will be understood by and perhaps be convincing to his colleagues in other traditions."[39] In concluding a discussion by Polish intellectuals about *The Acting Person*, Wojtyła implicitly confirmed the validity of this claim by stating "that in his study he brings about some sort of translation from one philosophical language to another."[40]

Reflecting on the Council

As *The Acting Person* is a philosophical work, religious concerns do not overtly intrude upon the text. Wojtyła's 1972 book, *Sources of Renewal*, however, endows certain ideas expressed in *The Acting Person* with a religious character. Its primary purpose was to introduce participants in the Kraków diocesan synod to the Council's documents. To use Wojtyła's own description, "it is not a commentary on the Council documents. . . . This book is rather to be thought of as a *vade-mecum* introducing the reader to the relevant documents of Vatican II" (SR 11).

This may explain why few commentators have given *Sources of Renewal* much attention. The book consists largely of extensive citations from conciliar documents. At many points, Wojtyła simply provides linking passages that carry him safely from one quotation to the next. On these grounds, Hebblethwaite claims that the book does not really provide a glimpse into how Wojtyła interpreted the Council and which of its insights were most important to him.[41]

If, however, *Sources of Renewal* is considered in the context of other Wojtyłan writings, it does provide clues as to where Wojtyła was likely to synthesize his ethical-anthropological ideas with the Council's broader

---

39. A. Wilder, O.P., "Community of Persons in the Thought of Karol Wojtyła," *Angelicum* 56, no. 2/3 (1979): 215.
40. "Słowo końcowe" [Closing Remarks], *Analecta Cracoviensia* 5/6 (1973/1974): 257.
41. See P. Hebblethwaite, *Pope John Paul II and the Church* (Kansas City: National Catholic Reporter, 1995), 84.

themes. The book highlights, for example, *Gaudium et Spes*'s statements about human activity with particular reference to its place in God's creative work (SR 48). As John Paul II, Wojtyła was to focus upon this theme in *Laborem Exercens* and invest it with identifiably Wojtyłan nuances. Throughout *Sources of Renewal*, a similar consonance between Wojtyła's ideas and *Gaudium et Spes* may be observed. Hence, although we need not examine it here in detail, *Sources of Renewal* provides us with useful reference points.

Man in an Incongruous World

The final Wojtyłan work to be considered here is the collection of twenty-two Lenten sermons delivered by Wojtyła to Paul VI and the Roman Curia in March 1976. Published under the title, *Sign of Contradiction* (1976), Wojtyła understands these words to be "a sign of our times, or at least the key to understanding the various symptoms displayed by modern life" (SC 7). The book, then, is especially significant as it reveals much about Wojtyła's view of modernity and which of its "signs" were significant to him shortly before he became pope.

Sign of Contradiction begins by considering man's encounter with the truth of God. This truth, Wojtyła suggests, is contradicted by "the world" and for that very reason needs to be affirmed by the Church as much as possible (SC 8). The three main themes permeating the text elaborate upon this point.

The first motif may be described as the insistence that there is a pre-ordained order, and that modern man's defiance of it is at the root of his problems. Wojtyła utilizes the Genesis narratives to explain why this is so. The creation stories, Wojtyła submits, stress that God is first cause, that He created being and good (SC 21). Wojtyła adds that the covenant which God makes with man in Genesis is based on "God's love for man. At the same time, it is built on truth, rooted in what is real, that is to say, true." In other words, it is based upon an objective order. Wojtyła portrays the tree of knowledge in Genesis as symbolizing this pre-existent order; it signifies that created man is not set beyond the limits of good and evil, "as Nietzsche and other propounders of the autonomy of man would have it" (SC 23).

In the Genesis stories, man did indeed eat of the tree. Wojtyła points out that man did so because the serpent held out for him the prospect of becoming like God (SC 30). This leitmotif of man's hubris is regarded as having special significance for the modern world. "Even in the apparent simplicity of the biblical description," Wojtyła states, "we cannot fail to be struck by the depth, and present-day relevance, of this problem" (SC 31). The world has become "a terrain of rebellion rather than of collaboration with the Creator . . . a terrain for struggle between man and Creator. . . . This is the great drama of history, myth and civilization" (SC 31–32). Such a view puts Wojtyła at odds with those who view history as an "inevitable" progression towards an enlightened humanistic future. Indeed, to Wojtyła's mind, the attempts of Karl Marx and Ludwig Feuerbach to "give everything to man," independently, as it were, of the objective order of good established by God, are merely modern versions of the serpent's temptation (SC 34–35).

But with man "free" of the objective order, Wojtyła proposes that there is nothing to prevent man from being regarded purely as a "mere tool" (SC 34). This is, of course, reminiscent of Dostoevsky's pronouncement that "if there is no God, then everything is permissible." To "abolish" God in order to glorify man is, from Wojtyła's perspective, a nonsense. To this end, he cites de Lubac's argument that the tragedy of atheistic humanism is that it strips man of his transcendental character, thereby destroying his ultimate significance as a person (SC 16),[42] as well as *Gaudium et Spes*'s statement that "forgetfulness of God leaves the creature itself devoid of understanding" (SC 34).[43]

It is, of course, the business of the Catholic Church to inveigh against human attempts to usurp God's place. But, as Tony Judt notes, *Sign of Contradiction* goes much further.[44] Wojtyła uses the arguments outlined above as the basis for his second theme—the contemporary crisis of human knowledge. Looking at the modern world, Wojtyła states, one cannot but marvel at "the speed and acceleration [the word used by the Council] of its progress." In the midst of this, however, he suggests that human thought is becoming disorientated. For despite man subduing the earth to a degree unprecedented in history, Wojtyła states, "when he has extended so very far the 'horizontal' thread of his knowledge, what strikes one most forcibly is a lack of balance in the relation to the 'vertical' component of that knowledge" (SC 11)—that is, cognizance of the transcendental. When it comes to the latter, *Sign of Contradiction* regards modern man as having positively deteriorated.

For one thing, Wojtyła refers to "the problem of the 'divinization' of

---

42. See H. de Lubac, S.J., *The Drama of Atheistic Humanism* (London: Sheed and Ward, 1949).

43. Citing GS 36.

44. See Judt, "Holy Warrior," 11.

matter." Both philosophical and everyday materialism are "doing their best to turn matter into an absolute in human thought" (SC 13). Moreover, Wojtyła maintains that unlike the biblical writers and the thinkers of antiquity who spoke of the Creator or the Prime Mover respectively, "[p]resent-day man . . . does not think things through to the end, does not seek the fundamental reasons *why*." According to Wojtyła, modern man understands reason essentially in terms of "empirical knowledge." What was hitherto accepted as transcendental realities—truth, beauty and goodness—are now dismissed as scientifically unverifiable. In short, man no longer understands the meaning of wisdom. Instead, human knowledge has "chosen to branch off laterally along a minor road, abandoning the main trunk routes" (SC 12). To distinguish wisdom from empirical knowledge, Wojtyła recalls Aquinas's formula: that wisdom goes beyond the empirical by seeking answers to the most essential questions. Metaphysics is therefore the purest expression of wisdom (SC 12–13).

What, then, does Wojtyła consider to be the results of thinking limited to the empirical-material dimension? One consequence is the ambivalent character of modern progress. "Nowadays," he states, "one need only consider the progress made in nuclear physics alongside the attendant folly of armaments" (SC 34). These words suggest that man's refusal to acknowledge the pre-given order of being and goodness has left him morally unhinged. *Any* development produced by science, regardless of its consequences, is considered a priori to be good. In this moral universe, there is no difference between the possible benefits ensuing from greater knowledge of nuclear physics, and the potentially disastrous repercussions of creating nuclear weapons: scientific results are their own justification.

The other major consequence is genuine degeneration. "The word 'progress' is," Wojtyła posits, "on everyone's lips and in everyone's thoughts; but real life confronts us with so much loss, calamity and ruin that one wonders whether, broadly speaking, regress is not triumphing over progress" (SC 156). Manifold examples are provided: abuse of natural resources (SC 156), the West's obsession with material goods, and Third World poverty (SC 157). "There is no lack of literature," Wojtyła submits, "bearing sad witness to 'our century of progress', which has become the age of a new enslavement, the age of the concentration camp and the oven" (SC 157). To explain the essential cause, Wojtyła cites St. Paul: " 'And since they declined to consider knowing God, God left them open to perverse ways of thinking, so that they commit acts that run counter to every law' " (SC 156–157).[45]

It is presumably these criticisms of modern progress which lead Hebblethwaite to describe *Sign of Contradiction* as "an austere, pessimistic work, very conscious of the power of evil, and [marking] a break with the optimism of *Gaudium et Spes*."[46] Certainly, *Sign of Contradiction* contains few positive comments about the modern world. Yet one should remember that the Pastoral Constitution is not a boundlessly optimistic document. Its opening chord refers not only to man's "joy and hope" but also his "grief and anguish" (GS 1). Nor did the Council minimize man's propensity to defy God: "He lifted himself up against God and sought to attain his goal apart from him." Indeed, it spoke of "the whole life of men, both individual and social, [showing] itself to be a struggle, and a dramatic one, between good and evil" (GS 13). *Sign of Contradiction* thus has more in common with *Gaudium et Spes* than Hebblethwaite admits.

In any case, to view *Sign of Contradiction* as thoroughly pessimistic is to ignore its third theme: that man is *not* doomed by the modern world's cognitive disorientation. Man can affirm his fundamental dignity in the face of evil by freely choosing to *live in truth*:

> The dignity proper to man, the dignity that is held out to him both as a gift and as something to be striven for, is inextricably bound up with truth. Truthful thinking and truthful living are the indispensable and essential components of that dignity. (SC 119)

Man's capacities to ascertain what is true and to strive for it through truthful actions, then, are central to resisting evil.[47] But where is the truth to be found? One source, Wojtyła says, is God: "Truth has a divine dimension; it belongs by nature to God himself" (SC 120). The figure and teachings of Christ are highlighted as especially important in this respect. Interestingly, Wojtyła cites the ex-Marxist philosopher, Leszek Kołakowski, in support of this point:

---

45. Citing Rom. 1:28–31.

46. P. Hebblethwaite, *Paul VI: The First Modern Pope* (London: HarperCollins, 1993), 658.

47. The parallels here between Wojtyła's thought and that of certain Central European intellectuals are profound. In 1975, Havel not only posited "living in truth" as the best way to resist the lies underpinning Communist systems, but also traced modernity's problems to its denial of a pre-given natural order. See V. Havel, "It Always Makes Sense to Tell the Truth," *Open Letters* (London: Faber and Faber, 1991), 94–95.

[Christ] proved himself capable of forthrightly expressing the truth, of uncompromisingly defending it all the way, of resisting to the very end the pressures of the establishment that refused to accept him. . . . Thus he was an example of that radical authenticity to which every human being can, with his or her own values, truly devote his or her life. (SC 106)

Another way to find truth is to adopt the attitude of love. God's love, Wojtyła states, was the motive for creation. It is therefore the source of the objective order of good and evil that man encounters in creation (SC 20). Love and truth are thus inseparable, and, Wojtyła believes, can prevail in even the most barbaric instances.

To prove this, Wojtyła refers to the example of the Catholic priest, Maximilian Kolbe. Kolbe was a prisoner in Auschwitz and, as noted, the concentration camp is, in this book, a kind of metaphor for important features of the twentieth century.[48] Wojtyła recalls that Kolbe died "of his own free choice, offering his own life in exchange for that of a fellow prisoner." "And with that particular revelation," Wojtyła states, "there passed through that hell-upon-earth a breath of fearless and indestructible goodness" (SC 51). In giving his life, Kolbe "emasculates" Auschwitz by showing that love of others and the truth is more basic to man than his instinct for physical survival. It is a testament to the power of personal human agency. Thus, in all areas of life, Wojtyła maintains that

we must always rediscover the law of gift. With this principle as basis it will be possible, patiently, but also effectively, to overcome all that has engendered and still does engender the Anti-Love . . . [which] lies at the root of all the ruthless exploitation of men by other men. (SC 58–59)

This advocacy of the power of free choice for truth and love resonates throughout John Paul's encyclicals. So too do many of *Sign of Contradiction*'s concerns about the modern world.

3.4 Catholic Intellectuals in a Marxist State

Most of the works surveyed above were written by a Catholic cleric living

---

48. Meditation on Auschwitz figures in several Wojtyłan articles. See, for example, "Wymowa Oświęcimia" [The Eloquence of Auschwitz], *Notificationes e Curia Metropolitana Cracoviensi* 3/4 (1965): 81–83.

in a Marxist-Leninist state. In a way, this testifies to the unusual nature of Poland's post-war situation. A Communist regime held political power. It co-existed alongside the Catholic Church, to which over ninety percent of the population in some sense belonged and strongly identified with Polish nationhood. Faced with this reality, it is not surprising that, compared to many Communist governments, successive Polish regimes never systematically persecuted the Church.[49] The Catholic episcopate was nevertheless aware of Poland's unfortunate geo-political position. An uneasy, but never ruptured, relationship between church and state was thus maintained, even during Cardinal Wyszyński's detention between 1953–1956.[50] According to Gregory Baum, these unusual circumstances facilitated a dialogue between some Catholic intellectuals and their Marxist counterparts.[51] We intend to clarify here Wojtyła's place in this discussion.

Znak and "Mounier–Personalism"

Jan Kalvoda points out that Wojtyła's encounters with Marxism took place on two levels. As a bishop, he dealt with the reality of a Communist power-structure. But like other Catholic intellectuals, Wojtyła was also confronted with Marxist philosophy.[52] Baum submits that this situation evoked two responses to Marxism from Polish Catholics. Some utterly rejected it, whilst others appreciated certain positive elements in Marxism.[53]

Those who adopted the latter approach, Baum argues, engaged with Marxism from a viewpoint akin to that of the French Catholic thinker Emmanuel Mounier. In Baum's view, Wojtyła was close to this group who wished "to correct and enrich Marxism with the help of personalist insights," and protected them from criticism by anti-Marxist Catholics. Baum suggests that this explains Wojtyła's "Mounier-like" approach to Marxism as pope.[54] He even contends that Wojtyła's own philosophical approach was "*inspired* by the French personalist Emmanuel Mounier, and

---

49. See P. Michel, *Politics and Religion in Eastern Europe* (Cambridge: Polity, 1991).
50. See R. Monticone, *The Catholic Church in Communist Poland* (New York: Columbia University Press, 1986); cf. B. Szajkowski, *Next to God . . . Poland* (London: Pinter, 1983).
51. See Baum, *The Priority*, 3.
52. See J. Kalvoda, "Karol Wojtyła, Marxism, and the Marxist-Leninists," *Nationalities Papers* 10, no. 2 (1982): 203.
53. See Baum, *The Priority*, 3–4.
54. Baum, *The Priority*, 4.

German phenomenologists such as Max Scheler."[55]

The preceding survey of Wojtyła's writings reveals *no* evidence of Wojtyła paying any significant attention to Mounier's thought. Nor is Mounier cited in any Wojtyłan texts. Baum himself provides little evidence to support his thesis.[56] Instead he refers his reader to an article by Mounier biographer John Hellman. Here Hellman claims that Wojtyła had links to what he describes as "[t]he two chief personalist-orientated reviews in Poland, the monthly *Znak* and the weekly *Tygodnik Powszechny*,"[57] both published by the Kraków-based "Znak" Catholic intellectual movement.

Mounier visited Poland in 1946, and later wrote about Poland's "unique opportunity" to reconcile Catholicism and Marxism.[58] In Hellman's view, Mounier's impact upon many Polish Catholic intellectuals was immense because his version of personalism allowed them to engage in dialogue with Marxism: "personalism became of great importance, as one Pole later put it, 'in aiding us to better respond to the fundamental question which was imposed upon us after the war—the attitude of Catholics vis-à-vis the socialist reality.'"[59] These personalists saw "Communism [as] a partially correct response to the injustices of an old feudal order, and the fragmenting individualism of capitalism." According to Hellman, they "called attention to the humanistic values which ran through the writings of the young Karl Marx and juxtaposed them to the aberrations of Stalinism."[60]

Znak or Więź?

Valid points are made in Baum and Hellman's respective articles. Wojtyła was close to the Znak group,[61] which published many of his articles in *Znak* and *Tygodnik Powszechny*. Moreover, when tensions

---

55. Baum, *The Priority*, 15. Italics added.
56. In a later article, Baum concedes that a study of Marxism's impact on the pope's thought requires a reading of Karol Wojtyła's writings. See G. Baum, "The Impact of Marxism on the Thought of John Paul II," *Thought* 62, no. 244 (1987): 26. He then neglects, however, to follow his own advice.
57. J. Hellman, "John Paul II and the Personalist Movement," *Cross Currents* 30, no. 4 (1980/1981): 409.
58. See E. Mounier, "L'ordre regne-t-il a Varsovie?," *Esprit* 6 (1946): 970–1003.
59. Hellman, "John Paul II," 414.
60. Hellman, "John Paul II," 416.
61. See, for example, Kwitny, *Man of the Century*, 124–125.

emerged between some Catholic intellectuals and Cardinal Wyszyński, Wojtyła produced a carefully worded memorandum clarifying the responsibilities of intellectuals vis-à-vis the Church, which largely mollified both parties to the dispute.[62]

But Baum and Hellman's summations of Catholic intellectuals' engagement with Marxism in Poland and Wojtyła's role in it are somewhat misleading. Norbert Zmijewski points out that Znak "never had a consistent and unanimously accepted program on political and social questions,"[63] an interpretation confirmed by *Tygodnik Powszechny* editor, Jerzy Turowicz.[64] Znak's membership, according to Zmijewski, embraced Catholic "conservatives," "liberals," "personalists," and mavericks who defied easy labeling.[65] Znak was also very "[reluctant] to create a bridge between the Marxist and Catholic ideological positions."[66] In *Tygodnik Powszechny*'s first edition, Jan Piwowarczynk suggested that while Catholics had no desire to reconstruct pre-war Polish economic realities, they had no need of Marxist analysis to comprehend reality.[67] Indeed in 1948, a *Tygodnik Powszechny* editorial argued that Mounier's ideas would find little support amongst Catholics precisely because adherence to his personalism could be interpreted as support for Marxism.[68]

If there was a group of "Mounier-inspired" personalists interested in dialogue with Marxists, it was the *Warsaw*-based Więź circle. According to Zmijewski, this organization "followed Mounier's ideas . . . seeking cooperation between groups of different persuasion."[69]

---

62. See "Apostolstwo świeckich" [The Apostolate of the Laity], *Ateneum Kapłańskie* 71, no. 5 (1968): 274–280; cf. G. Blazynski, *Pope John Paul II* (London: Sphere, 1979), 99–101.

63. N. Zmijewski, *The Catholic-Marxist Ideological Dialogue in Poland, 1945-1980* (Sydney: Dartmouth, 1991), 31.

64. See J. Turowicz, *Chrześcijanin we współczesnym świecie* [The Christian in the Modern World] (Kraków: Znak, 1963), 174.

65. See Zmijewski, *The Catholic-Marxist Ideological Dialogue*, chp. 2.

66. Zmijewski, *The Catholic-Marxist Ideological Dialogue*, 73.

67. See J. Piwowarczynk, "Ku Katolickiej Polsce," *Tygodnik Powszechny* 1, no. 1 (1945): 1.

68. See "Redakcyjny," *Tygodnik Powszechny* 4, no. 25 (1948): 5. Nor were Znak members afraid to highlight French Catholicism's twentieth-century failures. In *Znak*'s first edition, Stanisław Stomma compared the evident strength of Polish Catholicism throughout society with French Catholicism's weakness in this area. Despite its intellectual accomplishments, Stomma stated, French Catholicism had plainly failed to inspire the masses. See S. Stomma, "Maksymalne i minimale tendencjé społeczne w Polsce," *Znak* 1, no. 1 (1945): 12.

69. Zmijewski, *The Catholic-Marxist Ideological Dialogue*, 74. See also T. Mazowiecki [Więź founder and first post-war non-Communist Polish prime minister], *Rozdroża i*

The Polish left-liberal, Adam Michnik, presents a similar picture. He portrays Znak as primarily interested in creating a "space" for people that was not dominated by party propaganda.[70] It remained, then, open to the world. Nevertheless its leaders, Michnik adds, remained skeptical of the willingness of non-believers to take seriously the views of anyone who believed in God.[71] Confirmation may be found in Turowicz's suggestion that the logic of any non-believer's position inevitably leads them to hope that "all those false convictions, all that mystification so inseparably bound up with religion and the Church, should finally get out of the path of reason and progress once and for all."[72] The preface to the book in which Turowicz made this comment was, incidentally, provided by the then-Archbishop Wojtyła. Więź, on the other hand, are depicted by Michnik as interested in dialogue with Marxist intellectuals, but gradually becoming very critical of Marxist thought.[73]

Both Baum and Hellman's presentations, then, of Znak as a "personalist" grouping are very dubious. They may have even confused Znak with Więź. This naturally raises questions about many of the presumptions underlying their picture of Wojtyła.

Other evidence suggests that neither Wojtyła's mindset nor his approach to Marxism can be labeled that of a "Mounier-personalist." It cannot be said that the "Marxist" writings cited in Wojtyła's works are used in such a manner. We have already seen that *Sign of Contradiction* cites Kołakowski's 1965 article, "Jesus Christ: Prophet and Reformer"[74] to underline the need to live in truth. Wojtyła did not, however, endorse in the process any aspect of Kołakowski's Marxist thought. In any case, by 1965, Kołakowski was more than mid-point in his journey from being a self-described "personal enemy of God" to viewing Catholicism as one of the few surviving guarantors of objective norms.[75]

Another instance is to be found in Wojtyła's 1977 article, "Participation or Alienation." Here Wojtyła cites a work by the Polish

wartości [Crossroads and Values] (Warszawa: Więź, 1970).

70. See A. Michnik, *Letters from Prison and Other Essays* (Berkeley: University of California Press, 1986), 46.

71. Michnik, *Letters*, 127.

72. Turowicz, *Chrześcijanin*, 25.

73. See A. Michnik, *The Church and the Left* (Chicago: University of Chicago Press, 1993), 183–185.

74. See L. Kołakowski, "Jezus Chrystus—prorok i reformator" [Jesus Christ: Prophet and Reformer], *Argumenty* 51/52 (1965): 19–26.

75. See Michnik, *The Church*, 190–191; J. Tischner, *Marxism and Christianity* (Washington, D.C.: Georgetown University Press, 1987), 129–137.

Marxist revisionist, Adam Schaff, to support his claim that transferring the question of alienation beyond man to his products actually increases alienation.[76] This use of a Marxist's ideas to challenge the general Marxist understanding of the nature of alienation hardly constitutes a case of "enriching Marxist insights."

As far as the impact of Catholic-Marxist dialogue upon Wojtyła is concerned, the subject is only mentioned twice in his writings, and neither instance lends support to Baum and Hellman's contentions. In *Sign of Contradiction*, Wojtyła recalls that he could

> remember several publications, typical of the early post-war years in Poland, in which Catholic intellectuals in argument with Marxists demonstrated that matter cannot have the character of any absolute. Arguments of that type have died down . . . although the Marxist *weltanschauung* and system go on asserting that matter constitutes the be-all and end-all of man. (SC 13)

The literature suggests that Wojtyła was referring to the responses of Kazimierz Kłósak, Stefan Świeżawski and other Thomists from the Jagiellonian's Theology Faculty and the Catholic University of Lublin, to dialectical materialist theses promoted by Kołakowski and Schaff.[77] In *Crossing the Threshold of Hope*, the Pope recalls how Kłósak comprehensively refuted Marxist dialectical materialism in the post-war years.[78] In short, it would seem that part of the Catholic-Marxist dialogue served to convince Wojtyła that Marxism suffered from profound epistemological flaws.

The second reference to Catholic-Marxist engagement occurs in *Crossing the Threshold of Hope*. Here John Paul briefly mentions that his "concern for 'the acting person' did not arise from the disputes with Marxism, or, at least, not as a direct response to those disputes."[79] One is, of course, bound to wonder if this disputation (a more polemical word than "dialogue") with Marxism shaped *The Acting Person* more than John Paul recalls. It should be understood, however, that by the time of this book's

---

76. See "Participation or Alienation," *Analecta Husserliana* 6 (1977): 72–73 n.9 referring to A. Schaff, *Markism i jednostka ludza* [Marxism and the Human Individual] (Warszawa: PWN, 1965), 176–195.

77. See Zmijewski, *The Catholic-Marxist Ideological Dialogue*, chp.1; Tischner, *Marxism*, chp.15.

78. See *Crossing*, 198.

79. *Crossing*, 199.

publication (1969), fewer and fewer Polish intellectuals were taking Marxism seriously. Tischner claims that in the Poland of the mid-1960s, "in the broader humanistic education, especially at the universities, nothing was left of Marxism but the label."[80] Nothing more poignantly symbolized this than Kołakowski's famous Warsaw University lecture of October 1966, in which his assessment of Marxism was so critical that he was expelled from the Party.

The same period was marked, in Tischner's view, by an intense resurgence in Catholic intellectual activity:

> the post-conciliar period brought an extraordinary revival of philosophical and theological discussion. Christian thought embarked on a broad dialogue with the positive sciences, reaching out to phenomenology and hermeneutics, drew life from the ideas of existentialists, made use of positivist methodology. . . . Against the background of a severe paralysis of Marxist thought still struggling and searching for self-identity, Christian thought had the attraction of wide-open horizons.[81]

In light of the preceding outline of Wojtyła's writings, it would appear that many of the openings to which Tischner refers, were more significant to Wojtyła than an engagement with a Marxism repudiated by some of its previously most prominent advocates.

The Lublin Influence

Another problem with Baum and Hellman's theses is that they ignore Wojtyła's Lublin background. The Catholic University of Lublin was the only non-state university in the Communist bloc. It was also the home of the Lublin school of philosophy, which Schaff described as "the greatest threat to Polish Marxism."[82] According to Andrew Woźnicki:

> *Lublin Thomism, Lublin Existentialism,* or *Lublin Existential Personalism* is a striking synthesis of . . . (1) Thomist realist metaphysics, as interpreted by Etienne Gilson and Jacques Maritain and (2) the best insights of contemporary phenomenological existentialism and hermeneutics.[83]

---

80. Tischner, *Marxism*, 75.
81. Tischner, *Marxism*, 75.
82. A. Schaff, cited in A. Woźnicki, *A Christian Humanism* (New Britain: Mariel Publications, 1980), v.
83. A. Woźnicki, Translator's Foreword, in M. Krąpiec, *I-Man: An Outline of Philosophical*

The Lublinists' attention to Aquinas did not therefore entail simply the repetition of Thomist principles. It was creative and willing to incorporate contemporary insights, and thus in the spirit of Leo XIII's *Aeterni Patris*.

In his account of Wojtyła's contribution to "Lublinism," Stefan Świeżawski—a Lublin historian of philosophy—states that Poland's experiences during World War II forced Catholic intellectuals to ask what made man capable of both profoundly evil acts and superhuman examples of love. This created a preoccupation with that fundamental anthropological question: *Quid est homo?*[84]

According to Świeżawski, the attempts of many Catholic scholars to provide an answer produced an awareness of "the philosophical poverty of idealistic and materialistic systems, on the one hand, and the need for reflecting on fully authentic reality on the other."[85] This suggests that they were dissatisfied with Kantian idealism as well as its materialist "corrective" epitomized by Marx. The effect, Świeżawski claims, was that many Polish Catholic intellectuals

> called into question the value of the whole subjective current of European philosophizing in the modern age and directed keen interest toward classical philosophy, both ancient and medieval. Medieval thought ceased being merely an interesting area for historical research and began to attract various minds precisely because of its decidedly objective character.[86]

The center for Catholic thinkers committed to this "return" to premodern thought was the Catholic University of Lublin. Świeżawski states that Wojtyła was specifically recruited to its philosophy department because his "ethical, anthropological, and metaphysical interests predisposed him completely to our circle."[87] As a group, the Lublin philosophers shared a commitment to affirming the primacy of realistic metaphysics in philosophy, underlining the significance of philosophical anthropology, rediscovering the "true" Aquinas, and applying his ideas to

---

Anthropology (New Britain: Mariel Publications, 1983), v.

84. See S. Świeżawski, "Karol Wojtyła at the Catholic University of Lublin," in *Person and Community*, T. Sandok, O.S.M., ed. and tr. (New York: Peter Lang Publishing, 1993), ix–x. See also J. Seifert, "Karol Cardinal Wojtyła (Pope John Paul II) as Philosopher and the Cracow/Lublin School of Philosophy," *Aletheia* 2 (1981): 130–199.

85. Świeżawski, "Karol Wojtyła," x.

86. Świeżawski, "Karol Wojtyła," x–xi.

87. Świeżawski, "Karol Wojtyła," xii.

contemporary problems.[88] Wojtyła's specific contribution was to prevent Lublinism from becoming "distorted by focussing exclusively on the contemplative side and neglecting the whole sphere of activity."[89]

3.5 Conclusion

Though brief, the preceding summary of the Lublin philosophical school demonstrates that its basic commitments are reflected in Wojtyła's writings, as is its use of phenomenological and existential insights. In reviewing Wojtyła's major publications, we have seen that a fidelity to Thomist principles prevails throughout. It is also clear, however, that his thought was enriched by contemporary non-Catholic insights. Yet this openness to modern ideas did not inhibit Wojtyła from highlighting those aspects of modernity which troubled him.

We may say, then, that the ideas expressed in Wojtyła's writings are distinctive. This does not necessarily mean that they are "original." It may even be the case that none of his thoughts are original, or that others have articulated them in slightly different ways. But for our purposes, this is not important. The configurations of ideas and language in Wojtyła's writings are sufficiently specific for them to be identifiable as influences upon developments in Catholic social teaching.

In his study of Wojtyła's writings, Buttiglione suggests that Wojtyła's work is incomplete.[90] Perhaps if Wojtyła had remained a professor of ethics, he would have further refined his ideas. As it was, Wojtyła was called to another service—but one in which he could employ the same insights, though in a different context, and for a larger audience. This had particular consequences for Catholic social teaching about work.

---

88. Świeżawski, "Karol Wojtyła," xii–xiii.
89. Świeżawski, "Karol Wojtyła," xiv.
90. See Buttiglione, *Karol Wojtyła*, 306.

4
WORK:
THE KEY TO THE
SOCIAL QUESTION

4.1 Introduction

While classical moral thought dealt at length with responsibilities regarding property, it paid little attention to responsibilities regarding work.[1] Charles agrees, adding that labor was accorded greater respect in the Jewish world than in Romano-Hellenic cultures. Christianity, he suggests, inherited and maintained this regard throughout the ages.[2]

Catholic social teaching continues this tradition, with John Paul II commemorating *Rerum Novarum's* ninetieth anniversary with an encyclical on work in 1981. Here the Council's teaching about the creativity of work as well as work's effects upon man and his world are compared with corresponding statements in *Laborem Exercens*. We then assess the Wojtyłan influence upon identified developments in teaching.

4.2 Work, Genesis, and Creation

Notwithstanding Christianity's traditional emphasis on work's dignity, one is bound to ask why John Paul devotes an encyclical to the topic. The pope

---

1. See Grisez, *Living*, 754.
2. See Charles, *The Social Teaching*, 312–313.

himself indicates that he is responding to profound social changes. The world, he states, is "on the eve of new developments in technological, economic and political conditions which . . . will influence the world of work and production no less than the industrial revolution of the last century." Whilst noting that "it is not for the Church to analyze scientifically the consequences these changes may have on human society," the pope insists that it is the Church's task "to help to guide the changes so as to ensure authentic progress by man and society" (LE 1). A sense that man is loosing a proper understanding of what constitutes true progress permeates, we recall, Karol Wojtyła's later writings. It soon becomes apparent that *Laborem Exercens* underlines what John Paul regards as "fundamental truths" about work, as if to remind people what constitutes the most important progress that man ought to realize through work: the acquisition of moral good and dominion over himself as a person.

Nevertheless when *Laborem Exercens* appeared, some were unsure as to why John Paul had promulgated an encyclical on work. Hebblethwaite for one was puzzled. It was, in his opinion, "a long time since anyone has dared to address the Church and 'all men of good will' on a topic of such vast generality."[3] This statement is not, however, strictly true. Preconciliar magisterial teaching certainly considered work in detail.[4] The Council also examined the issue, placing it at the heart of *Gaudium et Spes*'s theological anthropology of man.

Man's Co-creative Activity

Gaudium et Spes's central teachings about work are contained in the chapter, "Man's Activity in the Universe." Though human activity is the focus of the Council's attention, work is the paradigm of activity considered. Work, as presented in this section of the Pastoral Constitution, allows man to fulfil his "double vocation"—the exercise of dominion over the earth and the direction of this dominion to affirmation of the Creator.

> Throughout the course of the centuries, men have labored to better the circumstances of their lives through a monumental amount of individual and collective effort. To believers, this point is settled: considered in itself,

---

3. Hebblethwaite, "The Popes and Politics," 85.
4. See J-V. Calvez, S.J., and J. Perrin, S.J., *The Church and Social Justice* (London: Burn and Oates, 1961), chp.X.

such human activity accords with God's will. For man, created to God's image, received a mandate to subject to himself the earth and all that it contains, and to govern the world with justice and holiness [refers to Gen. 1:26–27; 9:2–3]; a mandate to relate himself and the totality of things to Him who was to be acknowledged as the Lord and Creator of all. Thus, through the dominion of all things by man, the name of God would be made wonderful through all the earth.

This holds good also for even the most ordinary every-day activities. For, while providing the substance of life for themselves and their families, men and women are performing their activities in a way which appropriately benefits society. They can justly consider that by their labor they are unfolding the Creator's work, serving their brothers and sisters, and contributing by their personal industry to the realization in history of the divine plan. (GS 34)

The reference to Genesis in this extract is important. In Paul Ricoeur's view, "the 'Adamic' myth is *the* anthropological myth *par excellence*."[5] In any event, it certainly provides the text above with its understanding of man as the *imago Dei* given dominion over the world. This dominion, however, is not absolute, as the "mandate" given to man involves relating himself and all things towards the One who endows him with dominion. It is in realizing this dominion that work is critical. No matter how "ordinary" its character, work permits man to actualize his dominion over the world by unfolding the Creator's work. Human work is therefore understood as *proceeding from* and *co-operative with* God's creative Act.

The Truth about Work

Novak

Following *Laborem Exercens*'s promulgation, Michael Novak described it as rooting the magisterium's understanding of work "in the biblical category of creation or, more precisely, co-creation."[6] The preceding section shows, however, that this view of work was integral to magisterial teaching about work before *Laborem Exercens*. Indeed, to underline this encyclical's continuity with the Council, John Paul incorporates the first part of *Gaudium et Spes*'s paragraph 34 into his text under the heading, "Work as a sharing in the activity of the Creator" (LE 25).[7]

---

5. P. Ricoeur, *The Symbolism of Evil* (Boston: Beacon Press, 1967), 232.
6. M. Novak, "Creation Theology," in *Co-Creation*, 17.
7. Here one should note the French Catholic contribution to the conciliar magisterium's

[handwritten margin notes: "Theological underpinning", "using", "Genesis", "relate work to creation"]

Like the Council, John Paul defines work as a divinely ordained activity:

> work means any activity by man, whether manual or intellectual, whatever its nature or circumstances; it means any human activity that can and must be recognized as work, in the midst of all the many activities of which man is capable. . . . Man is made to be in the visible universe an image and likeness of God himself [refers to Gen 1:26], and he is placed in it in order to subdue the earth [refers to Gen 1:28]. From the beginning therefore he is *called to work.* (LE 0)

The second half of this citation underlines the importance of Genesis's first chapter for *Laborem Exercens*'s statements about man and his work. Indeed, John Paul stresses how well "the very first pages" of Genesis encapsulate the truth about man:

> An analysis of these texts makes us aware that they express . . . the fundamental truths about man. . . . These truths are decisive for man from the very beginning, and at the same time they trace out the main lines of his earthly existence, both in the state of original justice and also after the breaking, caused by sin, of the Creator's original covenant with creation in man. (LE 4)

Laborem Exercens then focuses upon the two Genesis verses in which man is described as created "in the image of God . . . male and female" (Gen 1:27) and told to "Be Fruitful and multiply, and fill the earth and subdue it" (Gen 1:28). These verses, John Paul states, "indirectly indicate [work] as an activity for man to carry out in the world." They also specify that "[m]an is the image of God partly through the mandate received from his Creator to subdue, to dominate, the earth. In carrying out this mandate, man, every human being, reflects the very action of the Creator of the universe" (LE 4).

John Paul's position is thus the same as the Council's. As Alberto Gini

---

focus upon work. The French interest in work may be traced to figures associated with the *nouvelle théologie* of the 1940s and 50s, such as Chenu, Congar, de Lubac and Jean Daniélou, S.J.—all of whom played significant roles at the Council. Their attention to work arose from recognition of the Church's loss of the French working class, a desire to assist intellectually the French worker-priest experiment, as well as their belief that Catholics had to contribute more to discussion about a subject to which Marxism had directed much attention. On these matters, see M.-D. Chenu, O.P., *Pour une théologie du travail* (Paris: Editions du Seuil, 1955).

" co-creation" never used

states: "Although *Laborem Exercens* never uses the terms 'co-creation' or 'co-creator', John Paul II makes it clear that the divine action of creativity and human work are dynamically interrelated."[8]

It is, of course, theologically risky to link human work directly with God's activity. Karl Barth, for one, maintains that while man can in some sense participate in God's activity, this "does not mean that he becomes a kind of co-God."[9] To this, one may add that viewing human work as "co-creative" risks trivializing God's creative Act.

John Paul, however, avoids such objections:

> As man, through his work, becomes more and more the master [*dominus*] of the earth, and as he confirms his dominion over the visible world, again through his work, he nevertheless remains in every case and at every phase of this process within the Creator's original ordering [*ordinatio*]. And this ordering remains necessarily and indissolubly linked with the fact that man was created, as male and female, "in the image of God". (LE 4)

The message here is unambiguous. Man and his work remain dependent upon God because God is and remains first cause: *Actus Purus*. Thus there can be no question of a "co-Godship." Moreover, the extract above presents man's subordination to God and His divine order as a theological-anthropological truth about his nature as *imago Dei*. For if man is the *imago Dei* then, by definition, both he and his work remain subject to God's original ordering—indeed, this ordering permeates man's very nature. It follows that if human work is to reflect this truth about man, then it must at all times and in each instance conform to God's original ordering. While such a position is surely implicit to the Council's statements, John Paul uses it to underline the moral significance of *every* work-act for man.

Hauerwas gen?

In a piece critical of *Laborem Exercens*, Stanley Hauerwas asks why John Paul bases his arguments upon Genesis "when other texts of scripture might be equally relevant or even more appropriate."[10] Part of the answer should already be evident. The pope believes that these texts are fundamental if man is to arrive at a truthful understanding of his nature and his work. In this connection, there is much to suggest that Wojtyłan emphases have influenced *Laborem Exercens*.

rf to nature

Impt to focus

---

8. A. Gini, "Meaningful Work and the Rights of the Workers," *Thought* 67, no. 266 (1992): 230.
9. K. Barth, *Church Dogmatics*, Bk. 3, Vol. IV (Edinburgh: T. and T. Clark, 1961), 482.
10. S. Hauerwas, "Work as Co-creation," in *Co-Creation*, 43.

On nature and ordering

Creation and Truth

Though they do not refer to Genesis, Wojtyła's pre-conciliar writings explore the relationship between human and divine creativity. *Love and Responsibility* stresses that if man harmonizes his activity with God's created order, then he affirms his dignity and participates in God's eternal design:

> God is the Creator, and so all beings in the universe, creatures in general and man in particular, owe their existence to Him. Not only is God the Creator, the constant renewer of existence, but the essences of all creatures derive from Him and reflect the eternal thoughts and plans of God. . . . Man, by understanding the order of nature and conforming to it in his actions, participates in the thought of God, becomes *particeps Creatoris*, and has a share in the law which God bestowed on the world when He created it at the beginning of time. (LR 246–247)

Whilst Wojtyła's reasoning proceeds from a more overt natural law basis, it closely resembles that of *Laborem Exercens*. God is first cause of everything and has ordered all things, including man, in a particular way "from the very beginning." Man's uniqueness lies in the fact that he can understand this order of nature and thus his own place in it. He can therefore conform his actions to this original ordering. This confers upon man the ability to participate in God's thought and plans: the dignity of *particeps Creatoris*.

Though this expression does not quite conceptualize man as a "co-creator," it falls not far short of this. In "Thomistic Personalism," Wojtyła moves closer to this position:

> In creating we also fill the external material world around us with our own thought and being. There is a certain similarity here between ourselves and God, for the whole of creation is an expression of God's thought and being.[11]

Several of these pre-conciliar ideas mature in Wojtyła's post-conciliar writings. In *Sources of Renewal*, Wojtyła claims that for the Council

---

11. "Thomistic Personalism," 670–671.

[t]he idea that "material being does not depend on God" is basically at variance with the truth and message of creation, as if one were to say that "created things are not created." . . . The dogma of creation defines reality itself in the profoundest way. Not only does the concept of "creation" make no sense without that of a Creator, but the reality which we thus define cannot exist without Him who gave it life and continually keeps it in being . . . Hence the "autonomy of earthly affairs," if conceived as a negation of God the Creator, is at the same time a negation of creatures and a denial of their ontological character . . . this leads to a fundamental disorientation of man's cognitive and active powers. (SR 50–51)

On one level this passage suggests that logical inconsistencies underlie the rejection of God as first cause. But it also provides us with a clue as to why *Laborem Exercens* is so insistent upon this point: the denial of God as Creator leaves man bereft of a *truthful* understanding of what he *is*. This profoundly disorders human knowledge and acts.

Sign of Contradiction continues this assertion of a God-centered order via a commentary upon the same chapter of Genesis from which the Council derives its anthropology of human work. To grasp Genesis's significance for Wojtyła, one need only note his comment that

unless one does reflect upon that fundamental ensemble of facts and situations it becomes difficult—if not impossible—to understand man and the world. . . . I think it is true, that today one cannot understand either Sartre or Marx without having first read and pondered very deeply the first three chapters of Genesis. These are the key to understanding the world of today, both its roots and its extremely radical—and therefore dramatic— affirmations and denials. (SC 24)

The use of the word "fundamental" in regard to Genesis reappears in *Laborem Exercens*'s description of this text. Indeed, some of the "fundamental facts" that Wojtyła identifies in Genesis prefigure the encyclical's emphasis that man's dominion over the world does not mean that he is somehow "beyond" God's original ordering.

For a start, Wojtyła contends that Genesis 1:26 (cited by both the Council and *Laborem Exercens*) demonstrates that man's dominion is dependent upon God: "This dominion extends over all that man little by little succeeds in deriving from the earth." "But," Wojtyła cautions, "even when . . . man reaches the moon, he can only do this by virtue of the first covenant, from which and thanks to which he received the prerogative of dominion" (SC 23). Nor is there any doubt in Wojtyła's mind that Genesis underscores the "secondary" character of human acts:

> "And God saw that it was good." This divine "seeing" is in every way primary, because it creates being and good and also ensures their continuance within time: *conservatio est continua creatio*. Human seeing and human doing are always secondary because they are always concerned with something already provided: they always encounter pre-constituted being and value. (SC 21)

These words not only depict God as first cause, but stress that human reason and acts (seeing and doing) *always* encounter the pre-constituted order of good and being. This is precisely the position underscored by *Laborem Exercens* in relation to acts of work.

Given, then, John Paul's emphasis that man is eternally subject to God's original ordering, it is little wonder that he explains *how* man, through work, may freely conform to this order and thereby realize moral good. Whilst *Laborem Exercens*'s development of teaching on this matter owes much to *Gaudium et Spes*, distinctly Wojtyłan influences are also detectable.

4.3 Work: Inner Person and Outer World

In *Gaudium et Spes*, the Council explains that human work simultaneously shapes its immediate initiator as well as the world in which man lives:

> Just as human activity proceeds from man, so it is ordered to man. For when a man works, he not only alters things and society, he develops himself as well [*se ipsum perficit*]. He learns much, he cultivates his resources, he goes outside of himself and beyond himself [*extra se et supra se*]. Rightly understood, this kind of growth is of greater value than any external riches which can be garnered. It is what a man is, rather than what he has, that counts. (GS 35)

perfectly

Chenu interprets this passage as indicating that in building up the world, man can simultaneously perfect himself.[12] He omits to specify, however, that work's transforming effect upon man is considered more important than its external impact. Recognition of this priority is crucial. It suggests that the true "building of the world" can only proceed from man's struggle

---

12. See Chenu, "A Council for All Peoples," 21.

for personal perfection.

Precisely what the Council believes man should "become" through work is obviously more than "personal development." It involves some degree of transcendence (*extra se et supra se*) "beyond" himself. As previously observed, the Council has in mind man's self-actualization of the goods of his own nature: dignity, communion, and freedom (GS 39).

4.4 The Person: The Subject of Work

The Council's attention to the good attained through work is replicated in *Laborem Exercens*. According to John Paul, work is "probably the *primary* [*primarium*] *key*, to the whole social question, if we try to see that question really from the point of view of man's good" (LE 3). But *how*, one may ask, does man become good through work?

In this respect, the encyclical's description of the creative process whereby man confirms his dominion through work becomes important. According to the pope, this process is

> *universal*: it embraces all human beings, every generation, every phase of economic and cultural development, and *at the same time* it is a process which takes place *within each human being*, in each conscious human subject. (LE 4)

Here John Paul indicates that by working, each man may realize dominion not only over the world but also *over himself*: the "conscious human subject."

Laborem Exercens's use of the adjective "conscious" in this context is revealing. It suggests that man cannot help being *aware* of his work's internal and external effects. This, of course, underlines man's responsibility for his work and its impact on himself and the world. The encyclical goes on to state that the ethical value of work "remains linked to the fact that the one who carries it out is a person, a conscious and free subject, that is to say a subject that decides about himself [*de se ipso deliberans*]" (LE 6). Thus it is not only the fact that man is a knowing subject, but also the reality that this subject makes *free choices about himself* when working, that makes work morally significant for man and responsible for himself. This is critical for comprehending John Paul's teaching on how man shapes himself through work. Before explaining this, however, it is necessary to distinguish between what the pope calls work's "objective" and "subjective" dimensions.

Work in "the Objective Sense" and the Object

Laborem Exercens initially describes work in the objective sense as "[w]ork understood as a 'transitive' activity, that is to say an activity beginning in the human subject and directed towards an external object" (LE 4). Whilst these words parallel *Gaudium et Spes*'s position that work shapes the outside world, they add precision to the teaching about how this occurs. The identification of man as subject distinguishes man as the *support* and *predicate* of his work.[13] It is on these ontological and logical premises that one can say, as the Council does, that "work proceeds from man." Moreover, John Paul's specification that work's transitive dimension involves its direction to an external object, indicates that work proceeds from the human subject when he freely chooses an object, perhaps from a range of possible objects.

Paragraph 5 of *Laborem Exercens* elaborates upon the meaning of work as a "transitive" activity. Here the pope speaks of "the meaning of work in an objective sense, which finds expression in the various epochs of culture and civilization." He then details how man has gradually progressed through history to cultivating the earth and transforming its products through agriculture, industry, service enterprises, and his use of technology (LE 5).

Work in the objective sense, then, expresses man's dominion over the world and the ensuing material progress. *Laborem Exercens* itself denotes work's transitive-objective dimension as presupposing "a specific dominion by man over "the earth," and, in its turn, it confirms and develops this dominion" (LE 4). It is therefore something to be valued.

Work in "the Subjective Sense" and the Subject

Laborem Exercens then considers what may be called work's *intransitive* dimension: work in the subjective sense.

·

13. See D. Bigongiari (ed.), *The Political Ideas of St. Thomas Aquinas* (New York: Hafner Press, 1981), Glossary, 214: "Subject: In the logical sphere it is that concept of which something must be predicated and which itself cannot be a predicate. In its ontological sense it is correlative to accident; the support of an accident, be that support another and more basic accident, or, ultimately, the substance, is called *subject*." The use of subject in LE conforms to both senses of the word. Man is the "support" of work; at the same time, work is "predicated upon" man.

Man has to subdue the earth and dominate it, because as the "image of God" he is a person, that is to say, a subjective being [*animans subiectivus*] capable of acting in a planned and rational way [*capax ad agendum ratione praestituta et rationali*], capable of deciding about himself [*capax ad deliberandum de se*] and with a tendency to self-realization [*eoque contendens ut se ipsum perficiat*]. *As a person, man is therefore the subject of work.* As a person he works [*opus facit*], he performs various actions [*actiones*] belonging to the work process; independently of their objective content, these actions must all serve to realize his humanity, to fulfil the calling to be a person that is his by reason of his very humanity [*vocationi, ex qua est persona quaeque vi ipsius humanitatis eius et propria*]. (LE 6)

This paragraph is crucial. First, it grounds work's "interior effect" in Genesis's dominion motif. Secondly, it explains that man's work has an "intransitive" effect upon him, an effect which begins with man's use of his unique capacities as a person and a subjective being; that is, *acting* (the property of a subject) as his *reason* tells him and making decisions, or what one may call exercising his *will* (properties of a person). In other words, when the person-subject acts, he not only chooses an external object; he simultaneously makes a choice about himself.

The above extract also indicates that fulfilling oneself through work-actions is not doing whatever one wills. Free will is certainly important because man is identified as only having a "tendency to self-realization." However, *Laborem Exercens* also defines self-realization in terms of man attaining that which is his by virtue of his very humanity—"his calling" to be *a person*. To use an Aristotelian-Thomistic analogy, self-realization through work involves man as the subject of work actualizing his potential as a person. It means *always* choosing to do what one *ought* to do as a person, as the *imago Dei* called upon to realize dominion over the world and oneself.

The word "person," of course, features in Catholic social teaching long before *Laborem Exercens*. What is significant, however, about the above extract is its emphasis upon the link between man's status as the subject of work and his status as a person. Not only do the human subject's acts of work suddenly assume a significance beyond their objective effects, but the reader is reminded that man's spiritual dimension—of which his intellect and free will are aspects (see GS 14, 15, 17)—is part of the subject from which work-acts proceed. One might say then that the human subject's work-acts are always an act of the person. Indeed, John Paul makes precisely this point: "Since work in its subjective aspect is always a personal action, an *actus personae*, it follows that *the whole person, body and spirit*, participates in it" (LE 24).

This attention to man's nature as the person-subject is not as evident in *Gaudium et Spes*'s teaching on human activity. For John Paul, however, it serves to deepen understanding of why work's "inner-subjective" dimension (what the Council calls "developing oneself") is more important than its "outer-objective" aspect (the Council's "altering of things"). To cite him at length on this matter:

> the basis for determining the value of human work is not primarily the kind of work being done but the fact that one who is doing it is a person. The sources of the dignity of work are to be sought primarily in the subjective dimension, not the objective one. . . . This does not mean that, from the objective point of view, human work cannot and must not be rated in any way. It only means that *the primary basis of the value of work is man himself* who is its subject. . . . Through this conclusion one rightly comes to recognize the pre-eminence of the subjective meaning of work over the objective one. (LE 6)

In light of these statements, we may say that since the human subject's work in the intransitive-subjective sense always involves the formation of man's character as a person, it is *always* more significant than work's transitive-objective dimension. Man's achievement of dominion over himself through work is, in short, more important than the same work's effects upon the world. As if to underline the point, John Paul states that "in the final analysis it is always man who is the purpose [*scopus*] of the work, whatever work it is . . . even if the common scale of values rates it as the merest 'service,' as the most monotonous, or work which puts one on the margins of society" (LE 6).[14]

These words are consistent with the Council's insistence in *Gaudium et Spes*'s paragraph 35 that just as activity proceeds from man, it is also ordered towards him. They also suggest that, besides being the subject of work, man is also its final object. For when the subject freely directs his work to an object, he simultaneously makes a choice which is "directed to" himself as a person, as it is only by "passing through" the subject that an act of will is able to "reach" an object.

In *Laborem Exercens*'s ninth paragraph, the pope specifies that man's

---

14. The English translation uses the words "even the most alienating." This is misleading. Alienation is different from marginalization. The Italian translation is better, using the word *emarginante*. In any case, the Latin is clear enough: "*in societatis partes secundarias potissimum detrudente*."

Moral growth & goal

self-realization as a person through work involves the acquisition of moral good. John Paul begins by stating that Genesis 3:19 "refers to *the sometimes heavy toil* that . . . has accompanied human work." This aspect of Genesis is mentioned by neither the Council nor Paul VI. Whilst it features in the teachings of Pius XI and Pius XII about work, their emphasis is upon explaining toil in terms of the consequences of original sin.[15] Whilst John Paul does not ignore this aspect (LE 27), he also places it in the context of acquiring virtue:

> in spite of all this toil—perhaps, in a sense, because of it—work is a good thing for man. Even though it bears the mark of a *bonum arduum* in the terminology of St. Thomas [refers to ST, I-II, q.40, a.1c; I-II, q.34, a.2, ad 1], this does not take away the fact that, as such, it is a good thing for man. It is not only good in the sense that it is useful [*bonum utile*] or something to enjoy [*bonum fruedum*]; it is also good as being something worthy [*dignum*], that is to say, something that corresponds to man's dignity, that expresses this dignity and increases it. If one wishes to define more clearly the ethical meaning of work, it is this truth that one must particularly keep in mind. Work is a good thing for man [*bonum hominis*] . . . because through work man *not only transforms nature* . . . but he also *achieves fulfillment* as a human being [*se ipsum ut hominem perficit*] and indeed, in a sense, becomes "more a human being."
>
> Without this consideration it is impossible to understand the meaning of the virtue of industriousness, and why . . . industriousness should be a virtue: for virtue, as a moral habit, is something whereby man becomes good as man [refers to ST, I-II, q.40, a.1c; I-II, q.34, a.2, ad 1]. (LE 9)

"Toil" in this context indicates that the person's self-realization through work in the subjective sense is not easy. Nevertheless, partly because of the toil, the good achieved through work is precious. The good, however, that the pope has in mind is more important that the utility or pleasure that work may bring. Work *itself* is understood as a good because in and of itself it lets man fulfil himself as he meant to: that is, by freely choosing to develop virtues, understood in the Thomist sense of the word, such as industriousness. These moral-spiritual goods are the most worthy [*dignum*] of man, because they express man's potential for perfection.

Summarizing, then, *Laborem Exercens*'s contribution to the teaching on work, one may say that Williams's contention that this encyclical is built to an extraordinary degree on scriptural revelation and not natural

---

15. See Calvez and Perrin, *The Church*, 227.

law thinking[16] requires strong qualification. The two sources would actually seem to complement each other. Even John Paul's use of Genesis has a strong natural law undertone. But to list the primary developments of teaching about the effects of work:

- *Laborem Exercens* specifies that in achieving dominion over the earth through work in the objective sense, man can realize dominion over himself through work in the subjective sense.

- By stressing that man is the free human subject of work, John Paul deepens the teaching about how work proceeds from man: i.e., work is logically predicated upon man and, ontologically speaking, he is its support. John Paul's attachment of the word "conscious" to the phrase "human subject" emphasizes that man—again by reason of what he is— is aware of what occurs inside and outside him when he works. This underlines man's responsibility for his work.

- Having characterized work as an act of the human subject, John Paul directs attention to the role played by the spiritual qualities of free will and reason in this action, both of which are facets of man's personhood. This endows each work-act proceeding from the human subject with a significance greater than its objective effect. The greatest value of the human subject's work-acts lies in their capacity to contribute to man's struggle to fulfil himself as a person by developing morally virtuous habits. It is for this reason that work in itself is described as "a good thing for man" and an *actus personae*. Every work-action, no matter how marginal, involves man making choices about himself and therefore either confirming or diminishing his self-dominion. Work in the intransitive-subjective sense, then, is always more important that its transitive-objective dimension. / *One takes priority* . . .

- John Paul's distinction between "object" and "subject" adds precision to magisterial teaching about how work is simultaneously directed to the world and man's inner dimension. The subject's act of work is directed to external objects, but, in the final analysis, the subject from whom the work proceeds is always the work's ultimate object.

---

16. Williams, "John Paul II on Church, State and Society," 475.

An Unusual Language

Looking at *Laborem Exercens*'s teachings, one must agree with Baum when he says that, for a Catholic document, the encyclical's use of the terms "subjective" and "objective" is unusual.[17] Catholic thought tends to look upon the world as a given: as the objective reality. To know the truth, the mind has to discern what constitutes objective reality. Conversely, "subjective" is often used to describe the purely personal and idiosyncratic.[18] As the subjective may be an obstacle to ascertaining the truth, it must be minimized. In this context, it is normal to speak of the priority of the objective over the subjective.

On one level, *Laborem Exercens*'s particular employment of these expressions proceeds from its use of the words subject and object. "Objective" reflects the idea of work being directed to objects and shaping the objective reality around man. "Subjective" corresponds to the concept of work affecting the subject from whom it proceeds. If, however, we turn to Wojtyła's writings, it becomes apparent that the pope's use of these ₃rms reflects the influence of Wojtyłan ideas.

4.5　Work, Action, and Person

As a Polish Catholic thinker, Wojtyła was not alone in having an intellectual interest in work. In 1946, for example, Stefan Wyszyński, then a professor of social ethics, wrote a book which presented work in terms of man's participation in the act of creation.[19] More contemporarily, Tischner's *The Spirit of Solidarity* explored work from a variety of ethical and theological perspectives.[20]

It was not until the late 1970s that Wojtyła's writings began to focus upon work as opposed to human acts per se. Wojtyła did, however, compose poems about work in the 1950s, and these, along with his inquiries into the nature of human action, closely parallel aspects of *Laborem Exercens*'s teaching about work. To demonstrate the influence of these thoughts upon developments in magisterial social teaching, we will

---

17. See Baum, *The Priority*, 17–18.
18. See, for example, DH 2.
19. See S. Wyszyński, *Duch pracy ludzkiej* [The Spirit of Human Work] (Włocławek: Nakl. Katolickiego Osroda Wydawniczego 'Veritas', 1946).
20. See J. Tischner, *The Spirit of Solidarity* (San Francisco: Harper and Row, 1984), 13–39, 60–71, 84–91, 94–104.

examine the relevant Wojtyłan texts in three groupings: the poems about work; other relevant pre-conciliar writings; and the post-conciliar texts.

Images of Work

In one sense, poetry is "opposed" to philosophy. The latter takes the long way around, claims rationality, and does not eschew lengthy exposition. Poems work more directly through image and evocation. There is no reason, however, why ideas expressed in one medium cannot be articulated and deepened in another. Interestingly, Krzystof Dybciak notes that the cross-fertilization of literature and philosophy has always been a strong tradition in Polish intellectual life.[21]

Between 1946 and 1979, Wojtyła published many poems.[22] While one may describe them as "religious poetry," their phraseology is by no means devotional or superficially religious. The translator of Wojtyła's plays describes the poems as intensely personal and dealing mainly with the inner life and man's contemporary problems.[23]

Poetry, of course, arises from sources not always within the reach of logical discourse. René Darricau, however, argues that Wojtyła gradually "transcended" poetry in the sense that only some formal aspects like rhythm or line pattern remained.[24] The suggestion is that his poems evolved into philosophical and theological reflections in poetic form. If true, then it is all the more surprising that no commentator has considered magisterial development in light of these poems.

For present purposes, the most significant of Wojtyła's poems are those published under the collective title "The Quarry." Though written in 1956, the year in which the riots of workers in Poznań led to significant internal upheaval in Poland, these events seem not to have made an impression. Instead, "The Quarry" is more evocative of the four years that Wojtyła spent working in a limestone quarry and a chemical factory during the German Occupation.

When considering the patterns of images contained within "The Quarry," we discover a hymn to work of such profundity that one is no longer surprised that John Paul devotes an encyclical to the topic. In the

---

21. See K. Dybciak, *La grande testimonianze* (Bologna: CSEO, 1981), 167–186.
22. The following extracts are from *The Place Within: The Poetry of Pope John Paul II* (London: Hutchinson, 1995).
23. See B. Taborski cited in J. Oram, *The People's Pope* (Sydney: Bay Books, 1979), 96.
24. See R. Darricau, "La poesie de Karol Wojtyła," *Revue française d'historie du livre* 32, no. 3 (1981): 402–404.

first stanza of the first of these poems, "Material," Wojtyła writes:

> A thought grows in me day by day:
> the greatness of work is inside man.[25]

An obvious parallel may be made between these words and the stress upon the greater importance of work's internal effect in *Gaudium et Spes* and *Laborem Exercens*.

The second poem, "Inspiration," describes work's effect upon man and the world:

> Work starts from within, outside it takes such space. . . .
> Look—your will strikes a deep bell in stone,
> thought strikes certainty, a peak
> both for the heart and for hand.
>
> For this certainty of mind, this certainty of eye,
> for this vertical line
> you pay with a generous hand.
> The stone yields you its strength,
> and man matures through work
> which inspires him to difficult good.[26]

These sentences encapsulate various themes developed by *Laborem Exercens*. Work proceeds from man's interior and permits his will to shape the external world. But it also involves man's reason ("thought") and will "striking certainty": that is, *truth*. Although it is hard, even costly, this aspect of work has transcendental significance ("this vertical line"), as it enables man to mature and aspire to "difficult good." Parallels may be drawn between these words and *Laborem Exercens*'s teaching about toil and man's acquisition of virtue through work.

The theme of transcendence is echoed in "Material." Its closing verses depict man toiling, his "hands drooping with the hammer's weight." In the midst of this, however, man's "thought [is] informing his work." Thus,

> for a moment he is a Gothic building
> cut by a vertical thought born in the eyes.
> No, not a profile alone,

---

25. "Material," 63.
26. "Inspiration," 66.

> not a mere figure between God and the stone
> sentenced to grandeur and error.[27]

Through the toil of work shaped by the use of his inner faculties, then, man can transcend, if only for a short time, his position as a creature existing between God and matter, and dominate himself.

The third poem, "Participation," complements these motifs:

> The light of this rough plank,
> recently carved from a trunk,
> is pouring the vastness
> of work indivisible into your palms.
> The taut hand rests on this Act
> which permeates all things in man.[28]

What *Laborem Exercens* defines as objective-transitive work is captured here in the plank recently formed from a tree through work. Long after the act of carving, however, the same work-act continues to affect the man from whom it came. The similarity between these words and *Laborem Exercens*'s description of work's intransitive effect seems clear.

The attaching of a capital "A" to "Act" in the extract above seems odd, until one realizes that it recalls *the* Act: that is, God, the pure Act of being, free from all mere potentiality—*Actus Purus*. The insistence that this Act permeates all things in man anticipates John Paul's emphasis upon God as the first and continuing cause of man and his work. "Material" also contemplates this theme:

> Passerbys scuttle off into doorways,
> someone whispers: "Yet here is a great force."
>
> Fear not. Man's daily deeds have a wide span,
> a strait riverbed can't imprison them long.
> Fear not. For centuries they all stand in Him,
> and you look at Him now
> through the even knocking of hammers.[29]

---

27. "Material," 65.
28. "Participation," 68.
29. "Material," 64.

Modern work, then, is not to be feared. Like all true work throughout the centuries, it proceeds from God ("Him") and reflects His work. The words above even hint at work's co-creative character and imply that work expresses man's nature ("you look at Him now") as *imago Dei*.

Nowhere in "The Quarry" are terms such as "subjective" employed. Conceptually, however, these poems encapsulate features of *Laborem Exercens*'s teaching on work, several years before *Gaudium et Spes* was even drafted.

Man and Action in the Pre-Conciliar Writings

Whilst work itself is not addressed in Wojtyła's other pre-conciliar writings, Wojtyła's long fascination with the human act has already been highlighted. One characteristic of Wojtyła's pre-conciliar texts are their efforts to integrate the modern notion of "consciousness" into an essentially Thomist anthropology of man and human acts.

As early as 1957, Wojtyła was using the phrase "conscious act" and placing it within a Thomist context. "A conscious human act," he stated, "is for St. Thomas not merely a stage upon which ethical experience is enacted. It is itself an ethical experience because it is an act of will."[30] The references to "experience" surely reflect Wojtyła's assimilation of Scheler's emphases. Nonetheless, Wojtyła is careful to ground the conscious act in man's will because this is the key to its moral significance. Another pre-conciliar article links consciousness with human reason. Here Wojtyła argues that in the Thomist tradition, "consciousness and self-consciousness are something derivative, a kind of fruit of the rational nature that subsists in the person. . . . The person acts consciously because he is rational."[31]

These two articles, then, seem to anticipate *Laborem Exercens*'s use of the word "conscious" to stress that man cannot help being aware of the significance of his work-acts. *Love and Responsibility* uses this word in a similar manner. It specifies, for example, that "man, acting in the way proper to him, consciously selects means and consciously adapts them to an end of which he is conscious" (LR 46). Here "conscious" highlights man's knowledge of his responsibility for his actions. This point is made more explicitly in an earlier piece in which Wojtyła states: "The

---

30. "Zagadnienie woli w analizie aktu etycznego" [The Problem of the Will in the Analysis of the Ethical Act], *Roczniki Filozoficzne* 5, no. 1 (1955/1957): 132.
31. "Thomistic Personalism," 669–670

consciousness of performing a determinate act, of which one is the author, carries with it a sense of responsibility for the moral value of this act."[32]

But there is much more in *Love and Responsibility* that prefigures *Laborem Exercens*. This is especially true of the former's use of the words "object" and "subject." "The word 'object,'" Wojtyła states, "means more or less the same as 'entity.'" However, this does not capture the full meaning of "object" because "an 'object,' strictly speaking, is something related to a 'subject.'" What, then, is a subject? Wojtyła says that while "[a] 'subject' is also an 'entity,'" it is nevertheless "an 'entity' which exists and acts in a certain way." Hence, he maintains, "[i]t would indeed be proper to speak of 'subjects' before 'objects'" (LR 21).

In these sentences, we find an understanding of subject and the relationship between subject and object that reappears in a modified form in *Laborem Exercens*. "Subject" describes that from which action proceeds—it is the "support" of action. Though Wojtyła does not specify here that the subject's acts are directed to external objects, this is surely implicit to his understanding of the relationship between subjects and objects. It is also clear that Wojtyła considers subjects to be objects, for the subject is defined as an entity, albeit one which acts. *Love and Responsibility* stresses this very point: "We must, then, be clear right from the start *that every subject also exists as an object, an objective 'something' or 'somebody'"* (LR 21).

Of course, it hardly need be said that Wojtyła regards man as a subject, for man is unquestionably an entity from which action proceeds. But he also specifies that "man is not only the subject, but can also be the object of an action (LR 24). The context of this remark is the claim that one person can make another person the object of his action. Thus Wojtyła has yet to depict man as the primary object of his own action as *Laborem Exercens* does. This transition occurs in Wojtyła's writings after the Council, spurred on, it seems, by *Gaudium et Spes*.

Having clarified the subject/object distinction, *Love and Responsibility* states that something else makes man distinctive as a subject of acts—the fact that man is a person. It is not enough, Wojtyła claims, to define man solely "as an individual of the species" (LR 22) (a phrase which recalls the medieval scholastic term "*suppositum*": that is, an individual subsisting in any given species).[33] As a subject and object, "there is something more to

---

32. "Problem oderwania przeżycia od aktu w etyce na tle poglądów Kanta i Schelera" [The Problem of the Separation of Experience from the Act in Kant and Scheler's Ethics], *Roczniki Filozoficzne* 5, no. 3 (1955/1957): 122.
33. See Bigongiari, *The Political Ideas*, 214–215.

[man], a particular richness and perfection in the manner of his being, which can only be brought out by the use of the word 'person'" (LR 22). *Laborem Exercens*, we recall, makes this very point when explaining man's uniqueness as a subjective being.

According to Wojtyła, man's personhood endows him with several special qualities as a subject of acts. The first is "the ability to reason." This makes man "the only subject of its kind in the world of entities." Another is the fact that "the person as a subject" has "a specific inner self, an inner life, characteristic only of persons" (LR 22). In Wojtyła's view, "*Inner life means spiritual life. It revolves around truth and goodness*" (LR 23). On this basis, Wojtyła intimates that reason and decision-making are aspects of man's spiritual dimension: "a person is a thinking subject, and capable of making decisions: these, most notably, are the attributes we find in the *inner self* of a person" (LR 26–27).

The last unique feature which the human subject derives from his personhood is, according to Wojtyła, "the power of self-determination, based on reflection, and manifested in the fact that a man acts from choice. This power is called free will"; it makes man "his own master" (LR 24). But what man *should* freely will, in Wojtyła's view, is not a matter of opinion. He specifies that since human reason is directed to objective good, "we must demand from a person, as a thinking individual, that his or her ends should be genuinely good, since the pursuit of evil ends is contrary to the rational nature of the person" (LR 27).

While these ideas could not be described as "new" for Catholic thinking of the time,[34] their configuration in *Love and Responsibility* anticipates lines of reasoning which pervade *Laborem Exercens*. By stressing that the human subject is also a person, both texts identify the

---

34. Maritain's thought may have been influential here. In a post-conciliar article, Wojtyła associates the term "subject" with the medieval-scholastic term *suppositum*. See "The Person: Subject and Community," 274. Maritain interprets *suppositum* in scholastic thought as denoting that which has an essence, that which exercises existence and action, that which subsists. In his view, it draws attention to a certain density subsisting in man's interior from which acts proceed. Maritain then states: "With man the *suppositum* becomes *persona*, that is, a whole which subsists and exists in virtue of the very subsistence and existence of its spiritual soul, and acts by setting itself its own ends." J. Maritain, *Existence and the Existent* (London: Geoffrey Bles, 1956), 70. Both Wojtyła and LE follow a similar line of reasoning. Each understands man's nature as person as inseparable from his existence as subject, a linkage which endows the human subject's freely willed acts with profound moral and spiritual significance. See also M. Serretti, "Etica e antropologica filosofia. Considerazioni su Maritain e Wojtyła," *Sapienza* 38, no. 1 (1985): 15–31.

acts proceeding from man-as-subject as central to his achievement of self-mastery as a person. Secondly, each text's attention to man's personhood highlights the critical role played by man's spiritual nature, specifically the qualities of reason and will, in directing the subject's acts to this end of self-dominion.

When it comes to the good which man may realize through human acts, Wojtyła directs attention to the acquisition of virtue. Wojtyła, we recall, was convinced that modern man is disinclined to this task because it is difficult, sometimes painful, and often means renunciation of pleasure (LR 35, 36, 143). In short, acquiring virtue involves what *Laborem Exercens* calls toil. It is therefore possible that John Paul's stress that the acquisition of virtue through work is difficult, but nevertheless rewarding, reflects this Wojtyłan conviction.

But more directly prefiguring *Laborem Exercens* is *Love and Responsibility*'s definition of self-fulfillment:

> The statement that something is really good and correct awakens a sense of duty in man and inspires him to act so as to realize that good. The superiority (transcendence) of the person in relation to its own dynamism and the objects of its endeavors brings about a realization of the good and hence the "self-fulfilling" of the person. (LR 305 n.54)

The free choice of true good is thus underlined as central to man's transcendence over himself and his acts: what *Laborem Exercens* understands as self-dominion. The extract above also defines man's fulfillment as his self-realization of goods truly worthy ("really good and correct") of the person. Aside from terminological similarities, the same logic underlies *Laborem Exercens*'s position that man may acquire goods worthy of him through work and thereby fulfil himself as a person.

Certain aspects of several developments in teaching occasioned by *Laborem Exercens* may thus be said to be anticipated in *Love and Responsibility* and other pre-conciliar Wojtyłan works. These texts do not, however, prefigure the encyclical's important differentiation between a work-act's subjective and objective dimensions. It is in Wojtyła's post-conciliar texts that this distinction is made in earnest.

Man and Action in the Post-Conciliar Writings

In the post-conciliar period, Wojtyła's writings on human action became more extensive and complex. To simplify matters, these will initially be considered in terms of their treatment of two broad topics: man as subject; and man's fulfillment through action. We then illustrate how Wojtyła's later post-conciliar texts began to translate his ideas about man and human acts into a Catholic philosophy of work.

1. Man as Subject

The Acting Person, we recall, begins by "relativizing" consciousness within the person. It does so because Wojtyła regards consciousness as useful in conceptualizing how acts shape man:

> man not only acts consciously, but he is also aware of both the fact that he is acting and the fact that it is he who is acting. . . . Consciousness accompanies and reflects or mirrors the action when it is born and while it is being performed; once the action is accomplished consciousness still continues to reflect it. (AP 31)

This, we suggest, partly prefigures *Laborem Exercens*'s use of the word "conscious": the fact that when man works, he is aware of the significance of these acts. However, consciousness is also used in the above extract to assist in explaining how the act's effect persists within man. This is less evident in *Laborem Exercens*, perhaps because discussions about consciousness are arguably beyond the magisterium's remit.

More significant in this regard is *The Acting Person*'s attention to man as subject. Wojtyła accepts the essential accuracy of Boethius's definition of the person: "*persona est rationalis naturae individua substantia*" (AP 73). But in Wojtyła's view, "neither the concept of the 'rational nature' nor that of its individualization seems to express fully the specific completeness expressed in the concept of the person" (AP 73–74). It does not adequately capture the person's "basic ontological structure" (AP 74). Nor does it sufficiently underline the significance of human acts for that person. For these reasons, Wojtyła employs the concept of subject because "[i]t is in the subject as a being that every dynamic structure is rooted, every acting and happening" (AP 72). Man as a person, according to Wojtyła, "is the subject of both existence and acting." He immediately qualifies this by specifying that the "existence proper to [man] is *personal* and not merely individual." Consequently, "the action . . . is also personal" (AP 74).

By drawing attention to the person's ontology as a subject, Wojtyła is able to rethink the nature of man in terms of being the support and author of actions which are of profound significance for him as a person. *Laborem Exercens'*s depiction of man as the subject of work reflects a similar reasoning. Apart from allowing the Pope to root work-acts even more firmly within man, it permits him to stress that because all work-acts proceed from the human subject, each work-act is significant for that subject as a person.

2. *Self-Determination and Fulfillment*

*The Acting Person'*s exposition of why human acts are important for man as a person appears to reflect contemplation of the Council's teachings concerning how one goes outside and beyond oneself through action. Fulfillment, Wojtyła claims, is "the person's transcendence in the doing of an action" (AP 149). Further explanation of what this means may be found in *The Acting Person'*s distinction between "horizontal" and "vertical" transcendence. The latter takes place in the context of the former and is central to fulfillment.

In a clear echo of the Council's words, horizontal transcendence is defined as man's capacity to "[reach] out and beyond the subject . . . or the directing of acts out of the cognizing subject beyond the objectifiable realm" (AP 179). It concerns man's ability to surpass his limits as subject and perceive, know, intend, and will objects beyond himself (AP 131). Both of these statements parallel *Laborem Exercens'*s definition of work in the transitive-objective sense.

The vertical transcendence which man may attain whilst "horizontally transcending" himself is understood as "the fruit of self-determination; the person transcends his structural boundaries through the capacity to exercise freedom; of being free in the process of *acting*, and not only in the intentional direction of willings towards an external object" (AP 119). It is the person's "ascendancy over his own dynamism" (AP 138) and "associated with self-governance" (AP 131).

In other words, vertical transcendence is the realization of what *The Acting Person* understands as freedom, previously identified as being achieved by man when he freely does what he ought to do. It also closely corresponds to *Laborem Exercens'*s understanding of what man can achieve through work in the subjective sense: the realization of dominion over oneself—"ascendancy over one's own dynamism"—by freely choosing moral good when working.

Turning, then, to *The Acting Person'*s discussion of action in the "transitive" and "intransitive" senses, it soon become apparent that this too has influenced *Laborem Exercens*'s distinction between work's subjective and objective dimensions. Here Wojtyła states:

> [action] is both transitive and intransitive with regard to the person. . . . In the inner dimension of the person, human action is at once both transitory and relatively lasting, inasmuch as its effects, which are to be viewed in relation to efficacy and self-determination, that is to say, to the person's engagement in freedom, last longer than the action itself. . . . [For] [h]uman actions once performed do not vanish without a trace: they leave their moral value, which constitutes an objective reality intrinsically cohesive with the person, and thus a reality profoundly subjective. (AP 150–151)

The importance of action's intransitive effect lies in its persistence within man long after the action has occurred. As observed, the same idea appears in Wojtyła's poem, "Participation." The text above primarily has in mind man's self-realization of freedom or lack thereof. But in a more general sense, it uses the word "intransitive" to indicate that every human act proceeding from man morally shapes him as a person. Their inner effect is an inescapable objective reality for man; yet because the person is also the subject of his acts, these acts simultaneously constitute a "profoundly subjective" reality.

Although these words foreshadow *Laborem Exercens*'s subjective-objective distinction, it should be said that the extract above essentially anticipates the encyclical's refinement of the Council's teaching that just as human activity proceeds from man, so it is ordered to him. Further evidence that this is the case may be found in one of Wojtyła's later post-conciliar writings:

> [the] [h]uman action or act has various aims, objects, and values towards which it is directed. Turning to these, man cannot fail in his conscious action to direct himself towards his own self as a goal, for he cannot refer to various objects of action and choose various values without determining himself and his value, through which he becomes an object for himself as subject. In this particular dimension the structure of the human act is auto-teleological.[35]

---

35. "The Person: Subject and Community," 282. Cf. "Rodzina jako 'communio personarum' " [The Family as a 'Communio Personarum'], *Ateneum Kapłańskie* 83, no. 3 (1974): 331: "man is a being capable of existing and acting 'for himself', that is, capable of a certain *autoteleology*, which means capable not only of determining his own ends but also of becoming an end for himself."

In part, this extract represents logical progression upon *Love and Responsibility*'s specification that while man is subject, he can also be the object of others' acts. The words above maintain that man cannot help being the primary object of his *own* acts, a claim similar to *Laborem Exercens*'s insistence that man is always the final end of his work.

Finally, it is also significant that Wojtyła's later post-conciliar writings defined fulfillment in terms of man's acquirement of virtue:

> I fulfil myself through good; evil brings me non-fulfillment. . . . Self-fulfillment is actualized in the act by its moral value, that is, through good which occurs only in the act as such (*per modum actus*). The experience of morality indicates further possibilities of further grounding and consolidating in the subject both good as a moral value and evil. The ethics of Aristotle and Thomas Aquinas . . . speak of habits which are moral abilities which may be either virtues or vices. In all this there are the manifold forms of self-fulfillment, or, on the contrary, of non-fulfillment of the self.[36]

Here we need only recall that in *Laborem Exercens*, fulfillment through work is understood as man self-realizing moral good, which John Paul associates with the development of virtue in the Thomist sense of moral habits.

3. A Catholic Philosophy of Work

Certain Wojtyłan post-conciliar texts apply many of the conclusions outlined above to contemporary theories about work. The significance of these texts is that they suggest that certain emphases in *Laborem Exercens* may also, in part, be broadly directed to this discussion. It involves pointing out where, from a Catholic viewpoint, certain conceptions of work are only partly correct because of their inadequate understanding of man.

In *Sign of Contradiction*, Wojtyła posits that "present day philosophy, Marxist especially . . . puts *praxis* before 'theory' and deduces all its explanation of reality—especially the reality of man—from that *praxis*, that is to say from the work by which man 'created himself' within nature" (SC 139).[37] Thus Marxist philosophy, as Wojtyła understands it, perceives

---

36. "The Person: Subject and Community," 287.
37. See also "Teoria e prassi nella filosofia della persona umana" [Theory and Practice in the Philosophy of the Human Person], *Sapienza* 29, no. 4 (1976): 377–384.

man as a creation of work—even the "material" of work. In stating this position, he indirectly highlights the materialist anthropology of man underpinning Marxism's understanding of work. As Martin Heidegger states: "The essence of materialism does not consist in the assertion that everything is simply matter but rather in the metaphysical determination according to which every being appears as the material of labor."[38]

Wojtyła then suggests that the Catholic view of work proceeds from different anthropological premises:

> Underlying the truth about man by the Church *usque ad sanguinem* lies the conviction that man cannot be reduced to matter alone. If he has mastery over matter, he has it solely thanks to the spiritual element which is inherent in him and which expresses itself in his knowledge and freedom, that is to say in his activity. So one could acknowledge that a partial truth is contained in the assertion that "work creates man." Yes, it does create; but it does so precisely because it is a work—an activity, a *praxis*—of man: *actus personae*. (SC 139)

The second point that *Sign of Contradiction* makes about work involves stressing its intrinsic moral worth:

> all human work, and all that it produces in any field of endeavor, shapes the human personality; but it does so not because of the objective worth of what it produces but because of its own moral worth—a distinctly human and personal element in all man's activity, man's *praxis*. (SC 139)

On one level, these words prefigure *Laborem Exercens*'s teaching that work's most important effect—what truly makes work in itself a good thing for man—is the moral impact of the work-act itself within the person. At the same time, they implicitly highlight inadequacies in Marxist thought about work. Not only is this suggested by the context in which Wojtyła makes these remarks (i.e., discussing Marxist ideas about praxis), but by similar statements contained in Wojtyła's 1977 article on human praxis. This expands upon the comments above by examining Marx's claim in his *Theses on Feuerbach* that man creates himself through his work. Responding to this assertion, Wojtyła declares that there is a decisive limit to Marx's idea that by transforming nature, man transforms himself. Marx, in his view, fails to recognize that it is not only or primarily

---

38. M. Heidegger, "Letter on Humanism," *Basic Writings* (New York: Harper and Row, 1977), 220.

transformed nature which conditions man. Rather, it is the very act of work which decisively shapes the subject from whom it proceeds. To explain this point, Wojtyła appeals to Aquinas:

> As I understand St. Thomas' thought, human activity is simultaneously *transitive* and *intransitive*. It is transitive insofar as it tends *beyond the subject*, seeks an expression and an effect in the external world, and is objectified in some product. It is intransitive, on the other hand, insofar as it *remains in the subject*, [and] determines the subject's immanent quality or value.[39]

For Wojtyła, the Marxist view is limited because it emphasizes only one of the two dimensions of action identified by Aquinas. Hence, Marx does not comprehend the significance of the moral effect of human acts *within* the human subject. Interestingly, however, Wojtyła adds: "I am not just engaging in a direct critique of the Marxist thesis that work produces or somehow is at the origin of man." More fundamentally, he wishes to stress that any discussion of work must recognize the importance of the scholastic principle that operation follows being: that "[w]ork . . . is possible to the extent that man already exists: *operari sequitur esse*."[40]

Taken together, the extracts from this article and *Sign of Contradiction* suggest that Wojtyła perceived Marxist thought as reversing the true relationship between work and man.[41] Whilst Wojtyła agrees that Marxist perspectives comprehend work's vital role in man's formation, they fail to recognize that work can only "create man" because, like any other act, work proceeds from man, more specifically his reason and will. From a Catholic viewpoint, these are part of the person's spiritual essence. It is on these grounds, we recall, that *Sign of Contradiction* insists that it is man's spiritual dimension that makes work an *actus personae* and gives him mastery over matter—a position incompatible with viewing man in purely material terms. This being the case, one may say that Wojtyła's writings about work underline a fundamental difference between Marxist and Catholic anthropologies of man: the latter's conviction that man is, by

---

39. "Constitution of Culture," 516. Here Wojtyła may be referring to Aquinas's *Quaestiones Disputatae de Veritate*, q.8, a.6c: "Action is of two sorts: one sort—action [*actio*] in a strict sense—issues from the agent into something external to change it . . . the other sort—properly called activity [*operatio*]—does not issue into something external but remains within the agent itself perfecting it."
40. "Constitution of Culture," 516.
41. See also P. Pollini, "Il problema della filosofia della prassi in Marx e Wojtyła," in *La filosofia*, 61–73.

nature, a partly spiritual being.

In this light, certain statements in *Laborem Exercens* begin to assume the character of a critique of Marxist conceptions of work and man. Both the encyclical's explanation of the priority of work's intransitive dimension and its highlighting of work's moral significance fall into this category. So too does *Laborem Exercens*'s use of the phrase *actus personae* to emphasize that work proceeds from a subject who, by nature, is a material and spiritual being. Whilst work does "create" man—this is the whole meaning of work in the subjective sense—this is only true because man as a person possesses the spiritual qualities of reason and free will which permit him to realize moral good when working. Of course, the encyclical's discussion of these matters makes no explicit reference to Marxist notions of work. One should therefore hesitate before reading too much of a critique of Marxism into the text. Nevertheless the Wojtyłan writings considered above indicate that this may have shaped aspects of *Laborem Exercens*'s teaching about work.

4.6 Conclusion

Given his evident willingness in the 1970s to engage with contemporary philosophical thought about work, one may speculate that if Wojtyła had not been elected pope, he might have eventually written a treatise on the topic. In many respects, *Laborem Exercens* may be understood as a realization of this end as well as the culmination of reflections traceable back to 1956. Although the encyclical builds, like *The Acting Person*, upon *Gaudium et Spes*, there is much to suggest that Wojtyłan emphases have been brought to bear upon *Laborem Exercens*.

But what possible significance could the topics considered here have for Catholic social teaching on more obviously political-economic questions? Surely most of what has been considered here belongs to the "abstract" order of anthropology, ethics, and theology.

Such questions rely, of course, on an artificial cloistering of disciplines—the view that the ethical, for example, can at best be of marginal relevance to the political. For a start, work is not done alone. It often involves interaction with others. Thus if the ultimate end of human work is man's self-dominion, then one must consider what political and economic arrangements allow all to pursue this. One might also inquire into the consequences of giving priority to work's objective dimension, which is the engine of material progress, over its subjective aspect, which is central to man's realization of virtue. In this sense, Hauerwas points out, John Paul's teaching about work challenges not only Marxists, but also "'liberals' and 'conservatives' [who have] become so enamoured with issues of distribution that they forget that work has a moral purpose."[42] Certainly, such concerns have influenced the pope's development of magisterial teaching about industrial relations. For, as Min notes:

> It is on the basis of "labor" and "co-labor" in society that the personalism of *The Acting Person*—which abstracts altogether from the actual content of man's historical experience despite its emphasis on the concrete, and remains on the high ground of generalities and principles—emerges as a full-blown, historically relevant social philosophy of Pope John Paul II.[43]

---

42. S. Hauerwas, "In Praise of *Centesimus Annus*," *Theology* 95, no. 768 (1992): 420.
43. Min, "John Paul II," 127–128.

5
INDUSTRIAL RELATIONS: PROTECTING THE PERSON

5.1 Introduction

When Leo XIII promulgated *Rerum Novarum*, his message was directed to nineteenth-century industrial Europe. According to Leo, one of industrial society's characteristics was its division into two classes between which there was an immense—and disturbing—abyss:

> On one side there is the party which holds power because it holds wealth; which has in its grasp the whole of labor and trade. . . . On the other side there is the needy and powerless multitude, sick and sore in spirit, and ever ready for disturbance. (RN 47)

Ninety years after *Rerum Novarum*, John Paul II issued *Laborem Exercens* in the midst of another "class-confrontation": that of Polish workers against the "owners" of People's Poland. As one historian states, Solidarity was "the *only* spontaneous and genuine working-class revolution which has ever occurred in history; it was directed against the socialist state governed by bureaucrats . . . and carried out under the sign of the cross and with the blessing of the Pope."[1]

---

1. M. Hauner, "Prague Spring," in *Czechoslovakia: Crossroads and Crises*, N. Stone and E. Stouhal, eds. (London: Basingstoke, 1989), 208. Laba's study suggests that Solidarity's emergence primarily resulted from the activities of ordinary workers along the Gdańsk coast during the 1970s. The intelligentsia's role was strictly secondary. See R. Laba, *The Roots of Solidarity* (Princeton: Princeton University Press, 1991)

In considering developments in teaching about industrial relations in John Paul's pontificate, it soon becomes apparent that the pope's desire to influence the Polish drama has contributed. Contextual matters, however, have not overshadowed the process of reflection on previous teaching that is central to magisterial development. It also becomes clear that distinctly Wojtyłan emphases have affected teaching about the three sub-areas to be considered: the causes of worker exploitation; the role of unions; and proposals for reforming the organization of work at an enterprise level.

5.2 Worker Exploitation

At the Root of Disorder

Considering the attention given to worker exploitation by pre-conciliar teaching, the Council has surprisingly little to say on this subject. Nevertheless, the Council did consider worker exploitation and explained it in terms of the actions of those organizing work:

> Since economic activity is . . . the fruit of the collaboration of many men, it is unjust and inhuman to organize and direct it in such a way that some of the workers are exploited. But it frequently happens, even today, that workers are almost enslaved by the work they do. So-called laws of economics are no excuse for this kind of thing. The entire process of productive work, then, must be accommodated to the needs of the human person. . . . Workers should have the opportunity to develop their talents and their personalities in the very exercise of their work. (GS 67)

Exploitation, then, occurs whenever the collaborative work that generates economic activity is organized in ways which deny the workers' personhood. In such instances, there is little possibility that workers may develop themselves through their work. Exploitation may therefore also be understood as proceeding from denial of the importance of what, as previously observed, the Council denotes as work's inner effect.

The "exploiters" are identified as those who direct collaborative work erroneously. Owners, employers and managers—both public and private sector—fall into this category by virtue of their directive role. The reference to "so-called laws of economics" implies that certain ideas have legitimized worker exploitation, though their precise character is not explained.

The Denial of Subjectivity

Laborem Exercens's analysis of worker exploitation flows naturally from its focus upon human work. As John Paul says, "it is well known that it is possible to use work in various ways *against man*" (LE 9).

Reflecting on this sentence, Baum states that as the pope views labor as the axis of man's self-making, he is bound to regard it as an activity in which man becomes particularly vulnerable. In itself, this is a reasonable contention. Baum adds, however, that John Paul understands the disorders connected with work as basically economic in nature.[2] This claim is more problematic. Like the Council, the Pope considers the origins of worker exploitation to lie in the moral failure to recognize man's personhood. *Laborem Exercens* explains this in terms of "the various trends of *materialistic and economistic* thought." Such ideas understand work "as a sort of 'merchandise' that the worker . . . sells to the employer." These notions are facilitated by "the development of a one-sidedly materialistic civilization, which gives prime importance to the objective dimension of work, while the subjective dimension . . . remains on the secondary level." This, the pope states, represents

> a reversal of the order laid down from the beginning by the words of the Book of Genesis: *man is treated as an instrument of production* [refers to Pius XI], whereas he . . . ought to be treated as the effective subject of work and its true maker and creator. (LE 7)

To a limited extent, this analysis builds upon *Gaudium et Spes* and *Quadragesimo Anno*,[3] specifically their condemnation of the treatment of workers as things. To this, however, John Paul adds several points. For a start, certain erroneous mind-sets—"materialism" and "economism"—are identified as underlying this exploitation. These deny the theological-anthropological truth that man is the creative subject of work. Such attitudes are regarded as symptomatic of a culture that reverses the priority of the "subjective" over the "objective."

---

2. See Baum, *The Priority*, 10.

3. The footnote reads: "Cf. Pius XI, Encyclical *Quadragesimo Anno*, AAS 23 (1931), 221 [QA 135]." QA 135 states: "very many managements treated their workmen as mere tools, with no concern at all for their souls . . . [Hence] bodily labor, which Divine Providence decreed to be performed . . . for the good . . . of man's body and soul, is being everywhere changed into an instrument of perversion."

Laborem Exercens adds historical-philosophical embellishment to this portrait of exploitation. It states that in the first period of industrialization

> the great *conflict . . .* emerged *between "capital" and "labor,"* that is to say between the small but highly influential group of entrepreneurs, owners, or holders of the means of production, and the broader multitude of people who lacked these means and which shared in the process of production solely by their labor. The conflict originated in the fact that the workers put their powers at the disposal of the entrepreneurs, and these, following the principle of maximum profit, tried to establish the lowest possible wages for the work done by the employees. (LE 11)

These words do not suggest that there was something inevitable about worker exploitation. The employers are portrayed as *choosing* to subordinate their employees' well-being to profit.

A different reflection on the passage above is offered by Gustavo Gutiérrez. *Laborem Exercens*, he believes, effectively endorses the Marxist view that the confrontation between "capital" and "labor" is a "structural conflict."[4] Yet the encyclical itself states that "[o]pposition between labor and capital does not spring from the structure of the production process or from the structure of the economic process" (LE 13). By any standard, this is a remarkably un-Marxist/un-structuralist proposition.

Instead, man's choice to violate the Genesis-ordained order in which "man is the master of the creatures placed at his disposal in the visible world" (LE 13) is regarded as facilitating the denial of man's personhood and subsequent worker exploitation:

> This consistent image, in which the principle of the primacy of person over things is strictly preserved, *was broken up in human thought . . .* labor was separated from capital and set in opposition to it, and capital was set in opposition to labor, as though they were impersonal forces, two production factors juxtaposed in the same "economistic" perspective [*prospectu "oeconomistico"*]. This way of stating the issue contained a fundamental error, what we call *the error of economism* [*oeconomismus*], that of considering human labor solely according to its economic purpose. This fundamental error of thought can and must be called *an error of materialism*, in that economism directly or indirectly includes a conviction of the primacy and superiority of the material, and directly or indirectly

---

4. G. Gutiérrez, "El Evangelio del Trabajo," in *Sobre el Trabajo Humano*, CEP, ed. (Lima: CEP, 1982), 53.

places the spiritual and the personal (man's activity, moral values [*bona moralia*] and such matters) in a position of subordination to material reality. (LE 13)

This lengthy extract indicates that economism's basic flaw is that it defies an anthropological truth about man: his possession of a spiritual and personal dimension which embraces his capacity to attain moral good [*bona moralia*] when acting. That is why the economistic perspective is linked with materialism. Put another way, having subordinated the transcendental to the material, man's thoughts become primarily instrumental in their orientation, and drift towards viewing other persons as an aggregate of material objects to be manipulated.

The consequences of such thinking for workers were, according to the pope, disastrous. Unlike the Council, however, John Paul places these in a specific historical-philosophical context:

the antinomy between labor and capital under consideration here . . . did not originate merely in the philosophy and economic theories of the eighteenth century; rather it originated in the whole of the *economic and social practice* of that time, the time of the birth and rapid development of industrialization, in which what was mainly seen was the possibility of vastly increasing material wealth, means, while the end, that is to say, man, who should be served by the means, was ignored. It was this practical error that *struck a blow* first and foremost against human labor, against *the working man*, and caused the ethically just social reaction. . . . The same error, which is now part of history and was connected with the period of primitive capitalism and liberalism, can nevertheless be repeated in other circumstances of time and place, if people's thinking starts from the same theoretical or practical premises. (LE 13)

Though John Paul does not identify the specific philosophies he has in mind, they seem to be associated with the Enlightenment. He may even be alluding to the thought of the Physiocrats. The references to the birth of industrialization and a vision of vastly increasing wealth (a phrase which resonates of Adam Smith's *Wealth of Nations*) suggest that Williams may well be correct in identifying eighteenth-century England as the place where the pope considers that labor was first systematically exploited.[5] In using the language of "means" and "ends" to conceptualize the problem, *Laborem Exercens* appears to add a certain Kantian flavor to this historical

5. See Williams, "Karol Wojtyła and Marxism," 372–373.

reflection. One should note, however, that John Paul's historical reading is very much directed to the present. The citation's last sentence stresses that working people will always be exploited whenever others act in accordance with economistic and materialistic premises.

The Shadow of Materialism

Many of the developments above show signs of being influenced by Wojtyłan ideas identified in previous chapters. One instance is *Love and Responsibility*'s discussion of the verb "to use." In Wojtyła's view, this phrase means "to employ some object as a means to an end" (LR 25). But "[i]s it permissible," Wojtyła asks, "to regard a person as a means to an end and to use a person in that capacity?" For example, "[d]oes an employer not use a worker i.e, a human person, for ends which he himself has chosen?" Wojtyła's answer is that "a person must not be *merely* the means to an end for another person. This is precluded by the very nature of personhood . . . [f]or a person is a thinking subject and capable of making decisions" (LR 26).[6] This insistence upon the impermissibility of stifling man's use of his unique faculties as a person and subject within the context of employer-worker relations reappears in *Laborem Exercens*.

The citations above also prefigure *Laborem Exercens*'s use of means/ends language. While the encyclical does not overtly affirm Kant's categorical imperative, its disapproval of employers using workers solely as means to attain material ends may reflect *Love and Responsibility*'s re-articulation of Kant's principle. In his discussion of "use," Wojtyła refers to Kant's imperative that one must "act always in such a way that the other person is the end and not merely the instrument of your action" (LR 27–28). Wojtyła re-states this principle as follows:

> Whenever a person is the object of your activity, remember that you may not treat that person as only the means to an end, as an instrument, but must allow for the fact that he or she, too, has, or at least should have, distinct personal ends. (LR 28)

Gaudium et Spes, we recall, also stressed that workers must be able to develop their personhood when working. Hence, one should not overestimate the influence of these Wojtyłan ideas. Nevertheless, the

---

6. See also "Kamień węgielny etyki społecznej" [The Cornerstone of the Social Ethic], *Tygodnik Powszechny* 12, no. 1 (1958): 7.

terminology employed in the citations above parallels aspects of *Laborem Exercens*'s characterization of worker exploitation: the reversal of means and ends, the use of persons solely as instruments, the tacit denial of man's personhood and subjectivity, a failure to recognize that man has personal ends, etc.

Another possible contribution of Wojtyłan thought to the encyclical concerns its attention to materialism. According to Świeżawski, materialism as a philosophical standpoint was given careful attention by the Lublin Thomists following the Second World War.[7] It underlaid, after all, the ideology of Poland's new masters.

In 1959, Wojtyła was invited, as a bishop and Catholic academic, to submit ideas for the Council's agenda. Amongst other things, he suggested that the Council needed to *confront* the growth of various materialisms.[8] It is not until the post-conciliar period, however, that Wojtyła's writings begin to concern themselves in detail with materialism. There is, of course, nothing extraordinary about a Catholic philosopher denouncing materialism. But for all that, Wojtyła's writings are strikingly insistent that materialism is an extremely powerful contemporary force. One article, for example, claims that although materialist outlooks are not new, never before has materialism "had so many means at its disposal and expressed itself in so many currents."[9]

As noted in chapter 3, *Sign of Contradiction* underlines the efforts of philosophical and everyday materialism to turn matter into an absolute in human thought as a major contemporary problem (SC 13). It then links materialistic attitudes with disdain for the spiritual. It is precisely such perspectives, described in Augustinian terms as *ad contemptum Dei*, that Wojtyła believes to lie "at the root of all the ruthless exploitation of men by other men: exploitation in industrial production . . . [and the division of] society into warring classes" (SC 58–59). The linkage here between materialism, disregard for the spiritual, and worker exploitation reappears in *Laborem Exercens*, albeit in a more systematically thought-out form.

Finally, the encyclical's conceptualization of exploitation in terms of

---

7. Świeżawski, "Karol Wojtyła," ix–x.
8. See "Consilia et vota episcopi K. Wojtyła," in *Acta et Documenta Concilio Vaticano II Apparando, Series I, Antepreparatoria*, Vol.II, Part II (Roma: Libreria Editrice Vaticana, 1960), 743–744.
9. "The Task of Christian Philosophy Today," *Proceedings of the American Catholic Philosophical Association* 53 (1979): 3–4. This text consists of those introductory paragraphs of the original 1976 Polish publication of "The Person: Subject and Community" which were not included in the 1979 English version of the same article.

the prioritization of work's transitive-objective dimension over its intransitive-subjective aspect also owes something to Wojtyłan thought. Addressing the topic of praxis, Wojtyła reiterates his conviction that "the intransitive is more important than that which is transitive."[10] He then states:

> If in our analysis of human praxis we wish to affirm this reality . . . we must radically reassess all formulations that speak of the transformation or modification of the world as the sole purpose of human praxis. More importantly, we must reassess all programs that view the whole of activity between the poles of production and consumption. While not denying the fundamentality of these categories as poles of economic thought . . . we must be careful in this way of thinking and speaking not to allow man to become an epiphenomenon and, in a sense, a product . . . we cannot agree to such an epiphenomenal, *economistic*, or productionistic view of man and human action.[11]

Wojtyła's suggestion that any accordance of primacy to the transitive dimension of human praxis risks reducing man to the status of a product is replicated in *Laborem Exercens*. So too is his use of the word "economistic" to describe those viewpoints which conceptualize man in precisely these terms. Although "economism" is not specifically linked to "materialism" per se, this is surely implicit in the text above inasmuch as economistic perspectives are associated with tendencies to view human work solely in terms of "production and consumption." One might add that economism, as depicted in both *Laborem Exercens* and the above citation, appears to constitute an instance of what *Sign of Contradiction* describes as modern man thinking in purely horizontal terms. The result, of course, is the same: a cognitive disorientation which leads to man being perceived primarily as a thing to be used. Having trivialized work's intransitive-subjective meaning, one is left with only that aspect of work which is directed to the material dimension of life. Though Wojtyła indicates in the extract above that thinking in terms of production and consumption can be useful for certain ends (such as theorizing about economics), he believes that such thought becomes destructive if it is regarded as providing a complete science of man.

When it comes, however, to *Laborem Exercens*'s placement of economism and materialism in a particular historical context, this is not

---

10. "Constitution of Culture," 515.
11. "Constitution of Culture," 517.

prefigured in any Wojtyłan text. But one should recall that *Laborem Exercens* emphasizes that this error is not restricted to any historical period or economic system. It can reoccur whenever human thought proceeds from the same premises. It represents, therefore, an indirect rebuff to those who identify worker exploitation with any one system or the dialectics of history: because man can choose, he remains responsible.

In any case, *Laborem Exercens*'s attention to history is not limited to some of the intellectual and economic transformations which contributed to modernity's emergence. Turning now to John Paul's teaching about trade unions, it becomes apparent that much of his development of teaching is directed to influencing events in the making.

5.3 Unions and the Workers' Struggle

Workers' Associations and Industrial Conflict

In 1891, *Rerum Novarum* endorsed what it described as "workingmen's associations" [*sodalitia artificum*] (RN 49). In part, this represented intervention in a discussion amongst Catholic social thinkers concerning the permissibility of such associations vis-à-vis combined worker-employer bodies.[12] Pope Leo affirmed the validity of both. Forty years later, Pius XI specifically underlined the worth of trade unions (QA 31–36). It is not surprising, then, that the Council is attentive to the role of workers' associations. In discussing socio-economic life, *Gaudium et Spes* speaks of unions in the following terms:

> Among the fundamental rights of the individual must be numbered the right of workers to form themselves into associations which truly represent them and are able to cooperate in organizing economic life properly, and the right to play their part in the activities of such associations without risk of reprisal. (GS 68)

Here unions are understood as having two functions: representing workers and contributing to the correct ordering of economic activity. Nevertheless, the Council hints that worker participation in unions has at times provoked reprisals, though from whom is not specified.

Nor does the Council pretend that collaboration between workers and employers is always smooth:

---

12. See Misner, *Social Catholicism*, chps. 8, 9, 10.

> In the event of economic-social disputes all should strive to arrive at peaceful settlements. The first step should be to engage in sincere discussion between all sides; but the strike remains even in the circumstances of today a necessary (although an ultimate) means for the defense of workers' rights and the satisfaction of their lawful aspirations. As soon as possible, however, avenues should be sought to resume negotiations and conversation for reconciliation. (GS 68)

Dialogue, then, is the favored approach for resolving industrial disputes. The strike is nevertheless legitimate, though only as a last resort, and only when discussion has failed to uphold workers' rights or realize their legitimate ambitions. In other words, a strike may only occur if the injustice is very serious and all other means of resolving the dispute are exhausted. Although workers may have a just complaint, this does not in itself necessarily legitimize strike action. Indeed, Nell-Breuning suggests that the Council's reference to "the circumstances of today" indicates a hope that strikes will no longer be necessary in the future.[13]

Gaudium et Spes does not, however, specify if union activity or strikes may enter the political sphere. This and other issues are addressed in Paul VI's *Octogesima Adveniens* (1971). Prominent amongst this document's themes are the spread of urbanization and industrialization (OA 8–12), and the relationship between politics and justice (OA 24–35). Modern trade unions are, of course, a result of industrialization, and, to varying degrees, are often involved in politics. After noting their important role, Paul states:

> Their activity is, however, not without its difficulties . . . the temptation can arise of profiting from a position of force to impose, particularly by strikes—the right to which, as a final means of defense, remains certainly recognized—conditions which are too burdensome for the overall economy and for the social body, or to desire to obtain in this way demands of a directly political nature. When it is a question of public services, required for the life of an entire nation, it is necessary to be able to assess the limit beyond which the harm caused to society becomes inadmissible. (OA 14)

This text elaborates upon the Council's teaching in several respects. First, strikes cannot be used by unions to achieve demands which cannot be met by the economy and society. Secondly, when strikes affect public services, a judgment must be made as to when the pursuit of a just claim

---

13. See O. von Nell-Breuning, S.J., "Socio-Economic Life," in *Commentary*, Vol. V, 305.

by striking will cause inadmissible social damage. Finally, un
use strikes to obtain demands of "a directly political nature."
that with these words, Paul "wants to deny unions any role in u~
sphere."[14] This is not the case. To deny that strikes may be used to dictate
overtly political demands is *not* the same as denying unions a political
role.

Unions and the Struggle for Justice

Laborem Exercens extensively considers the purpose of unions, their
relationship to politics, and the issue of strikes. According to John Paul,
history shows that unions are "an indispensable *element of social life*." The
word "indispensable" is stronger than Paul VI's statement that unions have
"an important role." John Paul's words suggest that the absence of unions
has profound ramifications for all.

He is careful, however, to disassociate the Catholic understanding of
union activity from what might be identified as a Marxist position.
"Catholic social teaching," the Pope states, "does not hold that unions are
no more than a reflection of the 'class' structure of society and that they
are a mouthpiece for a class struggle which inevitably governs social life."
Nevertheless, he adds, unions are certainly "*a mouthpiece for the struggle
for social justice*, for the just rights of working people . . . this struggle
should be seen as a normal endeavor 'for' the just good." For this reason,
"it *is not a struggle 'against' others*" (LE 20).

Although both the Council and Paul VI state that unions serve to
protect workers' rights, it is less apparent from their respective texts that
unions form part of a broader struggle for justice. John Paul evidently
considers this point to be important, because he specifies that

> if in controversial questions the struggle takes on a character of opposition
> towards others, this is because it aims at the good of social justice, not for
> the sake of "struggle" or in order to eliminate the opponent. It is
> characteristic of work that it first and foremost unites people. In this
> consists its social power: the power to build a community . . . both those
> who work and those who manage the means of production or who own
> them must in some way be united in this community. *In light of this
> fundamental structure* of all work . . . it is clear that, even if it is because of
> their work needs that people unite to secure their rights, their union remains
> a constructive factor of *social order* and *solidarity*. (LE 20)

---

14. Walsh, "Introduction," xvii.

From this viewpoint, it is clear that when union struggle is "in opposition towards others," it turns against them only to the extent that they obstruct justice. Struggle is thus *not* about achieving a "class victory," but rather the formation of a community which is inclusive of workers and managers/owners.[15] Even in conflictual situations, the struggle should take the form of "constructive opposition" which contributes to this end. In this sense, "opposition" is actually an expression of solidarity.

Echoing Paul VI, John Paul states that unions "must take into account the limitations imposed by the general economic situation of the country." To this, he adds that union "demands cannot be turned into a kind of group or class 'egoism', although they can and should also aim at correcting—with a view to the common good of the whole of society—everything defective in the system of ownership of the means of production or in the way these are managed" (LE 20). These words give a precise direction to the Council's teaching that unions should contribute to the correct ordering of economic activity: the reform of ownership/administration arrangements.

Proposals to change ownership arrangements inevitably have a political dimension. John Paul acknowledges this by stating that "[i]n this sense union activity undoubtedly enters the field of *politics,* understood as *prudent concern for the common good*" (LE 20). Unions, then, are permitted some forms of involvement in politics: specifically those essential for them to pursue their proper purpose. This position is consistent with *Octogesima Adveniens*'s teaching that unions are not to make overtly political demands.

Indeed, *Laborem Exercens* ensures that this distinction is understood by cautioning that "the role of unions is not 'to engage in political affairs' [*negotia politica gerere*] in the sense that the expression is commonly understood today." They "do not have the character of political parties seeking power" (LE 20). In other words, unions are different from political parties because they are concerned with their members' interests with a view—but not a direct and immediate concern—for the overall common good. Nor, according to John Paul, should unions

be subjected to the decision of political parties or have too close links to them. In fact, in such a situation they easily lose contact with their specific

---

15. See also G. Baum, "Class Struggle and the Magisterium: A New Note," *Theological Studies* 45, no. 4 (1984): 697–701.

role, which is to safeguard the just rights of workers within the framework of the common good of the whole of society; instead they become *an instrument used for other purposes*. (LE 20)

Finally, *Laborem Exercens* considers the matter of strikes. It refers to these "as a kind of ultimatum to the competent bodies," which is "legitimate in the proper conditions and within just limits." This position differs little from that of the Council. The pope adds that "workers should be assured the *right to strike*, without being subjected to personal penal sanction for taking part in a strike" (LE 20). This represents a variation on *Gaudium et Spes*'s teaching that workers should be able to participate in unions without fear of reprisals. The word "penal" implies that the state is a primary retaliatory body.

But if anything, John Paul is even more restrictive than Paul VI on the issue of the strike. He reiterates that the strike is "an extreme means" and insists that *"It must not be abused . . .* especially for 'political' purposes." In the case of essential community services, John Paul notes, "they must in every case be ensured, if necessary by means of appropriate legislation" (LE 20).

Most of the developments outlined above represent logical extensions of previous teaching. Even John Paul's teaching about struggle is not entirely new. Fifty years prior to *Laborem Exercens*, Pius XI stated that "if the class struggle abstains from enmities and mutual hatred, it gradually changes into an honest discussion of differences founded on a desire for justice" (QA 114). Nevertheless, one is struck by the detail into which *Laborem Exercens*'s teaching about unions enters. In part, this reflects Wojtyłan influences. Yet one suspects that specific situations are being addressed—especially when John Paul urges unions to remain a constructive factor of solidarity.

Solidarność

Laborem Exercens was originally scheduled for promulgation on 15 May 1981 (LE 27), but was delayed by the assassination attempt of 13 May. After further revisions (LE 27), the encyclical finally appeared on 15 September 1981. Although addressed to the entire Catholic world, it is plausible that John Paul anticipated that *Laborem Exercens* would be given close attention by the main participants in the drama which began with the Gdańsk strike of August 1980[16] and ended with the Polish regime's declaration of a "state of war" on 13 December 1981. Surprisingly few commentators have considered the magisterial developments outlined above in light of the Polish crisis. Typical is Ronald Preston's comment that "[t]he Polish political scene seems to condition what John Paul says about trade unions."[17] No explanation of the possible connection, however, is offered. Though it is difficult to prove definitive linkages, the following deductions have some validity.

The date of *Laborem Exercens*'s publication is not insignificant. The encyclical appeared whilst Solidarity was holding its first National Congress in Gdańsk between 5 September and 7 October 1981. Though it was the first assembly of a free trade union in the Soviet bloc, the congress was marked by growing disagreement among delegates over a long festering issue: the extent to which Solidarity should engage in political activity. Garton Ash summarizes the division as between:

- "fundamentalists": they viewed the Polish United Workers Party's monopoly of power as immoral, refused to accept the Party as a credible partner for Solidarity, and wished to pursue explicitly political ends; and

- "pragmatists": these referred cautiously to "supervising" the authorities, but did not question the Party's leading role. They did not wish to push the regime—or the USSR—towards using coercion to defend this central Leninist principle. Hence, they emphasized that the union was struggling for "bread" rather than political power.[18]

The Polish Episcopate's position hewed closely to that of the "pragmatists." Following the August 1980 strikes, Cardinal Wyszyński assured Solidarity's leadership of the Church's support. However, he also referred to a need for moderation and cautioned against using strikes as the only means of pressing demands.[19] Indeed in December 1980, the bishops

---

16. Many suggest that Solidarity's emergence owed much to the "psychological earthquake" experienced by Polish society during John Paul's 1979 visit. See T. Garton Ash, *The Polish Revolution: Solidarity* (London: Granta, 1991), 31–32.

17. R. Preston, "Pope John Paul II on Work," *Theology* 86, no. 709 (1983): 22.

18. See Garton Ash, *The Polish Revolution*, 226–227; cf. Szajkowski, *Next to God*, 141–142. The USSR's adherence to the Brezhnev doctrine meant that Soviet intervention to defend the Communist monopoly of power was always possible.

19. See "Cardinal Wyszyński Speaks to Solidarity Representatives," *Daily Report of the*

warned against actions being taken "which could endanger our motherland's independence and statehood"[20]—a probable reference to possible Soviet intervention in the wake of a national strike.

Zbigniew Pelczynski summarizes the Episcopate's approach throughout 1981 as one of counseling Solidarity to consolidate its gains, to focus on economic issues, but "to tread gently in the realm of political society."[21] Two days after *Laborem Exercens'* appearance, the bishops quoted the encyclical's statement about unions and politics in a text exhorting the Congress not to forget that the union's primary purpose was *not* political.[22]

It is possible, then, that *Laborem Exercens'* development of teaching on unions may have partly been directed to lending papal authority to those urging self-restraint upon Solidarity.[22] By stating that unions should neither engage in political affairs nor be linked to political parties, John Paul was making two points particularly relevant to the Polish situation. The first was that Solidarity had a right to an autonomous existence rather than being just another regime puppet. The second, however, was to dissuade Solidarity from adopting explicitly political ends.[24]

At the same time, the encyclical's affirmation that union activity *may* enter politics—insofar as it assists in reforming ownership arrangements with a view to the common good—was also pertinent to Solidarity's situation. It suffices at present to note that Solidarity did desire change in industry ownership arrangements. The "owner" of Poland's means of production was, of course, the state. Any negotiations, then, about ownership arrangements inevitably required Solidarity to enter the political arena.

Another development of teaching relevant to the Polish situation was *Laborem Exercens*'s characterization of union struggle as a form of

---

Foreign Broadcasting Information Service: Eastern Europe (Poland), 8 December 1980, G22.

20. See "Episcopate Meets, Urges Calm," *Daily Report*, 15 December 1980, G19.

21. Z. Pelczynski, "Solidarity and 'The Rebirth of Civil Society' in Poland," *Civil Society and the State*, J. Keane, ed. (London: Verso, 1988), 373–374.

22. See "The Episcopate on the Pope's Encyclical," *Daily Report*, 16 September 1981, G5.

23. The program adopted by the Congress referred to LE as "a new stimulus to work." *Tygodnik Solidarność* 29, special issue, 16 October 1981, 2.

24. Following a meeting in Rome with the Pope in January 1981, Lech Wałęsa stressed that Solidarity's purpose was not primarily political, but rather the protection of human rights. See Szajkowski, *Next to God*, 115. Solidarity's program specified that it "shall be independent of all political organizations and all organs of state administration." *Tygodnik Solidarność*, 1.

"constructive opposition." In a general sense, this may be understood as directed to Catholics tempted to confuse the struggle for justice with the interests of one group. But by specifying that the union struggle is for justice within the context of the common good, John Paul may have been indicating to Solidarity that its aim should not be the "destruction" of its opponents—which could have resulted in Soviet intervention—but rather building a community inclusive of managers as well as managed.

Two developments in the encyclical may also owe something to an effort on the pope's part to influence the Polish regime. One is the insistence that unions—specifically unions free from political parties—are indispensable. Here John Paul may have been intimating that to crush Solidarity would deprive the regime of an authentic representative of its discontented workers, not to mention society as a whole. Similarly, *Laborem Exercens*'s words concerning personal penal sanctions against strikers may have been composed with the Polish authorities in mind, given their past willingness to inflict such punishments.[25]

The Pursuit of Justice

Though a desire to influence a particular situation possibly shaped aspects of *Laborem Exercens*'s teaching about unions, certain developments may have been influenced by Wojtyłan thought. The previous chapter noted that Wojtyła spent much of the Second World War as an industrial worker. Less well known is that in 1947, Wojtyła used the vacation from his doctoral studies to minister to miners in Belgium. In the same period, Wojtyła also traveled to Marseilles, Paris, and Brussels to meet clergy involved in the worker-priest experiment.[26] The experience formed the subject of his first published article.[27] Although it focuses upon attempts to re-evangelize the French working-class, the article indicates Wojtyła's early interest in workers' problems.

On several occasions, John Paul has alluded to his youthful consciousness of social injustice. During his 1980 visit to Brazil, for example, he spoke of the powerful impressions made upon his mind when confronted with poverty. "As a young man," he stated, "I expressed these

25. See J. Lipski, *KOR: A History of the Workers' Defense Committee in Poland, 1976-1981* (Berkeley: University of California Press, 1984), 30–43.

26. See T. Szulc, *Pope John Paul II: The Biography* (New York: Scribner, 1995), 147–149.

27. See "Mission de France," *Tygodnik Powszechny* 5, no. 9 (1949): 1–2.

ideas in poetry and drama."[28]

One of Wojtyła's plays meeting this criterion is *Our God's Brother* (1945-1950). Set in Kraków in the 1880s, it is a study of Adam Chmielowski (1845-1916), a soldier and artist, who later took the religious name of Brother Albert and founded congregations of brothers and nuns which serve the homeless. In the play, Adam discovers the poor, an event which unsettles him. He consequently takes up work in a poorhouse. There then enters a character named "The Stranger"; the translator of Wojtyła's plays speculates that this might be Lenin, who lived in Kraków between 1912-1914.[29] In any event, the Stranger is certainly a Marxist who speaks the jargon of "consciousness-raising" and the "dialectics of history."[30] "Lenin" assures Adam that he is wasting his time. Radical change will only occur when the anger of oppressed factory workers, miners, and agricultural laborers[31] is harnessed. "[T]his anger," the Stranger states, "is just. What matters is that it should finally break out. . . . That act has to be speeded up, completed."[32] The oppressed "need only supply [their] anger, and forces will emerge that know how to control, use and direct it"[33]—a decidedly Leninist remark.

In response, Adam disputes neither the reality of oppression nor the justness of the anger. He knows "[a]bout anger. About great, just anger."[34] Adam insists, nonetheless, on the need "to rouse this anger in the right way. It is one thing to cultivate a just anger, make it ripen, and reveal itself as a creative power, and another to exploit that anger, use it as raw material and abuse it."[35]

The fourth of Wojtyła's poems from "The Quarry" expresses similar views. Entitled, "In Memory of a Fellow Worker," the poem reflects upon an industrial worker's death by accident:

> He wasn't alone. His muscles grew into the flesh of the crowd,
> energy their pulse, as long as they held a hammer,

---

28. "Homily at Mass for Youth (Belo Horizonte, Brazil)," *L'Osservatore Romano* (English Weekly Edition) 27 (1980), 1.

29. See B. Taborski, "Introduction to 'Our God's Brother,'" in *The Collected Plays and Writings on Theater* (Berkeley: University of California Press, 1987), 152 n.4.

30. *Our God's Brother*, in *The Collected Plays and Writings on Theater*, 190.

31. *Our God's Brother*, 235.

32. *Our God's Brother*, 190.

33. *Our God's Brother*, 235.

34. *Our God's Brother*, 266.

35. *Our God's Brother*, 243.

as long as his feet felt the ground.
And a stone smashed his temples
and cut through his heart's chamber.

They took his body, and walked in a silent line.

Toil still lingered around him, a sense of wrong.
They wore gray blouses, boots ankle-deep in mud.
In this they showed the end. . . .

They laid him down, his back on a sheet of gravel.
His wife came, worn out with worry; his son returned from
school.

Should his anger now flow into the anger of others?
It was maturing in him through its own truth and love.
Should he be used by those who come after,
deprived of substance, unique and deeply his own?. . . .

the man has taken with him the world's inner structure,
where the greater the anger, the higher the explosion of
love.[36]

The first half of this poem presents the worker's death as a blow to his
fellow laborers. It also conveys an atmosphere of exploitation,
compounded by the frazzled wife left to raise a child on her own.

The questions asked by both this poem and "Our God's Brother" are
evocative of Tolstoy's "What then must we do?" How should people
respond to injustice? Both play and poem warn against those who would
manipulate their anger. The meaning of the dead worker's life is not to be
submerged into class or history; as a person, he has a uniqueness that is
entirely his own. Instead, Wojtyła's answer is love. Whilst the workers'
anger is just, it must be transformed into love and, by implication, not
deteriorate into hate. This reminds us of *Laborem Exercens*'s insistence
that unions must not allow their struggle to degenerate into class egoism
but rather direct it towards building community.

Similar motifs pervade two short articles published the year following
publication of "The Quarry." In "Justice and Love" (1958), Wojtyła
argues that "[a] struggle does not have to be caused by hate. If it is caused

---

36. "In Memory of a Fellow Worker," *The Place Within*, 70–71.

by social or material injustice, then such a struggle is legitimate. The struggle for justice is inevitable wherever there is injustice, be it in relations between individuals or classes."[37] These words indicate an early acceptance on Wojtyła's part of the idea that struggle may proceed from injustice. One notes, however, that Wojtyła speaks of a struggle "for" rather than "against." Indeed, in his very next article, Wojtyła stated that "[s]truggle undoubtedly provides opportunities for acts of hate. But one cannot hate man. Therefore the struggle for justice must always be accompanied by the commandment of love, even love of one's enemies."[38] This motif is arguably implicit to *Laborem Exercens*'s position that struggle must ultimately be of an inclusive nature.

Naturally, one should be careful about attributing too much significance to these early Wojtyłan texts. Nevertheless, when considered as a collective whole, they do reveal a distinct view of the justice of the oppressed's cause, the legitimacy of struggle, maintaining the integrity of the struggle, and its proper ends. Like *Laborem Exercens*, then, these writings take a notion commonly associated with Marxist thought, and infuse it with profoundly Christian—and un-Marxist-Leninist—meaning.

In *The Acting Person*'s final chapter, however, we are on firmer ground, for here is to be found a systematic treatment of the "attitudes" of "opposition" and "solidarity." For contextual purposes, it is noteworthy that in the early twentieth century and the immediate post-war period, the concept of solidarity enjoyed a vogue among many Polish intellectuals, many of whom construed solidarity as an alternative to class-struggle.[39]

Wojtyła's theme that the attitude of opposition is consistent with that of solidarity is compatible with this tradition. "Opposition," as Wojtyła conceives it, cannot be construed as a class-struggle in the Marxist sense because it is concerned with realizing a greater share of the common good rather than promoting the interests of one particular group over others. Wojtyła states that "[t]he one who voices his opposition does not thereby reject his membership in the community; he does not withdraw his readiness to act and to work for the common good." This being so, it is "essentially an attitude of solidarity" (AP 342). Opposition aims at "the means employed to achieve the common good." Those who "stand up in

---

37. "Sprawiedliwość a miłość" [Justice and Love], *Tygodnik Powszechny* 12, no. 2 (1958): 7.

38. "Problem walki" [The Problem of Struggle], *Tygodnik Powszechny* 12, no. 3 (1958): 7.

39. See Zmijewski, *The Catholic-Marxist Ideological Dialogue*, 37–38, 84–85; W. Giełżyński, *Edward Abramowski, zwiastun solidarności* [Edward Abramowski, Harbinger of Solidarity] (London: Polonia, 1986).

opposition do not intend to cut themselves off from their community. On the contrary, they seek "a better, a fuller, and a more effective share of the communal life." For all these reasons, Wojtyła states, "[t]here can be no doubt that this kind of opposition is essentially constructive" (AP 343).

On one level, these comments may be understood as a subtle defense of those who opposed various policies of the Polish regime. This much is evident from one of Wojtyła's examples of "opposition": parents disagreeing with educational emphases in schools because their views concerning their child's education differ from that of the authorities (AP 286).[40] It alludes to the long battle of Polish Catholics to have religious education taught in schools during the Communist period.

However, much of the language and many of the concepts used here— "opposition," "constructive," "solidarity," "community"—seem to have been integrated into *Laborem Exercens*'s statements about union struggle. Though the encyclical does not describe opposition as "an attitude of solidarity," it insists that union oppositional struggle must remain a constructive factor which facilitates solidarity. And whilst *The Acting Person* does not refer to opposition as being directed to the realization of justice, it would seem to anticipate *Laborem Exercens* on this issue by contending that opposition is about attaining a fuller share of communal life for the one who opposes. Finally, though neither *The Acting Person* nor *Laborem Exercens* refers directly to Marxist notions of class struggle, there seems little question that each text implicitly disputes Marxist interpretations of the means and ends of opposition towards others. They also effectively underline the basic legitimacy of modern struggles for justice, whilst insisting that such struggles must be conducted in accordance with the principle of love of neighbor and directed to the common good of all.

5.4 Reforming Work-Place Relations

Unions, then, are considered by the magisterium to be critical contributors to justice in the industrial sphere. But industrial justice, according to the magisterium, also involves widening opportunities for all involved in a work-process to participate in its different dimensions. Again, John Paul's development of teaching in this regard may owe something to the

---

40. Cf. AP 343. Tymieniecka's version of AP's final chapter, published in the West and used above, is more forthright on this matter.

Solidarity factor. Nonetheless, there is much to suggest that Wojtyłan ideas have contributed as well.

Personalizing the Enterprise

The Council does not speak directly of work-place reform. It does, however, enunciate reform principles intended to undermine industrial conflict. These embrace the organizational forms through which economic activity occurs:

> In economic enterprises it is persons who work together, that is, free and independent human beings created to the image of God. Therefore, with due regard to the functions of each—owner, contractor, manager, or worker—and while maintaining the necessary unity of direction, the active participation of everyone in the running of [*actuosa participatio in curatione*] an enterprise should be promoted [refers to John XXIII, Pius XI, Pius XII, and Paul VI]. (GS 68)

In this extract, persons are presented as the foundation of economic enterprises. All members of these "work-groups" are understood to enjoy equal dignity by virtue of their personhood. The adjectives "free" and "independent" are important here. They indicate that recognizing the workers' personhood requires more than employers merely not treating workers as passive objects. As the enterprise consists, in the final analysis, of persons working together, it is reasonable that all persons have some say in all aspects of that joint activity (insofar as this is consistent with the enterprise's unity and the proper performance of the different functions). In this context, one would expect workers to have some say in deciding how their labor is used.

How, then, does the Council expect these principles to be realized within enterprises? The word *curatione* is important in this regard, and is highlighted in the footnote attached to the citation above.[41] As Nell-Breuning notes, it replaced—after much debate—the word *adminstratio* that was used in an earlier draft because some bishops viewed this word as too technical and definitive.[42] The footnote specifies that *curatione* is taken

---

41. The footnote reads: "Cf. John XXIII, *Mater et Magistra*, AAS 53 (1961), 408 [MM 32], 424 [MM 91–93], 427 [MM 109]; the word *curatione* used in the original text is taken from the Latin version of *Quadragesimo Anno* AAS 23 (1931), 199 [QA 65]. For the evolution of the question cf. also: Pius XII, *Allocution*, 3 June 1950, AAS 42 (1950), 484–488."
42. See Nell-Breuning, "Socio-Economic Life," 301.

from the Latin text of *Quadragesimo Anno*. Consequently, Nell-Breuning claims:

> it is at least hermeneutically legitimate to take it as having the same meaning as in the source, in which Pius XI recommended in very cautious terms that the status of the wage contract should be raised by some modification of company law; in this way, he suggests, employees would achieve "co-property" or "co-management," or some kind of "profit-sharing."[43]

Whilst Nell-Breuning's assessment of the significance of the Council's use of Pius XI's *curatione* is convincing, one should also take into account the other documents to which the Council's footnote refers. The first passage noted, from John XXIII's *Mater et Magistra*, states that "it is today advisable . . . that work agreements be tempered in certain respects with partnership arrangements, so that 'wage-earners and other employees participate in the ownership or the management, or in some way share in the profits.'"[44] The word "advisable" is important here. In the second passage cited from *Mater et Magistra*, John specifies that "[i]t is not, of course, possible to lay down hard and fast rules regarding the manner of such participation, for this must depend on prevailing conditions, which vary from firm to firm." Nevertheless, the same passage insists that there is a need to give workers an active part in the business of the company for whom they work (MM 91).

Important in this connection is the reference in the Council's footnote to the evolution of teaching on this matter. This indicates the Council's awareness of the controversy surrounding the issue of worker participation in enterprise management within social Catholic circles throughout the 1940s and 1950s. Put briefly, in 1948 some Austrian Catholic thinkers began asserting that *Quadragesimo Anno* held that workers had a "natural right" to the co-determination of an enterprise's affairs.[45] In the text cited by *Gaudium et Spes*, Pius XII refuted this view: "Neither the nature of the labor contract nor that of the enterprise in itself necessarily comprises a right of this kind."[46] At no point, however, did Pius condemn the idea of worker participation in management. In fact, he commended it on several

---

43. Nell-Breuning, "Socio-Economic Life," 301–302.
44. MM 32, citing QA 65.
45. For a historical overview, see J.-V. Calvez, S.J., *The Social Thought of John XXIII* (London: Burn and Oates, 1965), 37–40.
46. Pius XII, *Allocution*, AAS 42 (1950), 487 (original text in French).

occasions.[47] His point was that it could not be considered a natural right—
that is, an imprescriptible claim with all the absoluteness that this phrase
conveys.

Neither the teaching of the Council nor John XXIII dispute this
position. Instead, John describes worker participation as "advisable" and
states that it "should" occur. Likewise, the Council maintains that it
"should" be promoted. These words indicate that participation by all in the
running of enterprises in some form, though not a natural right, is
necessary.

Participation, Ownership, and Subjectivity

In broad terms, the Council's formulae for enterprise reform proceeds
from everyone recognizing the personhood of those with whom they labor.
John Paul's approach is similar, but with different emphases.

1. Ownership, Work, and Self-Realization

To understand John Paul's development of teaching on participation in
the enterprise/work-place, an outline of his position on two issues is
critical. The first involves the relationship between work and ownership.
On this matter, he states:

> When we read in the first chapter of the Bible that man is to subdue the
> earth, we know that these words refer to all the resources contained in the
> visible world and placed at man's disposal. However, these resources can
> *serve man only through work.* From the beginning there is also linked with
> work the question of ownership, for the only means that man has for
> causing the resources to serve himself and others is his work. And to be
> able through his work to make these resources bear fruit, man takes over
> ownership of small parts of the various riches of nature. . . . He takes them
> over through work and for work. (LE 12)

This text leaves one in little doubt that ownership arrangements must *serve*
work. Moreover, when the pope speaks of work "bearing fruit" for man,
one should remember that he has in mind not just material progress, but
also the moral goods that proceed from work's subjective dimension. This
point is stressed in *Laborem Exercens*'s teaching on private property:

---

47. See Calvez, *The Social Thought,* 39–40.

> The Church's teaching has always expressed the strong and deep conviction that man's work concerns not only the economy but also, and especially, personal values. The economic system itself and the production process benefit precisely when these personal values are fully respected. In the mind of St. Thomas Aquinas [refers to ST, II-II, q.65, a.2], this is the principal reason in favor of private ownership [*possessionis*] of the means of production. While we accept that for certain well-founded reasons [*certas gravesque causas*] exceptions can be made to the principle of private ownership—in our own time we even see the system of "socialized ownership" has been introduced—nevertheless the personalist *argument still holds good* both on the level of principles and *on the practical level*. If it is to be rational and fruitful, any socialization of the means of production must take this argument into account. (LE 15)[48]

Aquinas justified individual possession partly on the grounds that people are more careful to procure what is for themselves alone than that which is common, because people tend to shirk work which concerns communal goods. Put another way, private property encourages people to work and thereby become industrious and responsible for themselves. These, it would seem, are the type of "personal values" that John Paul insists that any property arrangement—private or socialized—must assist man to realize through work. In other words, property structures must facilitate man's work in the subjective sense.

The same principle underlies the second point to be clarified: the meaning of John Paul's phrase "the priority of labor." On one level, this refers to the fact that "labor is always a primary efficient cause, while capital, the whole collection of the means of production, remains a mere instrument" (LE 12). But in the next paragraph, the pope states that relations between workers and employers can be correct if they are shaped in accordance with "the principle of the substantial and real priority of labor, of the subjectivity of human labor and its effective participation in the whole labor process, independently of the nature of the services provided by the worker" (LE 13). The "real" priority of labor, then, involves ensuring that each individual's status—regardless of the precise character of their work—as a free and creative subject whose work-acts permit him to realize himself as a person, is the basic principle around which work-processes are organized. To cite John Paul at length on this matter:

---

48. The reference in this extract to ST, II-II, q.65, a.2 in LE's English edition is incorrect. It should be q.66.

When a man works, he wishes the fruit of this work to be available for himself and others, and he wishes to be able to take part in the very work process as a sharer in responsibility [*particeps onerum munerumque*] and creativity [*socius rerum auctor*] at the work-bench [*sedis operis*] to which he applies himself . . . it must be emphasized, in general terms, that the person who works desires *not only* due *remuneration* for his work; he also wishes that, within the production process, provision be made for him to be able to *know* that in his work, even on something that is owned in common [*in dominio quodam commune*], he is working *"for himself"* [*in re propria*] . . . as a true subject of work with an initiative of his own. (LE 15)

Because the person is a conscious human subject, he knows whether or not he is sharing in goods such as creativity and responsibility when working with others. It is not enough, then, just to pay each participant in a work process. Enterprises must be organized so that people may work "for themselves" in the sense that they are able to use the initiative which is theirs by virtue of being the subject of work, and thereby realize the personal values which people may attain through work in the subjective sense.

2. Proposals for Participation

In *Laborem Exercens*, the two themes outlined above are brought to bear upon the question of broadening participation in all aspects of an enterprise. Like *Gaudium et Spes*, *Laborem Exercens* allows great latitude for realization of this end. John Paul does, however, advance various proposals as worthy of consideration, most of which focus on ownership arrangements.

When it comes to ensuring "recognition of the proper position of labor and the worker in the production process," the pope "demands various adaptations in the sphere of the right to ownership." Given his reaffirmation of private ownership's effectiveness in assisting man to realize personal values, it is not surprising that John Paul states that the desired reforms "cannot be achieved by an *a priori elimination of private ownership of the means of production*"(LE 14). This only results in the means of production coming

under the administration and direct control of another group, namely those who, though not owning them, from the fact of exercising power in society *manage* them on the level of the national or the local economy. This group in authority may carry out its task satisfactorily from the point of view of the priority of labor; but it may also carry it out badly by claiming for itself a *monopoly of the administration and disposal* of the means of production. . . . [w]e can speak of socializing only when the subjective [*subiectiva*] character of society is ensured . . . when, on the basis of his work, each person is fully entitled to consider himself a part-owner [*compossessor*] of the great work-bench at which he is working with everyone else. (LE 14)

Careful nuances underlie these words. They do not, as John Paul earlier states, "exclude the *socialization*, in suitable conditions, of certain means of production," especially in light of the Church's teaching that property arrangements serve to realize "the universal destination of goods and the right to common use of them" (LE 14).[49] In the context of this encyclical, however, the stress is upon property arrangements facilitating man's acquisition of moral good through work in the subjective sense. To confine decision-making about the use of capital to a group who act "on behalf of society" does not, by definition, allow this to occur. To underline the point, John Paul states that man's awareness of working for himself "is extinguished within him in a system of excessive bureaucratic centralization, which makes the worker feel that he is just a cog in a huge machine, moved from above" (LE 15). In other words, the worker is treated simply as a commodity rather than as the creative subject of work with their own initiative. "Socializing," then, does not necessarily mean state-ownership.

Instead, John Paul recommends that attention be given to "the many proposals put forward . . . by the highest Magisterium of the Church [refers to Council and Pius XI]: *proposals for joint ownership of the means of work*, sharing by the workers in the management and/or profits of businesses, so-called shareholding by labor, etc" (LE 14). The references are to the section of *Gaudium et Spes* analyzed above as well as Pius XI's recommendations regarding the supplementing of wage contracts.[50]

Another way of ensuring the subjectivity of all within the work-process, according to John Paul, is to build community-like relations

---

49. In this sense, LE's use of the word "socialization" means the broadening of ownership so as to allow realization of the principle of common use. This is different to the meaning of the word "socialization" which appears in some English translations of MM. The Latin version of MM does not use "socialization" at all. Instead, expressions like *socialum rationum incrementa* [literally incrementing social relations] (MM 59) and *huismodi rationum socialium progressione* (MM 61) are used to describe the "increased complexity of social life."

50. It reads: "Cf. Pius XI, *Quadragesimo Anno*, AAS 23 (1931), 199 [QA 65]; Second Vatican Council, *Gaudium et Spes*, AAS 58 (1966), 1089–1090 [GS 68]."

within enterprise-bodies:

> A way towards that goal could be found by associating labor with the ownership of capital, and by producing a wide range of intermediate bodies with economic, social and cultural purposes . . . they would be living communities both in form and in substance, in the sense that the members of each body would be looked upon and treated as persons and encouraged to take an active part in the life of the body [refers to John XXIII]. (LE 14)

John Paul's recommendation that work-groups become communities may be viewed as logical progression upon the Council's teaching that enterprises, in the end, are made up of persons who ought to be treated as such. But the reference to *Mater et Magistra* is also revealing.[51] Here Pope John insists that "economic progress must be accompanied by social progress." What John has in mind is the need to ensure that everyone enjoys the benefits of economic growth (MM 73). Certainly, the extract above reflects this concern with its reference to broadening ownership. It is, however, in *Centesimus Annus* that the full import of John Paul's desire to see people who work together treating each other as persons—which is the "social progress" he primarily has in mind—becomes apparent. For unless material development is accompanied by growth in what the Council calls the "good" of brotherhood, man risks experiencing alienation.

3. Alienation

Acknowledging the consideration that Marxist thought has given to this decidedly modern expression, *Centesimus Annus* states that "Marxism criticized capitalist bourgeois societies, blaming them for the commercialization and alienation of human existence." John Paul adds, however, that "[t]his rebuke is of course based on a mistaken and inadequate idea of alienation, derived solely from the sphere of relationships of production and ownership" (CA 41). Alienation has, according to the pope, far more profound origins:

> Alienation is . . . found in work, when it is organized so as to ensure maximum returns and profits with no concern whether the worker, through his own labor, grows or diminishes as a person, either through increased participation in a genuinely supportive community or through increased

---

51. It reads: "Cf. John XXIII, *Mater et Magistra*, AAS 53 (1961), 419 [MM 73]."

isolation in a maze of relationships marked by destructive competitiveness and estrangement, in which he is considered only as a means and not an end.

The concept of alienation needs to be lead back to the Christian vision of reality, by recognizing in alienation a reversal of means and ends. When man does not recognize in himself and in others the value and grandeur of the human person, he effectively deprives himself of the possibility of benefiting from his humanity and of entering into that relationship of solidarity and community with others for which God created him. (CA 41)

These two paragraphs make the following concise points about alienation in work-relationships.

- Alienation's ultimate *cause* lies not so much in defects in man's relationship to the means of production, as posited by Marx. Instead it proceeds from the decisions of some not to treat others as persons, but rather as abstract entities to be used as a means to materialistic ends. It essentially amounts to a denial of the command to love one's neighbor as oneself. Again, John Paul uses Kantian means-ends language, this time to elaborate on how alienation occurs.

- Alienation is *experienced* by workers when others organize work in such a way that workers are unable to realize themselves as persons when working with others. Instead of growing through increased participation, they become more isolated within these relationships. John Paul's use of the word "alienation" underlines the profound inner derangement that results from such exploitation: man's *estrangement* from that which is intrinsic to his nature—his value and grandeur as a person. Alienation, then, has an anthropological dimension.

- The text above indicates that the converse of alienation is increased participation in a "work-community" in which people help others to grow as persons. By treating each other as persons, they affirm their own dignity as persons. Indeed, *Centesimus Annus* even states that "the purpose of a business firm is not simply to make a profit, but is to be found in its very existence as a *community of persons*" (CA 35).

5.5 Ownership, Subjectivity, and Alienation

While John Paul's development of teaching about reforming enterprises evidently build more or less directly upon previous teaching, in some instances further explanation is required. This is particularly true in regard to John Paul's attention to ownership arrangements. There is a strong likelihood that this reflects an effort to influence events in Poland. But when we consider John Paul's teachings regarding the real priority of labor and alienation, references to context are less illuminating. Here, attention to Wojtyła's post-conciliar writings is revealing.

Questions of Ownership

Many of *Laborem Exercens*'s statements concerning ownership seem to reflect the experience of one who has lived in a predominantly collectivized system.[52] Certainly, previous magisterial teaching had unreservedly condemned collectivization because of its suppression of private initiative.[53] Yet the pope's description of the exercise of monopolistic power over both capital and workers by a group who simply replace private owners is strikingly reminiscent of the ideas of dissident Eastern bloc writers. In *The New Class* (1958), for example, the Yugoslav revisionist intellectual, Milovan Djilas, contended that new elites based on membership of the Leninist party were exercising all the prerogatives of a monopolistic capitalist class in collectivist systems.[54] According to several commentators, this rang true of Poland between 1948 and 1989. Writing during the last decade of Communist rule, Garton Ash claimed that "[t]he [Polish] *nomenklatura* can accurately be described as a ruling class. . . . They may not individually own the means of production, but they do collectively control them. In the 1970s, they were popularly known as 'the owners of People's Poland.'"[55] *Laborem Exercens*'s particular critique of collectivist solutions may owe something to John Paul's direct experience of this situation.

It is also possible that John Paul addresses the question of socializing ownership in detail because of its relevance to Poland in 1981. Pelczynski notes that in June 1981, Solidarity activists began referring to the need to transfer control of factories from the state to democratically elected

---

52. Note, however, that Poland's agricultural sector was never fully collectivized. See Z. Pelczynski, "The Polish October," in *The History of Poland Since 1863*, R. Leslie, ed. (Cambridge: Cambridge University Press, 1980), 363.
53. See, for example, MM 55–58.
54. See M. Djilas, *The New Class* (London: Unwin Books, 1966), 37–123.
55. Garton Ash, *The Polish Revolution*, 8–9.

workers' councils.[56] Thesis 1 of the program approved by the union's Congress criticized the fact that "all economic power is concentrated in the hands of the party and bureaucratic apparatus." While Solidarity's program noted that "[t]he socialized enterprise should be the basic organizational unit in the economy," it insisted that "it should be controlled by the workers' council."[57] In its communiqué of support for Solidarity of 16 August 1981, the Polish Episcopate also spoke in favor of "expected structures of workers' responsibility in the management of their place of work." "Working people," the bishops affirmed, "rightly wish to have an opportunity to control what is jointly produced, and the manner in which the fruits of common work are shared."[58]

If these events and statements are viewed as a collective whole, then *Laborem Exercens*—particularly its emphasis that socialized arrangements must allow people to know that they are "part-owners" working "for themselves"—may be seen as indirectly lending support to Solidarity's demands for worker-participation in management and ownership. Similarly, the encyclical's suggestions concerning the various ways that a "non-state-collectivist" socializing of enterprises might be realized, could be interpreted as showing how this end might be achieved in a political system which viewed private ownership negatively.

The Priority of the Subjective

Polish considerations, however, less easily explain *Laborem Exercens*'s emphasis on ensuring that both man's uniqueness as the subject of work and the greater importance of work in the subjective sense are recognized in work-processes. On one level, this flows naturally from the encyclical's attention to these points. At the same time, one should note that in this regard, the encyclical parallels *The Acting Person*'s consideration of the fact that when people act, it is often with others.

The Acting Person's last chapter begins by asking "how . . . does man fulfil himself when acting together with others?" (AP 323). The key to realizing this end is what Wojtyła calls "participation." This is defined as "the person's transcendence in the action when the action is performed 'together with others'—transcendence which manifests that the person has

---

56. See Pelczynski, "Solidarity," 375.

57. *Tygodnik Solidarność*, 2.

58. "Statement of Main Council of the Polish Episcopate," 16 August 1981. Full text in P. Raina, *Poland 1981* (London: Allen and Unwin, 1985), 317.

not become altogether absorbed by social interplay, but stands out as having retained his very own freedom of choice and action" (AP 269).[59] We might say, then, that participation indicates that man, when acting together with others, is nevertheless able to realize the subjective value of his own acting.

But before relating this point to developments in magisterial teaching about the organization of work, it should be noted that Wojtyła goes on to describe participation as "a constitutive factor of community" (AP 332). *The Acting Person* identifies two types of community: "communities of being" and "communities of acting" (AP 334–335). The former includes "natural" communities such as the family. Communities of action are considered to be of a more temporary nature and never absorb man to the same degree as natural communities. Here Wojtyła may be drawing upon the German philosophical distinction between *Gemeinschaft* (community) and *Gesellschaft* (society).

Despite this difference, Wojtyła proposes that *any* community can be understood on two levels—its objective and subjective purposes. A team of laborers digging a trench, he suggests, is a community of acting. This "acting community" may be considered "from the point of view of the aim that its members are collectively striving for" (AP 335–336). In the laborers' case, the "aim" is the trench. "Hence," Wojtyła continues, "in the objective sense, a 'community of acting' may be defined according to the aim that brings men to act together." But from the viewpoint of the significance of such action to the person, Wojtyła argues that "it is not only the objective community of acting but also its subjective moment, which we have called here 'participation', that is important." The question, then, "is whether a man belonging to a community of acting . . . is in a position in his communal acting to perform real actions and fulfil himself" (AP 336).

Now as presented by Pope John Paul, enterprises certainly constitute acting rather than natural communities. But in the extracts above, the primary point is that the person must have a sense of "acting for himself" as the community strives to realize its "objective" goal. *Laborem Exercens*, of course, makes a similar point when it insists that each person must have a sense of "working for himself" when working with others ("the priority of the subjectivity of human labor"), and that ownership arrangements must serve this end.

---

59. The citation from Tymieniecka's version of AP's final chapter is used here because its meaning is clearer than the literal translation. Cf. AP 325.

Other legitimate correlations may also be made between *The Acting Person*'s last chapter and John Paul's teaching about enhancing participation in work processes. "As a member of a community," Wojtyła states, "a man has other men for neighbors" (AP 349). He then adds:

> The notion of "neighbor" forces us not only to recognize but also to appreciate what in man is independent of his membership in any community whatever; it forces us to observe and appreciate in him something that is far more absolute. The notion of "neighbor" is strictly related to man as such and to the value itself of the *person* . . . Thus the notion of "neighbor" refers then to . . . the broadest foundations of inter-human community. . . . Any community becoming detached from this fundamental community must unavoidably lose its human character. (AP 349–350) [italics added]

Neither *Laborem Exercens* nor *Centesimus Annus* speak of "neighbor" in this sense. But they do emphasize that it is fundamental that people working together recognize each other as persons. Though this position is surely implicit to the Council's teachings about enterprises, the text above may explain why John Paul stresses the point: without recognition of the basic anthropological truth that each member of a work-process is a person, the human character of that work-process will begin to disintegrate. As we know, the pope goes on to explain that the lack of recognition of personhood in work-relationships eventually results in people experiencing alienation. *The Acting Person* and associated Wojtyłan articles proceed in a similar manner.

Alienation: Denial of Personhood

Several of Wojtyła's post-conciliar writings appear to have provided *Centesimus Annus* with much of the conceptual framework used in its discussion of alienation. This term acquired philosophical currency with Hegel, but its most common usage is generally associated with the various systems of Marxist thought. Most Marxists understand the idea as indicating a disordered state of human life in society. Their emphasis, however, is invariably on man's defective relation to the fruits and instruments of his labor.[60]

---

60. See N. Lobkowitz, "Alienation," *Marxism, Communism, and Western Society*, Vol. 1 (New York: Herder and Herder, 1972), 88–93.

Writing in 1977, Wojtyła acknowledged the importance of the idea of alienation in modern philosophical discourse. "It seems," he claimed, "that the concept of alienation introduced into philosophy in the nineteenth century and taken up by Marx, is meeting with great success today." Wojtyła then indicated that he regarded the term as useful by stating that "the concept of alienation seems to be necessary in the philosophy of man." Its usefulness for Wojtyła, however, lay not so much in understanding the effects of man's relationship with things upon man. "Put to good account," he stated, "the concept of alienation could help in the analysis of the human reality, and that *not* from the point of view of external conditions on the side of the extra-human world, but within the scope of the strictly inter-human relations."[61] For Wojtyła, the idea of alienation was a way of conceptualizing the effects of negative inter-human relationships upon man as well as man's experience of non-fulfillment as a person.

Wojtyła's first major discussion of alienation occurs in *The Acting Person*. Like *Centesimus Annus*, *The Acting Person* reaches certain conclusions about alienation via a critique of the Marxist understanding of the word. It begins by stating that "[n]ineteenth and twentieth century philosophy has interpreted alienation as the isolation or separation of man from his very humanness . . . the value that we have here defined as personalistic" (AP 353). The point is reiterated by Wojtyła in an article published the same year as *The Acting Person*: "Alienation, when it occurs in life, involves estrangement from that which properly belongs to the human subject—his personhood."[62] Here we observe the anthropological aspect of alienation being brought to the fore—the sense of being separated from one's value as person—just as it is in *Centesimus Annus*.

Continuing its analysis, *The Acting Person* characterizes those views which hold that alienation's origin "lies chiefly in the system of things—man's relationship to nature, the system of production, civilization" as "prejudiced and misleading." *Centesimus Annus*, we recall, uses the word "inadequate" to describe this Marxist proposition. Wojtyła agrees that the "system of things" can contribute to human alienation: "it would be impossible," he states, "to reject this view entirely" (AP 353). But like the encyclical, Wojtyła does not consider it the primary cause:

---

61. "Participation or Alienation," 72.
62. "Problem teorii moralności" [The Problem of the Theory of Morality], in *W nurcie zagadnień posoborowych* [In the Current of Post-conciliar Considerations], Vol.3, B. Bejze, ed. (Warszawa: Polskie Towarzystwo Teologiczne, 1969), 243.

we have to remember that though man did not create nature, he is its master
. . . it is man who creates the systems of production, forms of technical
civilization, utopias of future progress, programs of social organization of
human life, etc. Thus it lies in his power to prevent civilization from
exerting a dehumanizing influence and causing alienation. That is why we
must assume that the alienation for which man himself is responsible is the
prime cause of any alienation resulting from the reference systems based
on things. (AP 353–354)

To claim, then, that alienation is ultimately caused by "systems of
things" is to deny man's ascendancy over the material world. If man is
indeed master, then he—and not things or structures—is the ultimate
cause of alienation. Thus, as Wojtyła explains, "[m]an's alienation from
other men stems from a disregard for, or a neglect of, that real depth of
participation which is indicated by the term *neighbor*" (AP 354). We recall
here that in *The Acting Person* to see another as our "neighbor" is to
recognize their value as a person. Although *Centesimus Annus* does not
use the word "neighbor," its point is the same: alienation ultimately stems
not from relationships of production, but man's failure to recognize and
treat others as persons.

Centesimus Annus, however, makes two points about alienation which
are less evident in *The Acting Person*: that people experience alienation
when their participation in work-relationships hinders their self-
realization, and/or results in them being used solely as a means to an end.
Other Wojtyłan writings, however, do use the concept of alienation in
these senses. One piece, for instance, speaks of people experiencing
"alienation" when they are deprived "in some respect of the possibility of
fulfilling themselves in community." In short, alienation is the obverse of
what *The Acting Person* defines as participation: the fulfillment of oneself
when acting together with others. In such circumstances, Wojtyła adds:

The social processes, which should lead to a true subjectivity of all, are
then checked or even turned back, for man cannot retrieve himself as
subject in this process. The social life is, so to speak, beyond him; it is not
only against him, but even "at his expense." Existing and acting "together
with others," he does not fulfil himself.[63]

This, one may suggest, anticipates *Centesimus Annus*'s teaching that
work-relationships directed solely towards profit rather than facilitating

---

63. "The Person: Subject and Community," 306.

the self-realization of all, progressively diminish the worker's sense of personhood, causing him to become isolated and unfulfilled even while working alongside others.

Other Wojtyłan writings foreshadow *Centesimus Annus*'s linkage of a reversal of means (things) and end (the person) to alienation. In one instance, Wojtyła suggests that this position is implicit to conciliar teaching:

> the Council calls attention to a certain danger . . . that the "order of things" will take precedence over the "order of persons". . . . In such a system, socialization may be diverted from its basic orientation towards the "welfare of persons". . . . In other words, Vatican II perceives in contemporary social processes—those connected with the enormous advance of technological, industrial, and material factors—the *danger of a fundamental alienation of human beings*. People can easily become tools in the system of things, the material system created by their own intelligence, and they can becomes objects of different kinds of social manipulation.[64]

In conciliar teaching, the word "socialization" is used only by *Gaudium et Spes*: "Socialization, as it is called, is not without its dangers, but it brings with it many advantages for the strengthening and betterment of human qualities and for the protection of human rights" (GS 25).

Though Wojtyła's words in no way condemn the modern world's material progress, they do place greater emphasis on the potential danger this represents to man than the Council. But for our purposes, one should note Wojtyła's description of alienation as resulting from man being treated as a tool by others. *Centesimus Annus* uses analogous and characteristically Wojtyłan Kantian-personalist language of reversal of means and ends to describe this aspect of the process of alienation.

5.6 Conclusion

Only three of the vast number of topics subsumable under the title of industrial relations have been examined here. Nonetheless, in each case John Paul has developed Catholic teaching. Most of these developments build upon statements of *Gaudium et Spes* and, in the case of unions, *Octogesima Adveniens*. Several, however, underline the importance of

---

64. "Rodzicielstwo a 'communio personarum'" [Parenthood and the 'Communio Personarum'], *Ateneum Kapłańskie* 84, no. 1 (1975): 29–30.

ensuring that man as a person and the subject of work is able to self-realize moral values when working: that is, the "priority of the subjective." In these instances, the influence of Wojtyłan moral-anthropological emphases has been significant. *Laborem Exercens*'s teachings about materialism and economism, for example, reflect thoughts articulated in Wojtyła's writings about the dangers of denying man's moral-spiritual dimension and the greater importance of the intransitive aspect of human acts. They may also owe something to *Love and Responsibility*'s use of Kantian-personalist terminology to describe relations between workers and employers.

There is much to indicate that all of these themes have conditioned in some way John Paul's statements about the nature of worker exploitation and the modern world of work which began to emerge in the eighteenth century. They also affect John Paul's analysis of how contemporary property structures may assist or inhibit man in realizing personal values when working with others.

Here we observe that *Laborem Exercens* does not avoid dealing with the fact that the socialized ownership of enterprises was prevalent in many nations, not least the Communist world, in 1981. John Paul's response, one notes, is not to condemn such arrangements outright. Apart from not excluding the permissibility of socialization in certain instances, he outlines the criteria which socialized arrangements must meet before their legitimacy can be affirmed: like any other property structure, they must actualize the principle of common use and facilitate man's acquisition of moral good through work. On these grounds, the pope articulates a fresh critique of state-collectivism based upon its unspoken denial of the subjectivity of the majority, whilst outlining ways in which property arrangements might allow all members of a work-process to know that they are working for themselves. In a certain sense, then, this may be viewed as a critical yet constructive engagement with what was a widespread modern reality in 1981, with Wojtyłan thought informing much of the reflection.

There is a case for suggesting that some of the developments identified throughout this chapter have been influenced by events in Poland. This is especially true of *Laborem Exercens*'s teachings about unions. Yet even here, identifiably Wojtyłan ideas seem to have affected the teaching, particularly *The Acting Person*'s analysis of the attitudes of opposition and solidarity. At the same time, the encyclical's teachings about struggle may have been influenced by Wojtyła's grappling in poetry, plays, and articles with the problem of how one should respond to injustice in the modern world. Like *Laborem Exercens*, these writings implicitly repudiate the Marxist understanding of the ends of struggle while simultaneously affirming the validity of modern struggles for justice which are permeated by an ethic of love of neighbor.

But Wojtyłan ideas have also influenced magisterial developments of little relevance to Solidarity's situation. Though *Centesimus Annus*'s statements about alienation represent logical progression upon the Council's understanding of worker exploitation, the encyclical's critique of the Marxist interpretation of alienation parallels that of Wojtyła's writings. Whilst acknowledging Marxism's attention to this decidedly modern concept, both the encyclical and Wojtyła's writings suggest that Marxist explanations for this phenomenon are inadequate. Both consequently modify the idea so that it underlines the importance of recognizing man's nature as a person. Alienation is also used in these texts to describe man's experience of estrangement when he is unable to realize himself as a person. In short, both John Paul's teachings and Wojtyła's writings imbue the idea of alienation with moral and anthropological themes, and, in the process of doing so, demonstrate a willingness to engage with modern ideas.

The background, of course, to modern worker exploitation is that of the rise of industrialization and capitalism. The next chapter illustrates that the magisterium's view of capitalism has always been mixed. Though John Paul's teaching is no different in this regard, it does identify new good and new problems in capitalist systems.

6
CAPITALISM:
TYPES, ENTERPRISE, AND CULTURE

6.1 Introduction

When Leo XIII spoke of the spirit of revolutionary change, he referred to its influence "in the cognate sphere of practical economy," including "the vast expansion of industrial pursuits" (RN 1). These words demonstrate that industrial capitalism's emergence in Europe substantially defined the world upon which *Rerum Novarum* reflected. In the twentieth century, the creation of many economies loosely identified as "capitalist" was presided over by Christian Democrats. Yet their views about capitalism were decidedly mixed. One post-war Italian prime minister, Amintore Fanfani, exemplifies this. While his book, *Catholicism, Protestantism and Capitalism*, rejected collectivization, Fanfani was extremely critical of the "capitalist spirit" because it "held that wealth is simply a means for the unlimited, individualistic and utilitarian satisfaction of all possible human needs."[1]

Throughout John Paul's pontificate, the topic of capitalism has received significant attention from the magisterium. One reason for this has been the collapse of collectivist economies. This has been accompanied by increased market liberalization throughout the world. Then there is the phenomenon, first commented on by Samuel Huntington,

---

1. A. Fanfani, *Catholicism, Protestantism and Capitalism* (Notre Dame: University of Notre Dame Press, 1984), 28–29.

that most of the countries embracing market economies since 1970 are located in predominantly Catholic regions such as Central-Eastern Europe and Latin America.[2]

Taken as a collective whole, these changes have caused Catholic thinkers to look carefully at capitalism in recent years. Some, often associated with Latin American theologies of liberation, have been extremely critical.[3] They suggest, among other things, that capitalism has produced widening wealth gaps, rising unemployment, etc. Others argue that the Church needs to appreciate capitalism's achievements. Novak, for example, maintains that capitalism's wealth-producing capacity has progressively increased living standards. He also contends that there is much consonance between the Catholic emphasis on creativity, and the dynamism of what he calls "democratic capitalism."[4]

Throughout this ongoing discourse, there has been much citation of papal documents. Karol Wojtyła is, of course, the first pontiff to come from a mostly collectivized country. Some portray him as "a good social democrat." In 1991, John Wyles wrote:

When all the speech-making is done and the writings published, it is quite possible that the most prominent advocacy of socialist democratic values in Europe this year will not come from the likes of Willy Brandt, Felipe Gonzáles or even Neil Kinnock, but from Karol Wojtyła, the Polish Pontiff whose frequently controversial views suggest a quiet loathing for aspects of liberal capitalism. . . . The Vatican is nervous about acquiring political labels, but John Paul II has long been one of Europe's leading socialists. . . The impression the Pope gives is that he can find little more to praise in liberal capitalism than in marxist communism.[5]

An analysis, however, of developments in teaching about capitalism during John Paul's pontificate suggests that the pope's position is more complex than Wyles suggests. To this end, this chapter considers three issues. The first involves the magisterium's statements regarding different "types" of capitalism. This leads to a consideration of the teaching about

---

2. See S. Huntington, "Religion and the Third Wave," *The National Interest* 24 (1991): 29–42.

3. See, for example, Gutiérrez, *A Theology of Liberation*, 39 n.18, 111–112, 127 ns.53 and 55.

4. See Novak, *Freedom with Justice*, 39–57, 96–107, 157–164.

5. J. Wyles, "Vatican Prepares Attack on Sins of Capitalism," *Financial Times*, 9/10 March 1991: Sec.2, 1.

two related matters: personal economic initiative and consumerist culture. Though John Paul's attention to contemporary transformations explains much development, Wojtyłan ideas have also contributed.

6.2 Capitalism?

In *Centesimus Annus*, John Paul poses the question of whether, following communism's demise, "capitalism should be the goal of the countries now making efforts to rebuild their economy and society?" Explaining his answer, the pope twice prefaces his statements with the phrase "If by 'capitalism' is meant" (CA 42). These words point to a difficulty in any discussion about capitalism. What, indeed, is "capitalism"?

For a start, the expression is fraught with semantic ambiguity. It originated in Marxist discourse to describe the societies which emerged following the shift in their economic base from land to capital. Yet capitalism is also associated with classical liberalism and texts such as *The Wealth of Nations*. The complexity is heightened by the fact that the adjective "liberal"—often attached to capitalism—is commonly appropriated in "Anglo-American" countries by advocates of government intervention, while those favoring "free markets" are sometimes referred to as "conservatives." Paradoxically, the latter term indicates an orientation towards preserving the past, an attitude incompatible in certain respects with entrepreneurial inventiveness.[6]

Further complicating interpretations of capitalism are the different cultural connotations attached to the word. Some Catholic thinkers maintain that the phrase is used more positively in predominantly "Protestant-Anglo-American" societies than in "Catholic-European" nations.[7] Even capitalism's association with democratic polities is not necessarily helpful. The instances of Chile and Singapore illustrate that free markets can co-exist alongside less-than-democratic political arrangements.

Attempts to identify capitalism with certain economic institutions are also problematic. Defining it as a "private property-based" economy, for example, can be misleading; other economies—medieval, mercantilist—

---

6. See F. von Hayek's "Why I Am Not a Conservative," *The Constitution of Liberty* (Chicago: University of Chicago Press, 1960), 397–411.
7. See, for example, R. Buttiglione, "The Free Economy and the Free Man," in *A New Worldly Order*, 65–66.

have enjoyed a private property basis. Likewise, associating capitalism with industrialization is questionable as industrialization has occurred in command economies. Indeed, contemporary "first world" capitalism is often more identified with financial services, stock markets, etc.

For our purposes, there is no pressing need to define capitalism. The magisterium itself does not rely upon any one interpretation. Instead it has tended, in one commentator's words, "to engage in sorting out and evaluating the conceptual and moral frameworks underlying capitalism."[8] It is, nevertheless, useful to be aware of the ambiguities surrounding the term.

6.3 Types of Capitalism

In discussing magisterial teaching about capitalism, Baum claims that *Gaudium et Spes* refers hopefully to welfare capitalism's humanizing tendencies.[9] The word "capitalism" is not, however, mentioned in the Pastoral Constitution. Nor is any other economic system. J. Bryan Hehir speculates that this reflects the Council's determination not to allow its statements to be construed as endorsing either of the economic systems then dominant in Western or Eastern states.[10]

Yet within the Council's consideration of economic activity are to be found various statements which, albeit indirectly, may be understood as expressing views about different capitalist systems. According to the Council, "it is necessary that the voluntary initiatives of individuals and of free groups should be integrated with state enterprises and organized in a suitable and harmonious way" (GS 65). This seems to indicate approval of "mixed" economies—those which recognize the value of free economic activity, but also allow a place for state enterprises whilst underlining the need for overall direction. Put another way, the Council hopes that private and state enterprise will complement each another through acceptance of some general social guidance.

However, the Council effectively comes out against another type of capitalism. It states that economic development should not "be left to the almost mechanical evolution of economic activity . . . Hence we must

---

8. D. Finn, "The Church and the Economy in the Modern World," in *Questions of Special Urgency*, 163.
9. See Baum, "Liberal Capitalism," 80.
10. See J.B. Hehir, "Papal Foreign Policy," *Foreign Policy* 78 (1990): 32.

denounce as false, those doctrines which stand in the way of all reform on the pretext of a false notion of freedom" (GS 65).

This is as close as the Council comes to speaking directly about a form of capitalism, that being its laissez-faire manifestation. In doing so, it reflects the firm stance of pre-conciliar magisterial teaching on this matter. Some of the strongest words come from Pius XI:

> the right ordering of economic life cannot be left to a free competition of forces. From this source . . . have originated and spread all the errors of individualist economic teaching. Destroying through forgetfulness or ignorance the social and moral character of economic life, it held that economic life must be considered and treated as altogether free from and independent of public authority . . . free competition, while justified and useful provided it is kept within certain limits, clearly cannot direct economic life—a truth which the outcome of this application in practice of the tenets of this evil individualistic spirit has more than sufficiently demonstrated. (QA 88)

Charles correctly cautions that this judgment was expressed during the 1930s depression.[11] This does not, however, detract from the force of Pius's central point: whilst competition is not only legitimate but productive of good results, history demonstrates the negative consequences of absolutizing economic freedom.

Populorum Progressio maintains the Council's approach, though with different emphases. For one thing, Pope Paul states that in order to avoid increasing wealth disparities, public authorities must "encourage, stimulate, supplement and integrate" the economic activity of individuals and intermediatory bodies (PP 33). This picture parallels the Council's "mixed economy," though more attention is given to the state's role: the provision of a framework—which includes intervention—for free economic activity so that the universal destination of goods is not compromised.

Unlike the Council, however, *Populorum Progressio* specifically refers to "capitalism." Reflecting upon the effects of industrialization, Paul states that it has contributed to man's "control over his own way of life" (PP 25). Yet he also associates this situation with some negative developments:

---

11. See Charles, *The Social Teaching*, 282.

certain concepts have somehow arisen out of these new conditions and insinuated themselves into the fabric of human society. These concepts present profit as the chief spur to economic progress, free competition as the supreme law of economics, and private ownership of the means of production as an absolute right, having no limits or concomitant social obligations. (PP 26)

It is not clear from this extract if these "certain concepts" proceed from industrialization itself. They do, however, link industrialization's emergence with the appearance of ideas which considered material gain to be the primary end of economic activity, subverted the principle of common use, and accorded competition an inviolate status. These concepts are collated under the heading of "unbridled *liberalism*." The encyclical then defines liberalism's association with industrialization as "a type of *capitalism*" which "has given rise to hardships, unjust practices and fratricidal conflicts that persist to this day" (PP 26).

But before claiming that *Populorum Progressio* "sternly condemns capitalism,"[12] one should note that Paul speaks of "a type" of capitalism. This implies that other, perhaps acceptable capitalisms have developed. At no stage does Paul identify profit, private property, or competition as erroneous in themselves. It is liberalism's *absolutization* of these which is problematic.

This leaves the magisterium free to affirm systems which maintain but "de-absolutize" these elements. Paul's words about the market move in this direction. "Its advantages," he states, "are evident when the parties involved are not affected by any excessive inequalities of economic power: it stimulates progress and rewards effort" (PP 58). Schall describes this statement as the magisterium's most positive assessment of the market before 1991.[13] Nevertheless, Paul also says that developed nations have recognized the benefits of restoring "balance to their own economies, a balance, which is frequently upset by competition when left to itself," not least by adopting policies which seek "to restore comparable opportunities to competing industries which are not equally prospering" (PP 60). In short, they have sought to keep the market "within limits so that it operates

12. C. Skok, "The Social Economics of *Gaudium et Spes*," *International Journal of Social Economics* 13, no. 9 (1986): 39.
13. See J. Schall, S.J., "To Defend and to Teach: The Intellectual Legacy of Paul VI," *Lay Witness* 15, no. 11 (1993): 5.

justly and fairly" (PP 61). Paul's words about "liberal capitalism" would therefore not appear applicable to "de-liberalized" forms of capitalism.

6.4 Capitalism and Capitalisms

Capitalism is accorded attention in each of John Paul's social encyclicals. When it comes to "types," however, *Laborem Exercens* and *Centesimus Annus* are the most illuminating.

Defining Capitalism

When *Laborem Exercens* appeared, an editor of *Fortune* magazine commented that it "displays once again the evidently invincible determination of the Church not to understand capitalism."[14] Analysis of the text, however, suggests that the encyclical attempts to understand capitalism not just in theoretical terms, but as a historical phenomenon as well.

For a start, John Paul defines those situations in which primacy is accorded to "the objective dimension of work" and where man's status as "the effective subject of work and its true maker and creator" is not sufficiently recognized, as capitalist: "whatever the program or name under which [this] occurs, should rightly be called 'capitalism' " (LE 7). "Capitalism," then, describes *any* system in which work's subjective dimension and man's nature as the creative subject is trivialized. Hence, one may say that a state-collectivist economy in which people are treated as objects is, strictly speaking, "capitalist." As the Pope states, "the error of early capitalism can be repeated wherever man is treated on the same level as the whole complex of the means of production" (LE 7).

Although John Paul provides a "strict" definition of capitalism, his reference to "early capitalism" demonstrates his willingness to consider this topic in its historical context. "Everybody knows," he states, "that capitalism has a definite historical meaning as an economic and social system as opposed to 'socialism' or 'communism' " (LE 7).

The encyclical's historical analysis begins with a reference to "the system of injustice and harm . . . that weighed heavily upon workers in [the] period of industrialization." *Laborem Exercens* maintains that

---

14. D. Seligman, "Unfair to Capitalism," *Fortune*, 2 November 1981, 63.

> [t]his state of affairs was favored by the liberal socio-economic system, which, in accordance with its "economistic" premises, strengthened and safe-guarded economic initiative by the possessors of capital alone, but did not pay sufficient attention to the rights of workers, on the grounds that human work is solely an instrument of production, and that capital is the basis, efficient factor and purpose of production. (LE 8)

Here John Paul attributes the workers' suffering to neither industrialization nor private economic initiative, but rather, like *Populorum Progressio*, to the "liberalism" that existed alongside them. Indeed, if anything, his words imply that the opportunity for economic initiative should be enjoyed by more people. John Paul goes further, however, than his predecessor by identifying the error at the heart of the liberal system—the economistic precept of viewing work primarily in terms of its objective dimension and neglecting its intransitive purpose.

Later paragraphs trace the error of reducing labor to the status of capital to "the philosophy and economic theories of the eighteenth century" and "the economic and social practices of that time" (LE 13). As mentioned, there are good reasons to think that the pope has Enlightenment ideas and early industrial England in mind. Significantly, he describes this error as "now part of history" and identifies it with "primitive capitalism and liberalism" (LE 13). Thus, we may infer that capitalism has changed. Indeed, John Paul indicates that it *can* change for the better, and in some instances has done so.

This change revolves around the question of ownership. The "position of 'rigid' capitalism," *Laborem Exercens* states, "continues to be unacceptable, namely the position that defends the exclusive right to private ownership as an untouchable 'dogma' of economic life." As noted, Paul VI also condemned this idea. John Paul, however, adds that the absolutization of private property denies "the priority of work and, thereby, man's character as a *subject* in . . . the dynamic *structure of the whole economic process*." Accordingly, the right to private ownership "should undergo a constructive revision" (LE 14).

In John Paul's view, this revision has happened in many instances: "profound changes" have been brought about, as a consequence of "worker solidarity, together with a clearer and more committed realization by others of workers' rights." Capitalism, in other words, has not remained static: "[v]arious forms of neo-capitalism [*novi capitalismi*] . . . have developed." Expressions of this include workers sharing "in running businesses and in controlling their productivity," and exercising "influence over work and pay and also over social legislation" (LE 8). In short, the efforts of workers, those sympathetic to their cause, and the state, have in many instances qualified liberalism's absolutization of property so that more people are able to assume responsibility for their work. Some capitalist economies have thus been modified to reflect the fact that workers, like everyone else, are free subjects of work with an initiative of their own.

In Praise of the Market

Prior to 1991, it is fair to say that there ran throughout magisterial teaching a parallel critique of the two political-economic paradigms dominating the twentieth century: "liberal capitalism" and "Marxist collectivism." Though, for example, *Gaudium et Spes* condemns laissez-faire capitalism, it also denounces those doctrines "which subordinate the basic rights of individuals and groups to the collective organization of production" (GS 65). Thus one may agree with Hehir that with communism's collapse, "the context for the ethical evaluation of socio-economic systems [by the magisterium] has shifted."[15] This is obliquely acknowledged by *Centesimus Annus*'s detailed historical and theoretical attention to the different forms assumed by capitalism.

According to John Paul, one result of the Second World War "was the spread of Communist totalitarianism over more than half of Europe and over other parts of the world." The response of the non-Communist world was varied. In some countries, there was "a positive effort to rebuild a democratic society inspired by social justice, so as to deprive Communism of its revolutionary potential." This was characterized by:

- "attempts . . . to preserve free market mechanisms." Coupled with the maintenance of "a stable currency," this provided "the conditions for steady and healthy economic growth in which people through their own work [could] build a better future for themselves and their families"; and

---

15. J.B. Hehir, "The Social Role of the Church: Leo XIII, Vatican II and John Paul II," in *Catholic Social Thought and the New World Order*, J. Houck and O. Williams, C.S.C., eds. (Notre Dame: University of Notre Dame Press, 1993), 46.

- efforts to "avoid making market mechanisms the only point of reference for social life" by subjecting them "to public control which upholds the principle of the universal destination of material goods." This took the form of "an abundance of work opportunities, a solid system of social security and professional training . . . the effective action of unions, [and] the assistance provided in cases of unemployment" (CA 19).

As a collective whole, this sounds like an affirmation of the "social market economy," usually associated with European Christian Democrat parties.[16] But whilst a historical reflection, this picture effectively encapsulates the principles and guidelines outlined by Paul VI. Like *Populorum Progressio*, it places the workings of competition within a broader framework provided by the public authorities which prevents competition from becoming absolutized.

Centesimus Annus then adds that another kind of response to Marxism was "the affluent society or the consumer society." This sought "to defeat Marxism on the level of pure materialism by showing how a free market society can achieve a greater degree of satisfaction than Communism, while equally excluding spiritual values." Although John Paul agrees that the affluent society highlighted Marxism's failure "to contribute to a humane and better society," it is nevertheless unsatisfactory. By denying "an autonomous existence and value to morality, law, culture and religion . . . it totally reduces man to the sphere of economics" (CA 19). We may say, then, that John Paul's "affluent society" is essentially based upon economistic-materialistic premises.

Looking, however, at the present, John Paul underlines an important shift in modern capitalism, the emergence of what he refers to as "the modern *business economy*." *Centesimus Annus* states that

> there are specific differences between the trends of modern society and those of the past. Whereas at one time the decisive factor of production was *the land*, and later capital . . . today the decisive factor is increasingly *man himself*, that is, his knowledge . . . his capacity for integrated and compact organization, as well as his ability to perceive the needs of others and satisfy them. (CA 32)

---

16. For a summary of Christian Democracy's normative principles, see D. Goulet, "Economic Systems, Middle Way Theories, and Third World Realities," in *Co-Creation*, 150–151.

In these words, John Paul appears, as Weigel claims, to identify a new "sign of the times."[17] Though the pope does not use this phrase, he refers earlier in the same paragraph to the "increasingly evident and decisive" role of "disciplined and creative *human work* and, as part of that work, *initiative and entrepreneurial ability.*" This, he states, is a "process, which throws practical light on a truth about the person which Christianity has constantly affirmed": that "besides the earth, man's principal resource is *man himself.* His intelligence enables him to discover the earth's productive potential and the many different ways in which human needs can be satisfied." This process, the pope adds, "should be viewed carefully and favorably" (CA 32).

As a modern development, then, one may say that capitalism's shift towards greater reliance upon the human resources of intelligence and knowledge meets with magisterial approval. John Paul indicates, however, that this change has not altered an important principle of magisterial teaching. *Populorum Progressio*, we recall, stated that market transactions are just when participants start from relatively equal positions of economic power. Hence, if the central element of economic power is increasingly man's "*possession of know-how, technology and skill*" (CA 32) —what some call "human capital"[18]—rather than possession of "material capital," then more people must acquire such knowledge if market transactions are to be just.

Indeed, it is the lack of "human capital" which *Centesimus Annus* identifies as a new problem: "many people . . . do not have the means which would enable them to take their place in an effective and humanly dignified way within a productive system in which work is truly central. They have no possibility of acquiring the creative knowledge which would enable them to express their creativity and develop their potential" (CA 33). But like Paul VI, John Paul does not view this as de-legitimizing the market. The issue, rather, is to help people "acquire expertise, to enter the circle of exchange, and to develop their skills in order to make the best use of their capacities and resources" (CA 34). Here, then, is an instance of the magisterium rearticulating its teaching in the context of new conditions. If market transactions are to be just, then more people must acquire the new currency of economic power so that they can participate in the circle of

---

17. See G. Weigel, *Soul of the World* (Leominster: Gracewing, 1996), 139.
18. See, for example, Novak, *The Catholic Ethic*, 106–107.

exchange on a more equitable basis.

Later sections of *Centesimus Annus* move away from these historical observations and focus upon the market in theoretical terms. On one level, John Paul underlines the market's empirical assets: it is "the most efficient instrument for utilizing resources and effectively responding to needs" (CA 34). But John Paul also specifies the market's limits:

- "there are many human needs which find no place on the market" (CA 34). One cannot, for example, purchase love.

- "economic freedom is only one element of human freedom" (CA 39).

- "there are goods which by their very nature cannot and must not be bought or sold" (CA 40). Human life would presumably qualify as such a good, since persons are not commodities.

Moreover, *Centesimus Annus* devotes considerable attention to the state's role vis-à-vis the market. *Populorum Progressio* referred to the state as coordinating, supplementing, and encouraging non-state economic activity. Though John Paul does not contradict this, he elaborates upon *how* the state goes about this task.

Having stated that "the activity of a market economy cannot be conducted in an institutional, juridical or political vacuum," *Centesimus Annus* maintains that the state must provide "guarantees of individual freedom and private property, a stable currency and efficient public services." It also has the task of "overseeing the exercise of human rights in the economic sector" as well as the "right to intervene when particular monopolies create delays or obstacles to development." Additionally, "the state has a duty to sustain business activities by creating conditions which will ensure job opportunities, by stimulating those activities where they are lacking or supporting them in moments of crisis." The encyclical also refers to the state exercising "a *substitute function*, when social sectors or business systems are too weak or just getting under way." These interventions, however, "must be as brief as possible" (CA 48).

Two basic guidelines underline this picture. One is that the state *does* have a role vis-à-vis the market: the guaranteeing of certain goods (rights, etc.) and an institutional-juridical framework without which free economic activity cannot occur. Secondly, the state should seek to stimulate such activity (by removing monopolies, etc.) rather than replace it. The emphasis, then, is upon preserving *and* promoting free economic activity *alongside* other moral goods.

But in the context of the present analysis, *Centesimus Annus* is perhaps most distinguished for asking a question which neither the Council nor Paul VI were in a position to answer. John Paul asks if, in light of communism's collapse, it can be said that "capitalism is the victorious social system," and if it should be the goal not only of "countries now making efforts to rebuild their economy and society," but also "countries of the Third World" (CA 42).

According to *Centesimus Annus*, "[t]he answer is obviously complex." It depends upon what one means by "capitalism." The pope's answer is affirmative if capitalism means a system which "recognizes the fundamental and positive role of business, the market, private property, and the resulting responsibility for the means of production, as well as free human creativity in the economic sector." He is, nevertheless, uneasy about attaching the phrase "capitalism" to this set of arrangements. This is evident from his statement that it would be more appropriately described as the "free economy" (CA 42). *Centesimus Annus* thus avoids using a word which *Laborem Exercens* defines, in the strict sense, as any system which only values work's objective dimension.

But *Centesimus Annus* also provides a negative answer to the posed question. Capitalism is not adequate if it means "a system in which freedom in the economic sector is not circumscribed within the service of human freedom in its totality" (CA 42). In other words, a system in which freedom is interpreted in economistic terms is unacceptable. The "consumer society" would seem to fall into this category.

6.5 A Post-Communist Imperative

To explain some of the developments outlined above, some commentators posit that identifiably Marxist emphases have been tacitly incorporated into magisterial teaching. Novak, for instance, suggests that *Laborem Exercens*'s definition of early capitalism as a system in which labor was viewed primarily as a commodity, accords with that of Marx.[19]

On one level, *Laborem Exercens*'s teaching does coincide with the Marxist view that capitalism emerged as a consequence of changes in the means of production and the treatment of labor as a commodity. Few, however, would actually disagree that these factors—alongside others—

---

19. See Novak, "Creation Theology," 20–21.

contributed to early capitalism's formation. At this point, one may add that the encyclical's strict definition of capitalism implicitly refutes the historical determinism underlying Marxist conceptions of capitalism.[20] The error of treating man as a commodity is specified as *not* being limited to any one historical period or economic system. It occurs whenever man *chooses* to adhere to economistic principles. We have already observed John Paul specifying that this easily occurs in collectivist economies—the type of economy which Marx's writings vaguely denote as one in which exploitation would be overcome.[21]

Would it then be more accurate to say that some of *Laborem Exercens'* teachings about capitalism have been influenced by Wojtyłan thought rather than that of Marx?[22] Capitalism itself is mentioned in only one Wojtyłan article. Discussing the relationship between man and society, Wojtyła comments:

> persons may easily place their own individual good above the common good of the collectivity, attempting to subordinate the collectivity to themselves and use it for their individual good. This is the error of individualism, which gave rise to liberalism in modern history and to capitalism in economics.[23]

It was, however, hardly unusual for a Catholic philosopher to link individualism to capitalism in 1961. Thirty years previously, Pius XI had referred to the "evil individualistic spirit" underlying laissez-faire economics. In any event, John Paul's encyclicals do not refer to individualism when discussing capitalism.[24]

Conceptually, however, *Laborem Exercens* does appear to integrate

---

20. For Marx's thinking on this matter, see Copleston, *Fichte to Nietzsche*, 321–329.

21. See R. Freedman, *Marx on Economics* (London: Penguin, 1960), 229–231.

22. Although Wojtyła was familiar with Marxist ideas about work, his writings provide no evidence of any study of Marxist prescriptions concerning political economy. See also A. McGovern, S.J., "Pope John Paul II on Human Work," *Telos* 57/58 (1983/1984): 215; Williams, "Karol Wojtyła and Marxism," 359–374.

23. "Thomistic Personalism," 674–675.

24. Some maintain that AP's criticisms of "individualism" (AP 329–331) may be viewed as an implicit critique of capitalism. See P. Hebblethwaite, "Thoughts of the Heart," in *The Pope from Poland*, J. Whale, ed. (London: Fount, 1980), 53; cf. Williams, *The Mind*, 212.

Buttiglione, however, notes that the connection does not necessarily follow: "many cultural positions are definitely individualistic while, at the same time, understanding themselves as anti-capitalistic. One can think of the emblematic motto of the Marxist existentialist, Jean-Paul Sartre: 'Hell is other people.'" Buttiglione, *Karol Wojtyła*, 171.

certain Wojtyłan ideas into magisterial teaching about capitalism. The encyclical's reference to the character of liberal-primitive capitalism as owing much to economistic thought is one instance of this. Another is its ahistorical definition of capitalism as a reversal of the primacy of work's subjective dimension over its objective-transitive aspect. The depiction of capitalism being modified to reflect the truth that all people are creative subjects and the higher importance of work's subjective dimension also falls into this category. In each of these instances, the language employed and emphases added may be described as proceeding from the application of Wojtyłan moral-anthropological thought about man and his work-acts to questions of political economy and economic history.

Unlike *Laborem Exercens*, *Centesimus Annus*'s teachings about types of capitalism display little sign of being shaped by Wojtyłan thought. John Paul's statements about the "modern business economy" reflect contemplation of the shift in some capitalist economies from an industrial to a post-industrial base. It would be remiss at this point not to mention the efforts of commentators such as Novak to enhance Catholicism's appreciation of the role played by entrepreneurship and knowledge in capitalist wealth creation processes.[25] One should, however, note that *Centesimus Annus*'s attention to the importance of human intelligence for wealth creation through work has precedents in magisterial teaching. *Populorum Progressio*'s discussion of industrialization, for example, states that "[b]y dint of intelligent thought and persistent work, man gradually uncovers the hidden laws of nature and learns to make a better use of natural resources" (PP 25). These words suggest that it is man's intelligence which endows him with the imagination that gives work its creative potential. One could say, then, that *Centesimus Annus* places this teaching in the context of broader historical-economic changes.

It appears, however, that other developments in teaching owe much to another, more sudden, transformation. During a general audience to mark *Centesimus Annus*'s promulgation, John Paul stated that "[o]ne event seems to dominate the difficult period in which we are living. . . . The Marxist system has failed."[26] Consequently, some countries are, as *Centesimus Annus* states, faced with "the radical re-ordering of economic systems hitherto collectivized" (CA 28).[27]

---

25. See, for example, M. Novak, *Will it Liberate?* (Mahwah: Paulist Press, 1986), chp. 10.
26. "Confronting the Challenges of Our Time," *L'Osservatore Romano* (English Weekly Edition) 18 (1991), 2.
27. Even before communism's collapse, several Polish Catholic intellectuals were

To John Paul's mind, such a re-ordering could take various forms, because it involves people making choices which reflect their understanding of man. This may underline *Centesimus Annus*'s contrast between "consumer capitalism" and "social market capitalism." The former reflected choices based on a view of man as *homo economicus*. The social market, conversely, grew from attempts to construct an economy around a non-economistic conception of man. In a sense, post-Communist and third world nations are, from *Centesimus Annus*'s viewpoint, faced with a similar choice.

Further evidence that this encyclical's teachings about types of capitalism are directed to providing guidance to these nations is found in its warning that communism's failure has created the risk that

> a radical capitalistic ideology could spread which refuses to even consider these problems [of material and moral poverty], in the *a priori* belief that any attempt to solve them is doomed to failure, and which blindly entrusts their solution to the free development of market forces. (CA 42)

In this light, John Paul's statements about the market and the state's role in the economy may be viewed as providing post-Communist and third world countries with a detailed outline of what a market economy can and cannot be expected to do. Tischner agrees. With reference to *Centesimus Annus*, he suggests that in post-Communist states, "there still live unrealistic myths about the functioning of a market economy—many dream of capitalist wealth without the capitalist effort. That is why a clear and comprehensive moral legitimation of the basic principles of a market economy is of the utmost importance."[28] To Western ears, some of John Paul's statements may sound rather basic; "everyone knows" that a market cannot properly function without property rights being judicially guaranteed. But to Central-East Europeans who have never experienced capitalism, let alone a modern market economy[29], such conclusions might

---

considering what type of market economy would be best for Poland. See, for example, R. Legutko, "Pokusa totalnego liberalizmu" [The Temptation of Total Laissez-faire], *Znak* 37, no. 8 (1985): 1077–1094.

28. J. Tischner, "A View from the Ruins," in *A New Worldly Order*, 167.

29. Several Central-East Europeans argue that their region lacks an indigenous tradition of widespread non-agricultural commercial activity. This, they suggest, is reflected in a long tradition of state-sponsored economic development *preceding* the Communist period. See J. Szücs, "Three Historical Regions of Europe: An Outline," in *Civil Society*, 291–332; cf. M. Vajda, "East-Central European Perspectives," in *Civil Society*, 333–360. An external

not seem so immediately obvious—not least because state institutions were often associated with usurpation of rights rather than their protection.

For these reasons, *Centesimus Annus*'s insistence that markets cannot function properly unless the state provides juridical guarantees, could be viewed as urging prudence upon post-Communist governments; that is, in the process of withdrawing the state from over-involvement in the economy, they should not compromise the state's capacity to perform certain essential functions. From this viewpoint, one may agree with Hittinger that with the closure of "the historical career of the Marxist state in Eastern Europe . . . the historical record of how these peoples can forge an appropriate political and legal order is still to be written. *Centesimus Annus* takes the gamble of recommending new institutional ways to engage that project."[30]

6.6 The Moral-Cultural Dimension

One thing emerging from the preceding analysis is the magisterium's attention to capitalism's moral dimension. Neo-capitalisms, for example, are praised for allowing more scope for all to realize themselves through work. Of course, a focus upon capitalism's moral-cultural character is not exclusive to magisterial teaching. Max Weber, for example, identified capitalism's "spirit" with "the Protestant ethic."[31] Though its conclusions are highly questionable,[32] Weber's study did suggest that capitalist systems cannot be understood solely in terms of objective economic techniques. To this we might add Michael Budde's point that capitalist economies not only require a number of moral and cultural inputs which they cannot create by themselves, but that they also shape the culture in which they operate.[33]

---

observer states: "Like most of Eastern Europe, Poland did not develop an indigenous bourgeoisie. In its first industrialisation periods from 1880 to the Second World War, Poland's capitalists tended to be Germans or Jews, both reflecting and contributing to the 'alien' reputation business activity acquired." D. Ost, Introduction, in *The Church and the Left*, 7.

30. R. Hittinger, "The Problem of the State in *Centesimus Annus*," *Fordham International Law Journal* 15, no. 4 (1991/1992): 996.

31. See M. Weber, *The Protestant Ethic and the Spirit of Capitalism* (New York: Charles Scribner's Sons, 1958), esp. 51–54, 176–178.

32. See, for example, J. Viner, *Religious Thought and Economic Society* (Durham: Duke University Press, 1978), 151–189.

33. See M. Budde, *The Two Churches: Catholicism and Capitalism in the World System*

Any consideration, then, of developments in teaching about capitalism requires closer analysis of the magisterium's treatment of capitalism's moral-cultural dimension. To this end, we will consider two matters touched upon in preceding sections. One is teaching about consumerism and the consumer society; the other, magisterial statements about personal economic initiative and entrepreneurship.

6.7 The Good of Economic Initiative

From Enterprise to Creative Subjectivity

Gaudium et Spes says little directly about personal economic initiative and nothing about the entrepreneur. This was much criticized by Nell-Breuning. Not only, in his opinion, do entrepreneurs play a role distinct from that of owners, managers, and workers, but Nell-Breuning believes that the Council fails to appreciate that the entrepreneur is the key figure in the modern economy.[34] Instead, the Council refers more generally to economic enterprise. "We must," it states, "encourage technical progress and the spirit of enterprise, we must foster the eagerness for creativity and improvement and we must promote adoption of production methods and all serious efforts of people engaged in production" (GS 64). One observes the emphasis upon enterprise's creative effect upon the world.

Nevertheless, when speaking about economic development, *Gaudium et Spes* insists that "[a]ll citizens should remember that they have the right and the duty to contribute according to their own ability to the genuine progress of the community and this must be recognized by the civil authority" (GS 65). This seems to indicate that, as far as possible, people should act upon their own initiative in the economic realm without being unduly impeded by the state. Again, the stress on the external benefits of such activity is noticeable.

Though John Paul's statements on personal economic initiative conform in essentials to previous teaching, they introduce particular—and now familiar—nuances into magisterial teaching. For a start, *Sollicitudo Rei Socialis* speaks explicitly of "the right of economic initiative":

(London/Durham: Duke University Press, 1992), 2–5.
34. See Nell-Breuning, "Socio-Economic Life," 291, 298–299.

It should be noted that in today's world, among other rights, *the right of economic initiative* [*inter alia iura etiam ius ad propria incepta oeconomica*] is often suppressed. Yet it is a right which is important not only for the individual but also for the common good. Experience shows us that the denial of this right, or its limitation in the name of an alleged "equality" of everyone in society, diminishes, or in practice absolutely destroys the spirit of initiative, that is to say *the creative subjectivity of the citizen* [*subiectivam videlicet effectricem civis*]. As a consequence, there arises not so much a true equality as a "leveling down." In the place of creative initiative there appears passivity, dependence and submission to the bureaucratic apparatus. (SRS 15)

Numerous commentators suggest that this text may be understood as implicitly highlighting state-collectivism's material and moral failures, and calling for economic reform in such systems.[35]

The text above, however, is also making a moral-anthropological point. It characterizes economic initiative as a right [*ius*]. This directs attention to its significance for the possessor of rights—man. The words "citizen" (used also by the Council) and "common good" suggest that John Paul (like the Council) views this right as possessing a correlative responsibility. But by associating economic initiative with man's creative subjectivity, *Sollicitudo Rei Socialis* also indirectly characterizes it as an *act of work* which flows from man as the *creative subject*. This has two effects. It deepens understanding of *why* economic initiative is a right: it expresses the truth that man is, by nature, the creative subject of work. Secondly, it indicates that economic initiative does more than create "things" and benefit others. As a work-*act* of the creative subject, economic initiative involves man's *self-realization* of moral good.

In the extract above, this last point has to be inferred from John Paul's insistence that the denial of economic initiative results in the opposite of personal growth—dependence, passivity, etc. *Centesimus Annus*, however, is more forthright on this matter. As noted, it states that in contemporary economic life "the role of disciplined and creative *human work* and, as an essential part of that work, *initiative and entrepreneurial ability* [is becoming] increasingly evident and decisive [refers to SRS 15]" (CA 32).

Not only do these words focus attention upon economic initiative and entrepreneurship as a work-act, but by referring to the extract from

---

35. See, for example, G. Baum, "Structures of Sin," in *The Logic of Solidarity*, 124.

Sollicitudo Rei Socialis cited above, they remind us of the importance of remembering that man is the creative subject of work when thinking about these activities. John Paul's reason for doing so becomes evident when he specifies that through entrepreneurship, one may acquire "important virtues . . . such as diligence, industriousness, prudence in undertaking reasonable risks, reliability and fidelity in interpersonal relationships, as well as courage in carrying out decisions which are difficult and painful" (CA 32). For John Paul, then, the fact that the human subject *self-realizes* virtue through *acts* of entrepreneurial work is at least equally important as any resulting material prosperity.

Promoting a Moral Imperative

In many respects, John Paul's statements on this topic represent logical extensions of previous teaching. He is not the first pope to refer to personal initiative in economic activity as a right. John XXIII, for example, stated that "man has the inherent right not only to be given the opportunity to work but also to be allowed the exercise of personal initiative in the work he does" (PT 18). The idea that man may acquire moral goods through creative work is, of course, articulated in *Gaudium et Spes*. Likewise, *Centesimus Annus*'s linkage of virtue to entrepreneurship has certain precedents in *Quadragesimo Anno*.[36]

On another level, John Paul's attention to entrepreneurial activity could be understood as constituting magisterial recognition that entrepreneurship has a character distinct from other economic roles such as ownership and management. Indeed, from Nell-Breuning's standpoint, *Centesimus Annus* goes some way towards underlining the importance of this economic function in modern capitalist systems.

There are, however, strong reasons for believing that the nuances of John Paul's teaching about entrepreneurship and economic initiative also proceed from particular emphases developed by *Laborem Exercens*. These involve the description of man as the creative subject, and the emphasis upon virtues such as industriousness that this subject realizes through his work-acts. For this reason, *Laborem Exercens* posits that work-acts are good in themselves inasmuch as they actualize man's free choice for moral good. The argument of *Sollicitudo Rei Socialis* and *Centesimus Annus* proceeds along similar lines: through entrepreneurial work-acts,

---

36. See QA 51; cf. Nell-Breuning, *Reorganization*, 116–117.

man as the creative subject may develop, often with much difficulty, various virtues including that of industriousness. In this sense, Buttiglione is correct to claim that *Centesimus Annus* may be understood as presenting entrepreneurship as a good in itself.[37]

Chapter 4 illustrated that each of these teachings in *Laborem Exercens* has been influenced by Wojtyła's thought about the moral significance of the subject's *acts* for man as a person, the linkage of fulfillment to the *difficult* task of acquiring *virtue*, and the insistence in his later writings that human work-acts possess their own moral worth. In this light, it would seem that John Paul's statements about personal economic initiative owe something to these Wojtyłan moral-anthropological emphases.

6.8 Consumer Capitalism

Inasmuch, then, that capitalism permits people to work in an entrepreneurial manner, John Paul views it favorably. This is surely implied by his listing of free human creativity amongst the elements of an acceptable capitalism. In considering, however, magisterial teaching about consumerism, we see that John Paul has grave reservations about another phenomenon normally associated with contemporary capitalism.

Unauthentic Humanism

These concerns owe much to previous teaching. When speaking about man's increasing mastery over nature, *Gaudium et Spes* refers to man's growing consciousness that "the forces he has unleashed are in his own hands and that it is up to him to control them or be enslaved by them" (GS 9). The Council adds that this predicament is actually "a symptom of the deeper dichotomy that is in man himself." Man is a creature aware of his transcendent future, but fallible: "Worse still, feeble and sinful as he is, he often does the very thing he hates and does not do what he wants [refers to Rm 7:14]" (GS 10).

The concept of man as a being torn between transcendent aspirations and sinful shortcomings is not new in Christian thought. The Council's reference to St. Paul acknowledges this. In the modern era, however, the Council is concerned that many are not only oblivious to this inner dichotomy, but identify fulfillment in strictly "this-worldly" terms. Often

---

37. See Buttiglione, "The Free Economy," 69.

"their vision is in fact blinded by materialism." Others set their hopes on "some future earthly paradise where all the desires of their hearts will be fulfilled" (GS 10).

Later sections of the Pastoral Constitution place these concerns in an economic context. The Council describes a widespread obsession with economic matters as characteristic of contemporary life: "[m]any people, especially in economically advanced areas seem to be dominated by economics; almost all of their personal and social lives are permeated with a kind of economic mentality" (GS 63). This "economic mentality" is therefore symptomatic of that slavery to which *Gaudium et Spes* earlier refers—subservience to what one produces. Its reference to "economically-advanced areas" implies that the wealthier the area, the greater the risk of such vassalage.

Many of these ideas are elaborated upon by *Populorum Progressio*'s statements about truly human development. These need to be outlined in some detail, as they provide the criteria for Paul's critique of "consumerism."

The encyclical begins by stating that human development "cannot be limited to economic growth alone. To be authentic, it must be well-rounded: it must foster the good of each man and of the whole man" (PP 14). But what is good for each and every person is not a matter of arbitrary taste. According to Paul, man "should of his own accord direct his life to God, the first truth and the highest good." This is the "highest goal of human perfection" (PP 16). God's existence is held to underlie "the proper scale of values" (PP 18), at the summit of which are "the higher values of love and friendship, prayer and contemplation [refers to Maritain]" (PP 20).

Paul's reference to Maritain[38] is indicative of the strong French Catholic flavor underlying these statements.[39] There are, for example, good reasons for supposing that the thought of Louis Lebret, O.P., particularly influenced *Populorum Progressio*. For the moment, however, it suffices to state that Lebret posited that a society is "more human" not when people "have" more, but when all its citizens are enabled to "be" more.[40] At a minimum, Paul's words indicate agreement with this

---

38. It reads: "Cf., for example, J. Maritain, *Les conditions spirituelles du progrès et de la paix*, in *Rencontre des cultures à l'UNESCO sous le signe du Concile Oecuménique Vatican II* (Paris: Mame, 1966), 66."

39. See also "Drafted in French," *The Tablet*, 1 April 1967, 359.

40. See D. Goulet, "The Search for Authentic Development," in *The Logic of Solidarity*,

proposition. *Gaudium et Spes* uses a similar expression: "It is what a man is, rather than what he has, that counts" (GS 35).

The French Catholic contribution is also evident from *Populorum Progressio*'s references to de Lubac's *L'drame de l'humanisme athée*.[41] While "man can organize terrestrial realities without God," Paul warns with a de Lubac quote that "closed off from God, they will end up being directed against man" (PP 42). The danger of such an eventuality is considered to be acute when man attaches excessive importance to material goods:

> Increased possession is not the ultimate goal of nations or of individuals. All growth is ambivalent. It is essential if man is to develop as a man; yet it can also enslave him if he comes to regard it as the supreme good and cannot look beyond it. . . . Avarice, in individuals and nations, is the most obvious form of moral underdevelopment. (PP 19)

Man, then, should not spurn his need for material things. But it should not dominate his vision. To paraphrase Lebret, "having" should not supplant "being."

Looking at the world, Paul implies that "wealthy nations" have, in many instances, forgotten to restrain their appreciation of material goods. Although affirming that these nations are in many ways successful, Paul adds that "they also provide the model for a way of acting that is principally aimed at the conquest of temporal prosperity" (PP 41). Although Paul does not identify these "wealthy nations" in terms of specific economic systems, he seems to have capitalist systems in mind. This becomes more evident in *Octogesima Adveniens*:

> Unlimited competition utilizing the modern means of publicity incessantly launches new products and tries to attract the consumer, while earlier industrial installations which are still capable of functioning become useless. While very large numbers of the population are unable to satisfy their primary needs, superfluous needs are ingeniously created. It can thus be rightly asked if, in spite of all his conquests, man is not turning back against himself the results of his activity. Having endeavored rationally to control nature, is he not now becoming the slave of the objects which he makes? (OA 9)

133–137.
41. See PP ns. 44 and 45.

Apart from stating that the creation of "superfluous needs" impedes realization of the universal destination of material goods, this passage asks whether certain features—which most would associate with modern capitalism (competition, aggressive advertising)—are encouraging man, in an echo of the Council, to become the slave of what he produces. Since Paul poses this as a question, one should note that he is *not* saying that such a state of affairs—which might be called "consumer capitalism"— has actually arisen. The rhetorical tone of Paul's question, however, indicates that he indeed thinks so.

A Consumerist Civilization

1. Truly Human Development

Many of Pope Paul's concerns are replicated in John Paul's encyclicals. But it is also necessary to precede analysis of John Paul's teachings on such matters with an outline of what he considers to constitute true human development. *Sollicitudo Rei Socialis* initially frames this issue in a manner analogous to *Populorum Progressio*: true development "*cannot* consist in the simple accumulation of wealth" (SRS 9). Rather, development "must be measured and orientated according to the reality and vocation of man seen in his totality" (SRS 29).

John Paul then demonstrates that the reduction of human development to a strictly this-worldly progress denies what man is by *nature*. In what amounts to a continuation of *Laborem Exercens*'s reflections upon Genesis, *Sollicitudo Rei Socialis* returns to the biblical paradigm and invests it with particular anthropological emphases:

> we must never lose sight of that *dimension* which is in the *specific nature* of man who has been created by God in his image and likeness (cf. Gen 1:26). It is a bodily and spiritual nature. . . .
> As the Genesis account says (cf. Gen 2:15), man is placed in the garden with the duty of cultivating and watching over it. . . . But at the same time man must remain subject to the will of God, who imposes limits upon his use and dominion over things (cf. Gen 2:16-17), just as he promises him immortality (cf. Gen 2:9; Wis 2:23). Thus man, being the image of God, has an affinity with Him too.
> On the basis of this teaching, development cannot consist only in the use, dominion over and *indiscriminate* possession of created things and the products of human industry, but rather in *subordinating* the possession,

dominion and use to man's divine likeness and to his vocation to immortality. (SRS 29)

In Walsh's view, this particular meditation on Genesis "confirms that the Pope [has] broken with the Thomistic philosophical tradition in which his predecessors had couched their own documents, and instead embraced a more biblical and theological approach."[42] It would, however, be more accurate to say that—like *Laborem Exercens*—*Sollicitudo Rei Socialis* uses the Genesis narrative to integrate what amounts to broadly natural law thinking with biblical-theological reflection. The words above specify that true development involves man recognizing the truth about his *specific nature*: that he is the *imago Dei*, a bodily and spiritual creature whose salvation lies in his free submission to the moral order which governs his dominion, possession and use of material things. As *Sollicitudo Rei Socialis* later states, man's "task is 'to have dominion' over the other created beings . . . This is to be accomplished within the framework of *obedience* to the divine law" (SRS 30). True development and dominion, then, are inseparable from man's recognition of, and free conformance to what *Laborem Exercens* denotes the original ordering of God which permeates not only the world, but man's very being.

2. *Problems of Development*

These elaborations in teaching about human development provide John Paul with a broader basis for critiquing modern consumerism. Unlike Paul VI, John Paul associates consumerism with Western capitalist nations. *Sollicitudo Rei Socialis* links "the West" with "a system which is inspired by the principles of . . . *liberal capitalism*" (SRS 20). The encyclical later states that "the West gives the impression of abandoning itself to forms of growing and selfish isolation" (SRS 23). One manifestation of this selfishness is what John Paul describes as "a form of *superdevelopment. . .* which consists in an *excessive* availability of every kind of material good for the benefit of certain social groups" (SRS 28).

The effects of "superdevelopment" are several. For one thing, it involves "so much 'throwing away' and 'waste'" as people discard objects already owned for something better, "with no thought . . . of some other human being who is poorer" (SRS 28). In other words, it trivializes the

---

42. Walsh, "Introduction," xx.

right of others to share in the universal destination of material goods.

Another effect may be termed "civilizational." Superdevelopment, *Sollicitudo Rei Socialis* states, easily makes "people slaves of 'possession' and of immediate gratification, with no other horizon than the multiplication or continual replacement of things already owned with others still better." Paul VI, we recall, asked whether this was becoming a widespread phenomenon. According to John Paul, it *is* a reality: "the so-called civilization of 'consumption' or 'consumerism'" which is characterized by "a crass materialism" facilitated by "the flood of publicity and the ceaseless and tempting offers of products" (SRS 28).

These statements suggest that, like his predecessor, John Paul views aspects of modern capitalism as contributing to a culture in which the only ideal is "more." *Centesimus Annus*, however, delineates how such a culture may be resisted. Referring to the problems of "advanced economies," particularly *"the phenomenon of consumerism,"* the encyclical states that "[o]f itself an economic system does not possess criteria for correctly distinguishing new and higher forms of satisfying human needs from artificial new needs." It is wrong then to blame "the market" in the first instance for consumerism. For this reason, *Centesimus Annus* states that people need to be educated "in the responsible use of their power of choice," so that "lifestyles [are created] in which the quest for truth, beauty, goodness and communion with others are the factors which determine consumer choices" (CA 36). Thus, while man's capacity for free choice is underlined as central to resisting consumerism, John Paul evidently believes that this will only occur if people's free choices *and* actions (their "lifestyles") are directed towards realizing those goods which reflect man's transcendent destiny and the moral-spiritual aspect of his nature.

John Paul's analysis of consumerism's effects also points to a more fundamental disorder than the self-enslavement predicted by Paul VI and the Council. The civilization of consumption is presented as facilitating "a *radical dissatisfaction*, because one quickly learns . . . that the more one possesses, the more one wants, while deeper aspirations remain unsatisfied and perhaps even stifled" (SRS 28). *Centesimus Annus* defines this as a contemporary form of *alienation*:

> The historical experience of the West shows that . . . alienation is a reality in Western societies. . . . This happens in consumerism when people are ensnared in a web of false and superficial gratifications rather than being helped to experience their personhood in an authentic and concrete way. . .

A person who is concerned solely or primarily with possessing and enjoying, who is no longer able to control his instincts and passion, or to subordinate them by obedience to the truth cannot be free: *obedience to the truth* about God and man is the first condition of freedom, making it possible for a person to order his needs and desires. (CA 41)

Here we see why John Paul stresses that true development is predicated upon man's free submission to the divine law. Unless man freely orders his needs and desires to the Revealed truth about himself, he is unable to experience his personhood. As the *imago Dei*, man naturally aspires to the higher values—identified by John Paul as "truth, beauty and goodness" (CA 36)—which prefigure his immortal vocation. Hence, if man fails to accord priority to the acquisition of these goods, his possession and use of material things will become an occasion of alienation for him.

6.9 A Mounting Critique

The preceding analysis demonstrates that John Paul's statements about consumerism owe much in thematic and conceptual terms to *Gaudium et Spes* and *Populorum Progressio*. Criticisms of modern consumerism, however, are hardly confined to Catholic social teaching. In *The Affluent Society* (a phrase used by *Centesimus Annus*), John Kenneth Galbraith refers to the role of competition and advertising in creating artificial needs and generating material waste.[43] Writing as a psychologist, Erich Fromm describes "affluent alienation" as no less dehumanizing than material impoverishment.[44]

But to put the critique articulated in John Paul's encyclicals in its proper context, one should note that in the early 1980s, many Catholic thinkers began articulating concerns about Western capitalist culture. During a series of interviews in 1985, for example, Cardinal Joseph Ratzinger, Prefect of the Congregation of the Doctrine for the Faith (CDF), described Western Europe and the United States as dominated by a culture in which "money and wealth are the measure of all things and where the model of the free market imposes its implacable laws on every aspect of life."[45]

Interestingly, Ratzinger specified that this view accorded with that of

---

43. See J. Galbraith, *The Affluent Society* (London: Penguin, 1991), 110–113, 129–131.
44. See introduction to *Socialist Humanism*, E. Fromm, ed. (London: Penguin, 1967), xii.
45. J. Ratzinger and V. Messori, *The Ratzinger Report* (San Francisco: Ignatius, 1985), 83.

prominent East European Catholic figures. He referred to Cardinal
Wyszyński's warning that the dangers of Western hedonism and
permissiveness were no less than of those of Marxist oppression, and
recalled that Cardinal Bengsch of Berlin saw Western consumerism as a
greater danger than Marxism. "Western culture," Ratzinger stated, "is
hellish when it persuades men that the sole aim of life is pleasure and self-
interest."[46]

Such concerns were not limited to Central-East European prelates. Lay
Catholic intellectuals from this region voiced similar reservations. In
1980, for example, Charter 77 spokesman, Václav Benda, spoke of the
materialist self-absorption encouraged by Western capitalism.[47] Five years
later, he praised the market economy but suggested that if Western nations
increasingly succumbed to a consumerist ethos, then the prosperity
ensuing from market activity would not become a resource for generosity
and creative investment, but rather an occasion for mass self-indulgence.[48]

No direct link between any of these ideas and John Paul's teachings is
being asserted here. They are simply illustrative of an emerging concern
common to several Catholic thinkers, some of whom have played
prominent roles in John Paul's pontificate, whilst others are from the
pope's own region of origin. These factors do, however, suggest that John
Paul was likely to have been aware of these growing apprehensions about
Western consumerism.

6.10   Genesis, Alienation, Consumerism

Turning, then, to Karol Wojtyła's writings, it soon becomes apparent that
Wojtyła shared many of the concerns outlined above. Indeed, certain ideas
expressed in Wojtyła's writings appear to have influenced aspects of John
Paul's teaching about consumerism. These concern the pope's words
about truly human development, consumerist alienation, and the
civilization of consumption.

---

46. Ratzinger, *The Ratzinger Report*, 187–188.
47. See V. Benda, "Katolicismus a politika" [Catholicism and Politics], in *Krestane a
Charta 77* [Christians and Charter 77], V. Precan, ed. (Munich: Opus Bonum, 1980), 266–
267.
48. See V. Benda, "The Curse of Social Equality," *Rozmluvy* 3 (1984): 37.

The Parameters of Dominion

In discussing human development, *Sollicitudo Rei Socialis* uses the Genesis narrative to stress that true development involves man's free obedience to the divine law. *Sign of Contradiction*'s meditation upon Genesis is especially relevant in this instance.

In exploring Genesis's portrait of God's covenant with man, Wojtyła suggests that it contains two interlinked elements. In Genesis 1:26, God gives man dominion over the earth. Wojtyła specifies, however, that this is linked to the obedience man owes to God. To this end, Wojtyła cites Genesis 2:16-17 which refers to God's commandment not to eat "of the tree of the knowledge of good and evil" (SC 23). From the beginning, then, man is faced with

> the tree which is a symbol of his human nature in that it is a sign of the limits implicit in his creaturely state and, at the same time, the frontier which development of the human person may not cross. The human person created in the image of God is not set "beyond the confines of good and evil." (SC 23)

But the tree of knowledge is not only an expression of man's subjection to God. It is also, Wojtyła specifies, "a symbol of being and value" and "linked symbolically with the tree of life (cf. Gen 2:9)" (SC 23).

Sollicitudo Rei Socialis replicates this reflection upon Genesis in its teaching on human development. While the encyclical does not mention "the tree," it refers to the same Genesis verses in the same order to make the same points as *Sign of Contradiction*: that whilst man is given dominion (Gen 1:26), he is also commanded to obey God's law (Gen 2:16-17), and this free obedience is the path to eternal life (Gen 2:9). Moreover, both book and encyclical state that recognition of the nature and purpose of man's dominion is central to ensuring that the person's development does not become disordered. *Sollicitudo Rei Socialis* goes beyond *Sign of Contradiction*, however, by applying these reflections on Genesis to the question of how man should order his use of material goods.

Consumerism and Alienation

Another possible Wojtyłan influence relates to *Centesimus Annus*'s specification that consumerism leads to alienation. Reflecting upon paragraph 10 of *Gaudium et Spes* in an article published in 1970, Wojtyła maintains that it underlines the need for priests to persist in preaching about the *bonum in se*. While acknowledging the difficulties involved in persuading people to pursue such good, Wojtyła insists that the Council's picture of man torn between his inclination to higher things and his numerous shortcomings makes such exhortations imperative. For unless people are reminded that they must strive for moral good, they may experience alienation:

> Every moral good makes its appearance in the world through a variegated state of being ranked with respect to manifold strivings and needs. It also experiences—as a consequence of this correct ranking—its own alienation in relation to it. . . .The essence of this alienation expresses itself in all forms of utilitarianism, especially consumerism. . . . Consumerism denies the deepest objective value of everything in order, in place of the *bonum in se*, to leave only pleasure and consumption as the measure of value. But man is destined for more than the endless consumption of material things. As a *person*, he is directed to choosing truth, good, and beauty. This is intrinsic to his nature as *imago Dei*. Thus, if man devotes himself to consumerist pleasure, he will become estranged from his personhood and condemn himself to an alienated existence. As a phenomenon, this form of alienation is increasingly apparent in the West.[49]

These observations are not placed in any particular economic context. Nevertheless, the parallels with *Centesimus Annus* seem clear. Apart from employing similar phraseology, both texts suggest that failure to pursue the higher values of truth, good, and beauty tends to lead to consumerist lifestyles. As a consequence, man experiences alienation because he denies his nature and destiny as a person. Moreover, like the encyclical, Wojtyła links the phenomenon of consumerism and consumerist alienation

---

49. "Notatki na marginesie konstytucji *Gaudium et Spes*" [Notes on the Margin of the Constitution *Gaudium et Spes*], *Ateneum Kapłańskie* 74, no. 1 (1970): 3, 5.

AP specifies that happiness (which Wojtyła calls "felicity") is not the same as pleasure, and that only man can experience happiness: "animals feel natural satisfaction and pain. . . Felicity . . . seems, however, to be the exclusive structure of the person which has no analogue in the world of nature" (AP 176). On this basis, one may posit that if man fixates himself on pleasure, he denies his uniqueness as person.

For an earlier exposition of Wojtyła's distinction between happiness and pleasure based on man's anthropological uniqueness, see "Właściwa interpretacja nauki o szczęściu" [The Proper Interpretation of the Teaching on Happiness], *Tygodnik Powszechny* 11, no. 36 (1957): 11.

with "the West"—a point upon which some of his later writings expand.

The Civilization of Consumption

The final Wojtyłan influence upon John Paul's teaching about consumerism concerns the pope's statements about the consumer society. Wojtyła's writings indicate that by 1976, he viewed consumerism and consumer societies not as possibilities but rather as modern realities—a point reiterated by John Paul's teaching. *Sign of Contradiction* speaks of modern man as "caught in the toils of consumerism and a prey to the hunger for status symbols that divides both the world and the hearts of men" (SC 51). Wojtyła even refers to Christ as "in every way a reproach to affluent, acquisitive societies" (SC 108).

Later in this text, Wojtyła places consumer societies firmly in the context of what he understands to be the modern world's mistaken understanding of "progress." He begins by questioning whether contemporary progress is being evaluated by the conciliar criterion that "[a] man's worth lies more in what he *is* than in what he *possesses*" (SC 156).

To Wojtyła's mind, it is not. This is evident from his equation of "the program of modern civilization" with "a program of consumerism and not of transcendental ends" (SC 199), and "our 'century of progress'" with "the age of a new enslavement" (SC 157). In this context, Wojtyła claims that "under the liberal regimes, where men have grown sick from too much prosperity, human life presents a saddening picture of all kinds of abuses and frustrating situations" (SC 157). This association of consumerist excess and resulting frustration (a word which hints at alienation) with the "liberal world" (which in 1976 could only mean Western Europe and North America[50]) foreshadows John Paul's

---

50. Some commentators claim that some of Scheler's political ideas may have influenced Wojtyła's negative comments regarding Western consumerism. To this end, both Williams and Hebblethwaite refer to a book written by Scheler to aid Germany's first World War effort entitled *Der Genius des Krieges und der deutsche Krieg* (*The Genius of War and the German War*). Apart from criticizing "Czarist societies," the book was extremely critical of what Scheler called "Anglo-American society and morality," and "Anglo-American utilitarianism, mercantilism, and consumerism." See Williams, *The Mind*, 139; Hebblethwaite, "Husserl, Scheler, and Wojtyła," 442.

Such suppositions should be treated with caution. There is no evidence that Wojtyła ever read what was, after all, a piece of German war propaganda. Nor does Scheler's *Der Formalismus*—which we know Wojtyła read—refer to "consumerism" or even "the West."

connection of consumerism with Western capitalist societies.

Some of these motifs are explored further in Wojtyła's 1977 article on culture and praxis. Here Wojtyła suggests that on a global level, the universal destination of material goods is far from being realized: "Alongside societies and people who have an overabundance of means, there exist societies and people who suffer from . . . an insufficiency of means." Hence, "it goes without saying that we should work toward a just distribution of goods."[51] But Wojtyła then suggests that this is as much for the good of those who have much as for those who possess little:

> A departure from the realization of this principle is a threat to the *humanum*. One might ask, however, whether the threat is not greater where *an overabundance of means*, a superfluity of what people *have*, obscures who they *are* and who they *ought* to be.
>   This is an especially critical question, perhaps the most vexing one, for the future of culture in the Atlantic world.[52]

These words highlight the danger of what *Sollicitudo Rei Socialis* defines as "superdevelopment"—an "overabundance of means"—for man: a loss of knowledge of what he *is*, and what, as a consequence, he *should* become. The extract above also associates this problem with, at a minimum, Western Europe and North America.

Wojtyła then outlines the "civilizational" nature of the problem faced by "the Atlantic world":

> So many works, so many products of human activity, are equally susceptible to the necessity of passing away. For a while they sparkle in the arena of the human world, and then they grow dim and wither away. . . Many of man's products bear the mark of something to be used up, something to be consumed, and cannot rise above this level in the hierarchy of values. A civilization that gives such products priority, *a civilization that is somehow completely focussed upon consumption*, is a civilization of the death of humanity.[53]

The terminological parallels of this extract with *Sollicitudo Rei Socialis* are obvious. It also anticipates the encyclical's insistence that a civilization

---

51. "Constitution of Culture," 518–519.
52. "Constitution," 519.
53. "Constitution," 522.

according priority to the production and consumption of consumable goods reflects man's denial of his transcendental vocation to eternal life.

To resist such tendencies, Wojtyła insists that man must go "beyond all the confines of the various kinds of utilitarianism and discover within the full richness of human praxis its deep relation to truth, goodness, and beauty."[54] Though the correlation is not exact, *Centesimus Annus* makes a similar point. Consumerism can be overcome if people orientate their lifestyles, that is, their daily decisions and actions—in short, their *praxis*—towards the pursuit of truth, good, and beauty.

6.11 Conclusion

John Paul's statements about consumerism are, of course, only one aspect of his teaching about capitalism. Though his words present consumerism as a regrettable phenomenon of Western capitalist societies, they should not be understood as typifying his development of teaching about a system which defines so much of the modern world. As demonstrated, if modern capitalism means certain things, John Paul is willing to recommend it as a model for nations to follow.

In developing the teaching in these directions, John Paul stresses the role of personal moral agency. This is especially true in regard to his statements about early capitalism's origins as well as how consumerism may be resisted. The pope also invests the teaching with moral-anthropological emphases: the denial of the priority of work's subjective dimension and man's status as the creative subject of work is presented as underlying early capitalism's deficiencies; the right of economic initiative is grounded in man's subjectivity; the importance of man correctly understanding his own nature is stressed; and consumerist alienation is defined in terms of man's estrangement from the truth of his own nature.

In extending previous teaching on each sub-issue, John Paul both responds to particular events and continues the magisterium's on-going reflection on longer-term phenomena. Communism's collapse has been identified as leading him to integrate various facets of previous teaching so that post-Communist and third world nations understand precisely what the Church regards as acceptable and unacceptable as they embrace capitalism. Likewise, an evident conviction that consumerism has become a widespread problem in Western capitalist nations seems to have

---

54. "Constitution," 522.

contributed to John Paul's updating of Paul VI's teaching on this matter. Similarly, John Paul's teachings about economic initiative may be viewed as part of his ongoing critique of modern statist economies. The increasing prevalence of personal initiative in economic life is, however, also welcomed for other reasons. Not only is entrepreneurship presented as a modern expression of the truth that man is the creative subject of work, but John Paul regards entrepreneurial acts as allowing man to acquire virtue.

There is also much to suggest that Wojtyłan ideas about man and human acts have been integrated into magisterial teaching about capitalism. This is certainly true in the case of *Laborem Exercens*'s application of the subjective-objective distinction and the concept of economism to explain primitive capitalism's character, as well as its understanding of the emergence of neo-capitalisms. A Wojtyłan influence is also discernible in regard to John Paul's grounding of the right of economic initiative in man's status as the creative subject. Nor, as we have seen, does magisterial teaching about "consumer capitalism" escape the effect of Wojtyłan emphases.

One of the magisterium's objections to consumerism is that it militates against realization of the universal destination of material goods. The global implications of this have not escaped the attention of Catholic social thinkers. In her 1977 address to the Roman Curia, for example, Barbara Ward characterized the affluent waste of prosperous capitalist nations as morally inexcusable in light of the third world's material deprivation.[55] Her comments reflect the attention of post-conciliar Catholic social teaching to the relationship between developed and developing nations. It is a matter to which the first pope from the "second world" brings a fresh perspective.

---

55. See B. Ward, "Looking Back at *Populorum Progressio*," *Catholic Mind* 76 (1978): 17–18.

7
JUSTICE AMONG NATIONS

7.1 Introduction

The twentieth century has witnessed Catholicism's transformation from a predominantly European church to one whose numerical basis lies increasingly in the third world.[1] Given Catholicism's growth in developing nations, the magisterium could not but become more conscious of their needs. But just as the phenomenon of worker penury in nineteenth-century Europe contributed to *Rerum Novarum*'s promulgation, so too has awareness of the contrast between third world privation and the developed world's prosperity facilitated an "internationalization" of Catholic social teaching. As Ratzinger states, "[t]he moral challenge of poverty and oppression [in the third world] presented itself in an ineluctable form at the very moment when Europe and North America had attained a hitherto unknown affluence."[2]

Here we compare the teachings of the Council and Paul VI concerning relations between developed and developing nations with those of John Paul II. We first examine their statements concerning how the relationship contributes to the developing nations' difficulties. Attention is then given to their respective treatments of the principle of solidarity which, in magisterial teaching, is considered central to the correct ordering of these relations. The developments identified are shown to have been shaped, in part, by consciousness of historical changes since *Populorum Progressio* (1967) as well as the magisterium's engagement with the "theologies of

---

1. See Budde, *The Two Churches*, 9–16.
2. Ratzinger, *The Ratzinger Report*, 178.

liberation." Yet despite the apparent remoteness of such global issues from Karol Wojtyła's philosophical pursuits, characteristically Wojtylan ideas have affected development.

7.2 Causes of Discord

The Council and the Third World

While concern about the international economic order manifests itself in Pius XI and Pius XII's teachings,[3] *Mater et Magistra* was the first encyclical to examine "the relationship between political communities that are economically advanced and those in the process of development" (MM 157). Given this document's lengthy treatment of the matter (MM 153–184), it would have been odd for the Council not to consider the issue. In any event, the presence at the Council's first session of 1,004 bishops (out of a total of 2,449) who worked in developing nations would have made the matter difficult to ignore.[4] On 25 November 1962, for example, the General-Secretary of the Latin American Bishops' Conference (CELAM), Bishop Helder Câmara, remarked in a well-publicized homily that with the relationship between developed and developing nations becoming critical to the modern world's future, it merited conciliar attention.[5]

Significant figures from the developed world were also determined to focus the Council's attention upon the third world's problems. In his plan for the Council, Suenens maintained that "[i]n the eyes of the underdeveloped countries, the Church must appear to be the Church of all and above all of the poor."[6] Almost identical words appear in Pope John's 11 September broadcast: "Faced with the developing countries, the Church presents herself as she is and wishes to be, as the Church of all and especially the Church of the poor."[7] In his intervention of 4 December 1962, Suenens went further and suggested that one of the major questions being asked of the Church by the modern world was "[w]hat is the duty of the rich nation to the third world nation suffering hunger?"[8]

---

3. See Calvez and Perrin, *The Church*, 312–314.
4. Figures from Hebblethwaite, *John XXIII*, 426–427.
5. See H. de Riedmatten, O.P., "Histoire de la Constitution Pastorale," in *L'église dans le monde de ce temps*, H. de Riedmatten, O.P., et al. (Paris: Editions St. Paul, 1966), 60–61.
6. Suenens, "A Plan for the Whole Council," 102.
7. John XXIII, *Radio-Television Message*, 682.
8. ASCV, 4 December 1962, 227.

New World, Old Disorder

It is not surprising, then, that references to the desire of "[d]eveloping nations . . . to share in the political and economic benefits of modern civilization" and the claim that "they are hampered by their economic dependence on the rapidly expanding richer nations and the ever widening gap between them" (GS 9) appear in the Pastoral Constitution's preface. The Council's detailed treatment of these issues occurs within the section of *Gaudium et Spes* that considers questions of war and peace (GS 77–90). The Council deliberated, of course, less than twenty years after World War Two and during a period of superpower tension. Nevertheless, the Council looked beyond these immediate circumstances when stating that "[t]he growing contrast between the economically more advanced countries and others could well endanger world peace" (GS 63).

Prominent amongst the inhibitions to what the Council calls "an authentic economic order on a world-wide scale" are "profiteering, nationalist ambitions, greed for political domination, schemes of military strategy, and intrigues for spreading and imposing ideologies." Here we see that sinful *actions* and *dispositions* on the part of men—greed, intrigues, etc.—are regarded as underlying the political, military, and ideological agendas which facilitate disorder. The Council also notes that "[m]aterial aid for developing nations will not be forthcoming unless there is a profound change in the prevailing conventions of commerce today" (GS 85). How such conventions obstruct this aid is not specified. Nevertheless, these words imply that certain practices have created obstacles to an international realization of the universal destination of material goods.

A Pope and Developing Nations

Given John Paul II's many international journeys, it is often forgotten that Paul VI inaugurated this form of papal visitation. According to Cardinal Casaroli (an architect of Paul's *Ostpolitik*), it was Paul's 1964 trip to India which inspired him to produce *Populorum Progressio*.[9] The encyclical itself dates Paul's interest in the third world to an earlier period:

Before We became Pope, We traveled to Latin America (1960) and Africa (1962). There We saw the perplexing problems that vex and besiege these

---

9. See Hebblethwaite, *Paul VI*, 483.

continents, which are otherwise full of life and promise. On being elected pope, We became the father of all. We made trips to Palestine and India, gaining first-hand knowledge of the difficulties that these age-old civilizations must face in their struggle for further development. (PP 4)[10]

Certain third world bishops were also determined to bring the developing nations' plight to Paul's attention. On 23 November 1965, for example, Paul addressed to Latin American bishops on the occasion of CELAM's tenth anniversary. After noting that by the year 2000, Latin America would contain more than half the world's Catholics, Paul stated that unless the developed world became more sensitive to third world poverty, Marxism's "social messianism" would become attractive and provoke "violent revolution."[11] In reply, CELAM's president, Bishop Manuel Larraín, spoke starkly of the developing nations' misery. "Every year," he stated, "more people die of hunger and disease in the Third World than perished in the six years of the Second World War."[12]

Direct awareness of the enormity of these matters may have contributed to the sense of urgency, the call for "bold transformations, innovations that go deep" (PP 32) that prevails throughout *Populorum Progressio*, distinguishing it from other magisterial documents of the 1960s that have, on the whole, the tone of treatises. Other influences, however, are also discernible. The encyclical reflects, for example, aspects of the thought of the economist-philosopher, Louis Lebret, O.P., whom Paul summoned to the Council as a *peritus*.[13] One statement in *Populorum Progressio* is a direct citation from Lebret's writings (PP 14).

Yet the significance of Lebret's thought should not be exaggerated. For a start, other contemporary authors are cited in the encyclical. Previously, it was noted that de Lubac enjoys this distinction. *Populorum Progressio* also refers to texts by Maritain, Chenu, Nell-Breuning, and the Australian economist Colin Clark.[14] The non-biblical text most cited, however, is

---

10. In 1960, Cardinal Montini visited Rio de Janerio, where he met Helder Câmara. From 19 July to 20 August 1962, Montini went to Southern Rhodesia, Upper Volta, Nigeria, and Ghana. See Hebblethwaite, *Paul VI*, 292, 301–302.

11. Paul VI, "Address to Latin American Bishops," AAS 57 (1965), 947.

12. See G. Gutiérrez, "Le rapport entre l'église et les pauvres, vu d'Amérique Latine," in *La réception de Vatican II*, G. Alberigo and J. Jossua, eds. (Paris: Cerf, 1985), 245.

13. See F. Malley, *Le Père Lebret: l'économie au service des hommes* (Paris: Editions Spes, 1968), 90–110. For Lebret's contributions to GS, see Moeller, "History of the Constitution," 39.

14. See PP ns. 17, 27, 29, 31, 44.

Gaudium et Spes.[15]

Another factor shaping *Populorum Progressio* may have been Paul's establishment of the Pontifical Commission *Iustitia et Pax* in 1966. Though neither provides any direct evidence, both Hebblethwaite and Novak suggest that the encyclical reflects the new Commission's input, specifically that of Catholic specialists in third world development such as Barbara Ward and George Jarlot.[16]

"The World is Sick"

Looking at the modern world in 1967, *Populorum Progressio* states that

> social conflicts have taken on world dimensions. . . . In certain regions, a privileged minority enjoys the refinements of life, while the rest of the inhabitants, impoverished and scattered, "are deprived of nearly all possibility of exercising personal initiative and responsibility, and quite often have to live and work in conditions unworthy of human beings." [citing GS 63] (PP 9)

The problem, then, is not just material deprivation, but the fact that this undermines the opportunity of many to use their initiative and acquire responsibility. Material deprivation, in short, hinders the capacity of people to grow as persons.

The origin of these problems, according to Paul, owes much to the character of relations between wealthy and poor nations. The colonial period receives special attention in this regard. Paul claims that colonizing powers not only often "furthered their own interests, power or glory [but] their departure left the economy of [developing] nations in precarious imbalance—the one-crop economy, for example, which is at the mercy of sudden, wide-ranging fluctuations in market prices" (PP 7).[17]

The encyclical also states that this colonial legacy benefits affluent

---

15. See also J. Schroeffer, "Continuity of the Conciliar and Pontifical Magisterium: From *Gaudium et Spes* to *Populorum Progressio*," *L'Osservatore Romano* (English Weekly Edition) 17 (1977): 6–7.

16. See Hebblethwaite, *Paul VI*, 484; Novak, *Freedom with Justice*, 134 n.42. Cf. J. Grémillion, "L'enciclica e la Commissione Giustizia e Pace," *L'Osservatore Romano*, 23 aprile 1967: 1–2.

17. Note, however, that Paul praises "those colonizers whose skills and technical knowledge brought benefits to many under-privileged regions" (PP 7).

nations and disadvantages developing countries:

> highly industrialized nations export manufactured goods, for the most part.
> Less developed countries, on the other hand, have nothing to sell, but raw
> materials and agricultural crops. As a result of technical progress, the value
> of manufactured goods is rising rapidly and they find a ready market. But
> the basic crops and raw materials produced by the less-developed countries
> are subject to sudden and wide-ranging shifts in market price. . . . This
> poses serious difficulties for the developing nations. They depend on
> exports to a large extent for a balanced economy and for further steps
> toward development. Thus the needy nations grow more destitute while the
> rich nations become even richer. (PP 57)

As an economic analysis, these statements have been criticized as
contrary to empirical evidence.[18] Whatever the merits of such arguments,
Paul uses this paragraph to explain what is wrong with what the Council
called "prevailing conventions of commerce." Given the differing
commodity bases of developed and developing economies, Paul states that
"the principle of free trade, by itself, is no longer adequate for regulating
international agreements." Whilst affirming the advantages of free trade,
Paul considers these to be predicated upon the parties involved being
relatively equal in economic power. But "when the nations involved are
far from equal . . . [m]arket prices that are 'freely' agreed upon can
produce unfair results" (PP 58).

On one level, Paul's picture is one of an economic order which
operates, without any apparent malice on the wealthy nations' part, to the
detriment of developing nations. Yet one must remember that Paul
presents it as being built, in part, upon the legacy of the developed nations'
colonialism. Moreover, his words imply that affluent nations effectively
acquiesce in this situation.

Thus, although there may be, as Hobgood claims,[19] a "structural"
element to Paul's analysis, *Populorum Progressio* indicates that past and
present decisions have made the international economic order what it is.
Indeed, the encyclical states that the world's "illness consists less in the
unproductive monopolization of resources by a small number of men than
in the lack of brotherhood among individuals and nations" (PP 66). The
ultimate source of the problem, then, is man's failure to love his neighbor.

---

18. See, for example, P. Bauer, "An Economist Replies: Ecclesiastical Economics is Envy
Exalted," *This World* 1 (1982): 65–74.
19. See Hobgood, *Catholic Social Teaching*, 187–188.

7.3 Unrealized Hopes: A Second World Pope

During a rare interview in 1993, Pope John Paul was asked what difference being Polish made to his pontificate. Part of his answer was, in many respects, surprising:

> Having lived in a country which had to struggle for its freedom, in a country vulnerable to the aggression and dictates of its neighbors, I have been led to sympathize with the plight of the countries of the Third World, which are also subject to another type of dependence, the economic one.[20]

Obviously these words reflect the feelings of one whose nation has endured a tragic history since its first partitioning in 1778. Yet while many Poles regard their historical struggle as having wider European or even religious significance,[21] it is unusual to hear such sentiments applied to the third world.

There is, however, evidence attesting to an empathy on John Paul's part for the developing nations which predates his pontificate. During the Council's first session in 1962, the then-Bishop Wojtyła composed seven poems under the overall title of "The Church." One of these was entitled "The Negro." Wojtyła addresses it to "My Dear Brother" (an unnamed African bishop) in whom he feels "the immense continent in which rivers dry up suddenly—and the sun burns the body like ore in a mill furnace." Wojtyła tells him that "I feel your thoughts like mine," "thoughts that differently flicker in your eyes and mine though their substance is the same."[22]

"The Negro," then, seems to convey Wojtyła's discovery of the third world. Though nobody in Africa was likely to read it, the poem expressed the same sense of brotherhood which reappears in the pope's 1992 interview. Interestingly, Wojtyła made a point of underlining the "ever-widening gap" between the first world and the impoverished third world nations during his Lenten Lectures (SC 157). Indeed, in the years following the Council, Wojtyła engaged in a significant amount of travel in third world nations such as Egypt, Jordan, the Philippines, and New Guinea (though not Latin America)—something unusual for Polish

---

20. J. Gawronski, "Io, il Papa tra l'Ovest e l'Est," *La Stampa*, 2 November 1993, 1.
21. See A. Walicki, "Polish Romantic Messianism in Comparative Perspective," *Slavonic Studies* 22 (1978): 1–15.
22. "The Negro," *The Place Within*, 103.

bishops at the time. Wojtyła also brought the third world to Poland by inviting Cardinal Zoungrana of Upper Volta to Kraków in 1975, as well as bishops from India and Tanzania.[23] Of course, as Pope John Paul, Wojtyła has visited numerous developing nations since 1978, with his first major journey being to Mexico in January 1979.

A Fragmented World

One may presume that these experiences contributed to John Paul's decision to promulgate *Sollicitudo Rei Socialis* in 1987 in commemoration of *Populorum Progressio*. Of his three social encyclicals, it is the most focused upon relations between developed and developing nations. While John Paul underlines many of the same problems as the Council and Paul VI, he employs somewhat different terminology in doing so. He refers, for example, to "the persistence and often the widening of the *gap* between the areas of the so-called developed North and the developing South" (SRS 14). Whilst Paul VI referred to massive inequalities between regions, "secular" expressions such as "North" and "South" are absent from *Populorum Progressio*.

Reflecting on changes in the circumstances of developing nations since 1967, John Paul insists that their situation has "become *notably worse*." He attributes responsibility both more widely and directly than Paul VI. For a start, John Paul refers to the "grave instances of omissions on the part of developing nations themselves, and especially on the part of those holding economic and political power" (SRS 16).[24] He also notes "the responsibility of the developed nations, which have not always, at least in due measure, felt the duty to help countries separated from the affluent world" (SRS 16).

Considering, then, relations between developed and developing nations, John Paul denounces

> the existence of economic, financial and social *mechanisms* which, although they are manipulated by people, often function almost automatically, thus accentuating the situation of wealth for some and poverty for the rest. These mechanisms, which are maneuvered directly or indirectly by the more developed countries, by their very functioning favor the interests of the people manipulating them. But in the end, they suffocate

---

23. See Szulc, *Pope John Paul II*, 220, 261; Kwitny, *Man of the Century*, 190.
24. SRS later refers to the existence of many "corrupt, dictatorial and authoritarian forms of government" in the developing nations (SRS 44).

or condition the economies of the less developed countries. (SRS 16)

On one level, these statements parallel Paul VI's analysis of the international economic order. Indeed, John Paul notes that *"Populorum Progressio* already foresaw the possibility that under such systems the wealth of the rich would increase and the poverty of the poor would remain [refers to Paul VI]" (SRS 16). The attached note refers to Paul's statement that free trade alone could never assure development and by itself tends to increase the wealth of the rich.[25] In the passage above, however, John Paul speaks more generally of "mechanisms" which are "manipulated" and "maneuvered" by affluent countries. This focuses greater attention upon the role of human agency in international economic affairs.

One mechanism singled out by John Paul are international loans. "Circumstances," he states, "both within the debtor nations and in the international financial market," have turned loans into "a *counter-productive mechanism*." Put briefly, debt-servicing has forced developing nations to export the capital they need for improving living standards. To underline continuity with past teaching, John Paul states that twenty years previously, *Populorum Progressio* warned that loans could have this effect (SRS 19).

Where, however, John Paul's analysis of the problems characterizing relations between developed and developing nations significantly differs from that of Paul VI, involves the former's attention to geo-political factors. *Sollicitudo Rei Socialis* refers to

> the existence of two opposing blocs, commonly known as the East and the West. The reason for this description is not purely political, but is also, as the expression goes, geo-political. Each of the two blocs tends to assimilate or gather around it other countries or groups of countries, to different degrees of adherence or participation. (SRS 20)[26]

Despite the fact that bloc-tension was probably more evident in 1965 and 1967, analogous statements appear in neither *Gaudium et Spes* nor

25. It reads: "Encyclical *Populorum Progressio*, 33." Here Paul states that "[i]ndividual initiative alone and the interplay of competition will not ensure satisfactory development. One must avoid the risk of increasing still more the wealth of the rich . . . whilst leaving the poor in their misery" (PP 33).
26. The second sentence cited has been described as a "generic euphemism" that allows the encyclical to collate those nations which adhere more or less freely to a bloc with those kept within a bloc against their wishes. See Novak, "The Development of Nations," 100.

Populorum Progressio.

In examining these blocs, John Paul states that "each bloc identifies itself with a system of organizing society and exercising power which presents itself as an alternative to the other." According to the pope, "[t]he political opposition, in turn, takes its origins from a deeper opposition which is *ideological* in nature." In the West there is "the *liberal capitalism* which developed with industrialization during the last century," whilst "[i]n the East there exists a system inspired by *Marxist collectivism.*" This *"ideological opposition"* in turn evolved "into a growing *military opposition* and [gave] rise to two blocs of armed forces, each suspicious and fearful of the other's domination" (SRS 20).

There seems little question that these words refer to the post-war confrontation between the United States and NATO, and the Soviet Union and the Warsaw Pact. What, however, has this to do with the developing world?

Gaudium et Spes, we recall, referred to the obstacles that political schemes, intrigues for imposing ideologies, and military strategies created for the evolution of a just economic order. In a loose sense, *Sollicitudo Rei Socialis* may be read as explaining how this occurs. According to John Paul, "[e]ach of the two *blocs* harbors in its own way a tendency towards *imperialism* . . . or towards forms of neo-colonialism" (SRS 22). Recently independent countries, he states, "find themselves involved in, and sometimes overwhelmed by, ideological conflicts which inevitably create internal divisions, to the extent in some cases of provoking full civil war" (SRS 21). Indeed, he refers to the blocs engaging in *"wars by proxy"* through the "manipulation of local conflicts" (SRS 20). More generally, bloc tension results in "investments and aid for development" often being "diverted from their proper purpose and in opposition to the interests of the countries which ought to benefit from them" (SRS 21).

Having directed attention to the negative impact of first and second world conflict upon the development of third world nations, John Paul places it and the mechanisms referred to above within the context of "A Theological Reading of Modern Problems." A world, the pope states, "which is divided into blocs, sustained by rigid ideologies, and in which instead of interdependence and solidarity different forms of imperialism hold sway, can only be a world subject to structures of sin" (SRS 36).

The expression, "structures of sin," allows John Paul to delineate, with greater precision than his predecessor, the exact relationship between personal moral error and the structures disordering relations between developed and developing nations. The pope specifies that structures of sin "are rooted in personal sin, and thus always linked to the *concrete acts* of individuals who introduce these structures, consolidate them and make them difficult to remove" (SRS 36). An unusually long footnote from John Paul's Apostolic Exhortation, *Reconciliatio et Paenitentia* (1985), is attached to this sentence. It indicates a desire to be clearly understood on this point:

> Whenever the Church speaks of *situations* of sin, or when she condemns as *social sins* certain situations or the collective behavior of social groups, big or small, or even of whole nations and blocs of nations, she knows and she proclaims that such cases of *social sin* are the result of the accumulation and concentration of many *personal sins*. It is a case of the very personal sins of those who cause or support evil or who exploit it; of those who are in a position to avoid, eliminate or at least limit certain social evils but who fail to do so out of laziness, fear or the conspiracy of silence, through secret complicity or indifference; of those who take refuge in the supposed impossibility of changing the world, and also those who sidestep the effort and sacrifice required, producing specious reasons of a higher order. The real responsibility, then, lies with individuals. A situation—or likewise an institution, a structure, society itself—is not in itself the subject of moral acts. Hence a situation cannot in itself be good or bad.[27]

All "structures of sin," then, are identified as the product of, and maintained by, *sinful personal acts*. This is the case because only persons are *subjects of moral acts*, and therefore are ultimately responsible for the social evil ensuing from the evil acts which proceed from man. This need not only take the form of choosing to act in an "overtly" evil manner. It can amount to choosing *not* to do good—by being lazy or indifferent. Whilst the structures maintained and consolidated by such acts can, in the pope's view, "influence people's behavior" (SRS 36), in the final analysis man "becomes bad" because he—the human subject—freely chooses to act wrongly.

Having clarified the relationship between personal and social sin via a moral-anthropological exposition of the origins of evil, John Paul states that two "very typical actions and attitudes opposed to the will of God" are "the *all-consuming desire for profit*, and . . . *the thirst for power*." At present, the pope claims, "we are faced with the *absolutizing* of human attitudes" such as these, and "not only [do] individuals fall victim to this double attitude of sin; nations and blocs can do so too." This, the pope

---

27. SRS 36 n.65. Apostolic Exhortation, *Reconciliatio et Paenitentia*, AAS 77 (1985), 217.

says, illustrates the usefulness of the concept of "structures of sin":

> If certain forms of modern "imperialism" were considered in the light of
> these moral criteria, we would see that hidden behind certain decisions,
> apparently inspired only by economics or politics, are real forms of
> idolatry: of money, ideology, class, technology. (SRS 37)

Though the pope offers no examples, his words suggest that the structures
negatively affecting developing nations are not based on "purely" political
or economic choices by nations or blocs. Rather, they involve the choice to
make idols of certain ends, such as profit or power.

7.4 A New Language

The developments outlined above may be understood as proceeding from
two primary sources. One is awareness of the emergence of new problems
in the twenty years since *Populorum Progressio* as well as greater
attention to the political complexities affecting relations between
developed and developing countries. The other concerns the
magisterium's efforts to engage with various theses commonly associated
with the theologies of liberation. In this latter case, Wojtyłan ideas appear
to have influenced John Paul's response.

John Paul's attention to the debt issue seems to fit the first category
noted above. The encyclical itself identifies it as "characteristic of the
most recent period" (SRS 19). By the late 1970s, more than one institution
was referring to the burdens that loan repayments imposed upon
developing nations.[28] In this sense, John Paul's references to the debt
problem indicate cognizance of the problem.[29] They also appear to reflect
concerns expressed by the Pontifical Commission *Iustitia et Pax* in its
1986 report, *At the Service of the Human Community: An Ethical
Approach to the International Debt Question*. With the Commission
directing attention to this matter just one year before *Sollicitudo Rei
Socialis*'s promulgation,[30] it is unsurprising that John Paul gives the issue
close attention. Indeed, the report is mentioned in both the encyclical's

---

28. See, for example, OECD, *Facing the Future* (Paris: OECD, 1979), 269–271.
29. CA 35 outlines principles and guidelines for resolving third world debt.
30. The Commission (now Pontifical Council) is not a source of doctrinal authority in the
proper sense, but serves the Church's magisterium by studying its social teaching. See Paul
VI, Apostolic Letter *Catholicam Christi Ecclesiam*, AAS 59 (1967): 25–28.

text and footnotes.[31]

As far as *Sollicitudo Rei Socialis*'s use of terms like "North" and "South" is concerned, this constitutes an instance of the magisterium using modern language commonly understood by all. Yet the same reasoning does not fully account for John Paul's introduction of a geo-political dimension into teaching on this matter. Certainly by the 1980s, the language of blocs was relatively common. This does not, however, explain the particular character of John Paul's analysis.

From whence, then, is *Sollicitudo Rei Socialis*'s geo-political analysis derived? In a general sense, it may be said to follow *Gaudium et Spes*'s references to the effects upon the international economic order of desires for *political* domination, schemes of *military* strategy, and intrigues for spreading *ideologies*. When it comes, however, to the specific form of John Paul's analysis, a cogent explanation is offered by Hehir. Writing in 1990, Hehir suggested that as a Pole, John Paul would be particularly conscious of how post-war U.S.-Soviet political, ideological, and military rivalry adversely affected the autonomy of other nations.[32] Confirmation that Eastern Europe's post-war fate has weighed on the Polish pope's mind may be found in *Centesimus Annus*. Here John Paul reflects that after 1945, "half of the [European] continent fell under the domination of a Communist dictatorship. . . . Many peoples lost the ability to control their own destiny and were enclosed within the suffocating boundaries of an empire" (CA 18).

If one adopts the analytical perspective of *Sollicitudo Rei Socialis*, then one may say that Central-Eastern European nations were the first to be dragged into the post-war U.S.-Soviet confrontation. One might even view the Warsaw Pact and Comecon as bloc-structures which locked these countries into place. In this sense, it would be quite natural for John Paul to conceptualize other nations' post-war history—especially as an arena for the blocs to carry out "wars by proxy"—in similar terms. This reasoning becomes even more convincing in light of the pope's willingness to draw parallels between Poland's fate and that of third world nations during his 1992 interview.

There is, however, another factor which may have influenced John Paul's geo-political analysis. *Sollicitudo Rei Socialis* refers to the fact that

---

31. See SRS 19 and SRS ns.38 and 40.
32. See Hehir, "Papal Foreign Policy," 27–48. See also F. Margiotta Broglio, "Il papato degli ultimi cinquant'anni. Dalla 'nuova cristianita' di Pio XII alla geopolitica di Karol Wojtyła," *Rivista di Studi Politici Internazionali* 56, no. 1 (1989): 47–56.

in the period following the publication of the encyclical *Populorum Progressio*, a new way of confronting the problems of poverty and underdevelopment has spread in some areas of the world, especially in Latin America. This approach makes *liberation* the fundamental category and the first principle of action. (SRS 46)

Assessment of the possible contribution of ideas associated with liberation theologians and documents produced by CELAM to John Paul's geo-political appraisal requires a preliminary outline of liberation theology. This is a notoriously difficult task, given the plethora of positions embraced by this phrase.[33] Here we limit ourselves to summarizing its origins and delineating some "liberationist" themes concerning relations between developed and developing nations.

7.5 *Liberación* Analyses: *Dependencia* Premises

The usual starting point of any study of liberation theology is CELAM's 1968 Conference held at Medellín, Colombia. Yet it would be absurd to imagine that the Latin American bishops "invented" liberation theology at Medellín. Conditions in Latin America during the late 1960s and 1970s— authoritarian regimes, vast wealth disparities, etc.—appear to have contributed to CELAM's re-expression of the Christian idea of salvation in terms of *liberación*: liberation *from* not only individual sins but also society's in-built "sinful structures." According to one liberation theologian, Hugo Assmann, liberation theology emerged as a demand for emancipation from the oppressive *status quo* dominant in Latin America. It signified an unwillingness to acquiesce in this situation and a commitment to transform it immediately.[34] The biblical metaphor commonly evoked was the Exodus story of Israel's liberation from bondage in Egypt.[35]

Liberation theology was derived, however, from more than

---

33. The CDF itself states: "As with all movements of ideas, the 'theologies of liberation' present diverse theological positions. Their doctrinal frontiers are badly defined" (LN III.3). In a non-magisterial capacity, the CDF Prefect, Cardinal Ratzinger, claimed that liberation theology consists of "a whole spectrum from radically marxist positions, on the one hand, to the efforts which are being made within the framework of a correct and ecclesial theology, on the other hand." Ratzinger, *The Ratzinger Report*, 174.

34. See H. Assmann, *Practical Theology of Liberation* (London: Search Press, 1975), 47.

35. See, for example, Gutiérrez, *A Theology of Liberation*, 291–296. For relevant texts by Gutiérrez and other Latin Americans before Medellín, see *Liberation Theology*, A. Hennelly, S.J., ed. (Maryknoll: Orbis, 1990), 1–84.

interpretations of scripture. Some liberationist ideas had precedents in magisterial teaching. *Populorum Progressio* spoke of building a world in which people "can live truly human lives, *freed from servitude* imposed on him by other men or by natural forces" (PP 47).[36] The notion of "liberation from oppression" was therefore present in pre-Medellín social teaching. Others[37] associate liberation theology with *Gaudium et Spes*'s statement that "man is often turned away from the good and urged towards evil by the social environment in which he lives." Here one should note the Council's qualification that "at a deeper level" economic, political and social problems "come from selfishness and pride" (GS 25). *Sollicitudo Rei Socialis* broadly conforms to this position. Whilst acknowledging that problematic conditions can negatively influence people, personal sin is identified as ultimately underlying these situations. The Council also specifies that "whenever [man] meets a situation where the effects of sin are to be found, he is exposed to further inducements to sin" (GS 25). The word "inducement" is important here. It suggests that though situations can tempt people, man remains responsible for his choice of evil—a point reaffirmed by John Paul.

Other observers suggest that many liberation theologies owed something to decidedly non-magisterial influences. Assmann singles out "[t]he language of the revolutionary movements of the left, the Marxist vocabulary of Latin American 'New Marxism'. . . . the terms used by student movements . . . the writings of Herbert Marcuse."[38] Ratzinger agrees. He refers to the influence of "various brands of neo-marxism," including "Bloch's marxism with its religious veneer and the strictly scientific appearance of the philosophies of Adorno, Horkheimer, Habermas and Marcuse."[39]

Whatever the origins of their thinking, most liberation theologians emphasized the importance of structures and the need to change them. Baum claims that in the 1960s, liberation theologians joined German political theologians such as Metz in demanding that people became conscious of the structures which produced marginalization. Their emphasis on this point is described by Baum as a reaction against what he describes as the Church's tendency to "moralize," that is, to create "the impression that if each person became more loving and generous, then

---

36. Italics added.
37. See, for example, Velásquez, *"Gaudium et Spes,"* 188.
38. Assmann, *Practical Theology*, 48.
39. Ratzinger, *The Ratzinger Report*, 177–178. For the magisterium's position on the use of Marxist analysis, see OA 34; LN VII.8.

social problems would straighten themselves out."[40] Thus, as Velásquez states, liberation theology was often "characterized by its emphasis on the *reform of sinful social structures* rather than on *conversion of the sinful individual*."[41]

According to Assmann, Medellín transformed the language used by many Latin American Catholics to describe the structural changes necessary in the international economy.[42] The word, "development," in the sense of gradual internal change aided by external forces, needed, in their view, to be replaced by "liberation": the abolition of the structural state of dependence in which they believed poor countries were kept by external forces, especially wealthy nations' economic power. Certainly, one Medellín document did refer to

> the implications for our countries of dependence on a center of economic power, around which they gravitate. For this reason, our nations frequently do not own their goods, or have a say in economic decisions affecting them. . . . We wish to emphasize that the principal guilt for the economic dependence of our countries rests with powers, inspired by uncontrolled desire for gain.[43]

In the same document, the Latin American bishops repeated *Populorum Progressio*'s statements regarding the detrimental effects of international trade upon developing nations.[44] The words above, however, speak more directly of others being morally responsible for the developing nations' situation than those of Paul VI. On this issue, some liberation theologians went further than the Medellín texts. In 1972, Gutiérrez suggested that

---

40. Baum, "Structures of Sin," in *The Logic of Solidarity*, 111. See J.B. Metz, *Zur Theologie der Welt* (Mainz: Matthais-Grünwald Verlag, 1968), 107–140. Metz's thought is closely analyzed by Gutiérrez in *A Theology of Liberation*, 221–225, 242–243.

The 1971 Synod of Bishops appears to have assimilated aspects of this structuralist emphasis when it stated that attempts to change the international order could not ignore "the objective obstacles which social structures place in the way of conversion of hearts" (*Iustitia in Mundo*, para. 16). Strictly speaking, these words simply acknowledge that there are structural obstacles to "a change of heart." This does not, however, downgrade the importance of personal conversion.

41. Velásquez, "*Gaudium et Spes*," 188; cf. Gutiérrez, *A Theology of Liberation*, 229–230.

42. See Assmann, *Practical Theology*, 45.

43. Second General Conference of Latin American Bishops, Medellín. "Document on Peace" (1968), paras. 8, 9, in *Liberation Theology*, 90–92.

44. See Medellín, "Document on Peace," para. 9.

only a class analysis enables us to see what is really involved in the opposition between oppressed countries and dominant peoples. To take into account only the confrontation between nations misrepresents and in the final analysis waters down the situation.[45]

Reformist efforts at development, in Gutiérrez's view, failed to realize that there could only be authentic change in the developing nations' circumstances if they are emancipated from the domination of capitalist countries.[46]

According to Hoy, Gutiérrez's arguments on this matter borrow heavily from "Marxist-derived dependency theory, which contends that the under-development of poor countries is the historical by-product of the development of other countries, and that Latin America is in a situation of dependency upon the external domination of world markets by capitalist nations."[47] In this light, *dependencia* propositions would seem to have influenced some liberationist analyses and perhaps even the Medellín document cited above. Their apparent effect, however, should not be exaggerated. Paul VI's synopsis of the problems affecting relations between developed and developing nations could not be described as "Marxist" or as utilizing a "class analysis." Yet *Populorum Progressio* parallels dependency theory insofar as both maintain that the developed nations' colonial legacy has contributed to the developing nations' problems.

7.6 Engaging with Liberationist Thinking

There is much to suggest that *Sollicitudo Rei Socialis*'s development of certain teachings represents, in part, indirect responses to several ideas associated with various liberation theologies: their *dependencia*-like analyses; the language of "idolatry"; and the attention to structures. To take the first of these, by stating that the geo-political conflict between two flawed political-military-ideological blocs is a major structural cause of developing nations' problems, *Sollicitudo Rei Socialis* indicates that the reasons for the third world's difficulties are more complex than suggested by some *dependencia* interpretations. For example, whilst attributing some

---

45. Gutiérrez, *A Theology of Liberation*, 87.
46. See Gutiérrez, *A Theology of Liberation*, 25–27, 82–84.
47. T. Hoy, "Gustavo Gutiérrez: Latin American Liberation Theology," *International Journal of Social Economics* 13, no. 9 (1986): 9. See also E. Hansen, *The Catholic Church in World Politics* (Princeton: Princeton University Press, 1987), 108–109.

responsibility to the "liberal capitalist" bloc for the situation, John Paul identifies the "Marxist-collectivist" bloc as *equally* culpable. This point does not figure in Gutiérrez's analysis, although Medellín did "denounce the imperialism of *any* ideological bias that is exercised in Latin America either indirectly or through direct intervention."[48]

One can, however, be more confident in suggesting that John Paul's use of the concept of idolatry to describe the sin at the base of contemporary imperialisms reflects assimilation of ideas underlined by some liberation theologians and articulated in CELAM documents. The condemnation of idolatry, in the sense of paying the same heed to things as one should to God, is hardly new in Christian thought: "you cannot serve both God and Money" (Lk 16:13). Donal Dorr, however, points out that the idea of idolatry as an absolutization of attitudes is a theme which figured prominently in the work of many liberation theologians.[49] As observed, *Sollicitudo Rei Socialis* defines idolatry in a similar manner.

Moreover, John Paul's specification that idolatry is at the root of blocs and modern imperialisms closely resembles ideas expressed in documents produced by CELAM at Puebla in 1979. Here the bishops described the idolatry of material goods as underlying both liberal capitalism and Marxist collectivism. They also described totalitarianism as being based upon the idolatry of power.[50] In other words, they were suggesting that idolatry can take on an almost systemic form. The same proposition appears in *Sollicitudo Rei Socialis*, but is used to explain the origins and nature of imperialistic blocs.

Lastly, John Paul's statements about structures of sin may be understood as responding to the liberationist attention to structures. As observed, the magisterium has never denied that economic processes can contribute to international injustice. Nevertheless, there was a concerted effort on the magisterium's part to delineate the precise relationship between personal sin and structural sin throughout the 1980s.

The two instructions produced by the CDF in 1984 and 1986 are particularly important in this respect, especially given that they represent a highly authoritative magisterial response to liberation theology. *Libertatis Nuntius* specified that one cannot "localize evil principally or uniquely in

---

48. Medellín, "Document on Peace," para. 10. Italics added.
49. See D. Dorr, *Option for the Poor* (Dublin: Gill and Macmillan, 1992), 330; cf. J. Segundo, S.J., *Theology of the Church* (London: Chapman, 1985), 55–65.
50. See Third General Conference of Latin American Bishops, Puebla (1979). "Evangelization, Liberation, and Human Promotion," paras. 4.4, 5.5, in *Liberation Theology*, 150–174.

bad social, political or economic 'structures' as though all other evils came from them." It then added that "[s]tructures . . . are the result of man's actions and so are consequences more than causes. The roots of evil, then, lie in free and responsible persons" (LN IV.15). This position was reiterated by *Libertatis Conscientia*: "the sin which is at the root of unjust structures is, in a true and immediate sense, a voluntary act which has its source in the freedom of individuals. Only in a derived and secondary sense is it applicable to structures, and only in this sense can one speak of 'social sin' [refers to John Paul II]" (LC 75). The parallels between these statements and *Sollicitudo Rei Socialis*'s definition of structures of sin are obvious. Indeed, the footnote attached to the last statement refers to the same paragraph of *Reconciliatio et Paenitentia* that is cited by the encyclical.[51]

7.7 Subjects and Structures

There is, however, one subtle difference between the CDF statements about structures and those of *Sollicitudo Rei Socialis*: the latter's use of the phrase, "subject of moral acts," to specify that structures in themselves cannot be good or bad. Although both CDF documents insist that because man alone is free and responsible, he alone is sinful, neither text uses this precise term.

It is, of course, a phrase much associated with Wojtyłan thought which, as we know, is much concerned with man's anthropological status as a subject of acts. Because the human subject is a person, *The Acting Person* posits that each of his acts involving the use of will and reason are of moral significance. Through such acts, man can respond to moral good and realize himself. In this context, Wojtyła warns that "too often man seeks and chooses what is not good for him. . . . Choices and decisions, which take as their object what is not a 'real good'—especially when contrary to what has been recognized as a real good—lead to the experience of 'guilt' or 'sin'" (AP 139).

If one applies this anthropology of man and his acts to a notion like "sinful structures," then the latter concept suddenly appears somewhat problematic. From Wojtyła's moral-anthropological perspective, a structure *cannot* be a subject of moral acts. Strictly speaking, acts cannot "proceed" from a structure: structures have no capacity to respond to

---

51. It reads: "Cf. Apostolic Exhortation, *Reconciliatio et Paenitentia*, 16: AAS 77 (1985), 213–217."

values; they cannot make choices about themselves; nor can they realize themselves. A structure cannot therefore "in itself," as *Sollicitudo Rei Socialis* states, be good or bad. To understand structures as having a moral capacity is, from the viewpoint of both Wojtyła and the encyclical, contrary to the anthropological fact that man alone is the subject of moral acts and thus ultimately responsible for good and evil. In a previous chapter, we noted that *The Acting Person* insists that while "systems of things" can contribute to man's dehumanization, man is ultimately accountable for the form taken by such systems. On these grounds, Wojtyła maintains that man is ultimately responsible for any alienation resulting from such systems. At a minimum, then, it may be said that Wojtyła's conclusion—that man, in the end, is responsible for problematic structures and their effects—accords with the position articulated in the CDF Instructions and *Sollicitudo Rei Socialis*.

Of course, if one delineates where the primary responsibility for problematic structures and systems lies, then one is more than halfway to outlining how people should respond to such situations. This is clearly John Paul's intent in *Sollicitudo Rei Socialis*. Referring to his teaching about the structures of sin, the pope notes:

> I have wished to introduce this type of analysis above all to point out the true nature of the evil which faces us . . . it is a question of *moral evil*, the fruit of many sins, which leads to "structures of sin." To diagnose the evil in this way is to identify precisely, on the level of human conduct, *the path to be followed* in order *to overcome it*. (SRS 37)

Whilst John Paul outlines several practical proposals for reordering relations between developing and developed nations, he insists that the key to change is realization of the principle of solidarity. So too do the Council and Paul VI.

7.8   The Solidarity of Mankind

In considering how to build a more just international order, the Council states that "[t]he present solidarity of mankind calls for greater international cooperation in economic matters" (GS 85). The precise meaning of solidarity is not delineated here. A clearer definition appears earlier in the paragraph of *Gaudium et Spes* headed "The Word Made Flesh and Human Solidarity." This states that "God did not create men for life in isolation, but for the formation of social union" (GS 32). Man, then, has a natural vocation to community. This is elaborated upon in an earlier statement: "God did not create man as a solitary. . . . For by their innermost nature human beings are social, and unless they relate themselves to one another they can neither live nor develop their gifts" (GS 12). People, in short, need each other not only to realize specific ends, but for fulfillment as persons.

How, then, is this human solidarity realized? In its teaching about solidarity, the Council maintains that Christ "clearly outlined an obligation on part of the sons of God to treat each other as brothers." Solidarity may therefore be said to involve fulfilling the basic duty to be just to, and love, one another. The Council then refers to solidarity as the rendering of "mutual service in the measure of the different gifts bestowed on each" (GS 32). This suggests that people should meet the obligation of brotherhood by serving each other in whatever way they are able to do so.

With the meaning of solidarity clarified, we are better positioned to grasp the precise inspiration underpinning the Council's proposals for re-ordering relations between developed and developing nations. The Council begins by stating that "it is now a necessity for the community of nations to organize itself in a manner suited to its present responsibilities, with special reference to its obligations to the many areas of the world where intolerable want prevails" (GS 84). Reference is made to the need to find "a common basis for a just world commerce" (GS 85) as well as the creation of international organizations "to promote and regulate international commerce, especially with less developed nations, in order to compensate for losses resulting from excessive inequality of power between nations" (GS 86). Solidarity, in this regard, involves the application of justice to economic relations so that poorer nations receive what they need in exchange for what they can supply.

The Council indicates that developed and developing nations have specific roles to play in this process. Developing countries are reminded that "their express and unequivocal aim is the total human development of their citizens" and that "progress is based, not only on foreign aid, but on the full exploitation of native resources and on the development of their own talents and traditions" (GS 86). Thus, developing nations are not only considered ultimately responsible for their own progress; they must also ensure that their development is more than material. Their acts of self-reliance must therefore be directed as much to their citizens' personal development as their material progress.

In this context, the role of "affluent nations is to help developing nations to fulfil these commitments" (GS 86). Hence, when the Council refers to developed nations aiding poorer nations in "the form of grants, loans, or investments" (GS 85), it means precisely that: *assisting* developing nations to act rather than treating them as passive recipients. One may say, then, that treating others as brothers involves allowing them sufficient opportunity to develop themselves.

7.9 Principles and Practices

The Council's general approach to changing relations between affluent and developing nations is replicated in *Populorum Progressio*, though with more precision. It begins by stating that "[t]here can be no progress towards the complete development of man without the simultaneous development of all humanity in the spirit of solidarity" (PP 43). Three dimensions of this spirit are outlined, and specific practical consequences attached to each.

The first dimension of the spirit of solidarity involves "the duty of human solidarity" itself. This particularly concerns "the aid that the richer nations must give to developing nations" (PP 44). The form of this aid must be both human and material (PP 48). This, according to Paul, represents an application of the principle that one's superfluous goods should be used to assist others in need (PP 49).

The second dimension concerns "the duty of social justice." This involves "the rectification of trade relations between strong and weak nations" (PP 44). Here Paul is somewhat more prescriptive than the Council. He recommends a specific form of regulatory action, that being "international agreements" to "establish general norms for regulating certain prices, for promoting production facilities, and favoring certain infant industries" (PP 61).

Thirdly, solidarity embraces the duty of "universal charity—the effort to bring about a more humane world community, where all can give and receive, and where the progress of some is not bought at the expense of others" (PP 44). The recommended actions correlating to this principle concern individuals from the developed world exercising personal solidarity towards people from developing nations. It is as if Paul wants to prevent the importance of person-to-person contact between developed and developing nations from being obscured by attention to programs, trade reform, etc. Universal charity involves, for example, businessmen from developed countries becoming "initiators of social progress and of human advancement in [developing] lands" (PP 70).

As we have seen, these expressions of the spirit of solidarity—

assistance, justice in trade relations, and love—are advocated by *Gaudium et Spes*. To maximize the effects of these actions, Paul encourages the creation of international bodies to "prepare," "coordinate," and "direct" the international collaboration generated by solidarity. With reference to the United Nations, *Populorum Progressio* expresses the hope that such institutions "will enjoy ever-growing authority" (PP 78).

Finally, it is noteworthy that Paul insists that "[n]ations are the architects of their own development, and they must bear the burden of this work" (PP 77). This implies that although developed nations must adjust their relations with the third world, they must not adopt a paternalistic attitude towards developing countries. Paul's concept of solidarity, then, embraces the Council's maxim that developing nations must be encouraged to act for themselves.

7.10   The Logic of Solidarity

Sollicitudo Rei Socialis's teaching about reordering relations between developed and developing nations is not as programmatic as *Populorum Progressio*. John Paul's "structures of sin" analysis indicates that he considers the essence of the problem to be personal sin. This implies, of course, that the key to change is personal reform. John Paul hints at this when he states that "for all who recognize the precise theological meaning of the word 'sin', a change of behavior or mentality or mode of existence is called 'conversion'." Structures, of course, cannot be "converted"—only people. It is therefore logical that the pope focuses upon

> the urgent need to *change* the *spiritual attitudes* which define each individual's relationship with self, with neighbor, with even the remotest human community . . . and all of this in view of higher values such as the *common good* or, to quote the felicitous expression of the Encyclical *Populorum Progressio*, the full development of "the whole individual and of all people." (SRS 38)

Here John Paul underlines the importance of a change of attitude on the part of individuals towards others—even the remotest human community such as other nations—so that they orientate themselves towards what is good for them and others: that being the total fulfillment of themselves and others. As previously noted, integral human development in magisterial teaching revolves around man's acquisition of higher values— love, truth, etc. In the citation above, however, John Paul singles out commitment to the development of others as well as oneself—*the common good*—as a "good" that individuals should include among the other higher goods they pursue as part of their effort to fulfil themselves. This position is consistent with the Council's stipulation that man is a social being who needs others if he is to fulfil himself.

Having stressed the importance of individuals pursuing the common good, John Paul then uses the word "solidarity" to conceptualize man's chosen commitment to the good of others as a specific moral *attitude* and *virtue*. It cannot be said that either the Council or Paul VI use this word in precisely the same way. Speaking of the "conversion" required, John Paul points to "the *positive* and moral value of the growing awareness of *interdependence* among individuals and nations." According to the pope, once this awareness is accepted "as a *moral category* . . . the correlative response as a moral and social attitude, as a 'virtue', is *solidarity*." This, he cautions, should not be mistaken for a vague feeling of compassion:

> On the contrary, it is *a firm and persevering determination* to commit oneself to the *common good*; that is to say to the good of all and each individual, because we are *all* really responsible for *all*. (SRS 38)

Solidarity, then, involves recognizing that every person and nation really has undeniable responsibilities towards each other (what the Council calls "obligations" and Paul VI "duties"). One meets these responsibilities by making a free and lasting choice to commit oneself to the common good.

The significance attached by John Paul to man's choice of solidarity soon becomes evident. He states that the "only" way to overcome the "structures of sin" and the absolutized "attitudes" underpinning them is for people to adopt "a *diametrically opposed attitude*: a commitment to the good of one's neighbor with the readiness, in the Gospel sense, to 'lose oneself' for the sake of the other instead of exploiting him" (SRS 38). The implication is that unless people choose freely and always to adopt the attitude of solidarity, the structures presently disordering relations between developed and developing nations will remain: the *personal* choice for the good of others, then, is the *prerequisite* to meaningful structural change.

On this basis, John Paul clarifies how the choice of solidarity may be actualized at an international level. He begins by explaining how this occurs within societies:

> The exercise of solidarity *within each society* is valid when its members recognize one another as persons. Those who are more influential, because

they have a greater share of goods and common services, should feel *responsible* for the weaker and be ready to share with them all they possess. Those who are weaker, for their part . . . should not adopt a purely *passive* attitude or one that is *destructive* of the social fabric, but . . . should do what they can for the good of all. (SRS 39)

All people are thus viewed as able to choose the good of others and thereby self-realize solidarity as a virtue. In the extract above, the "rich" actualize their choice of the good of others by following the principle that the use of their possessions is common, in the sense that they are ready to share them with others in need. The "weaker" actualize the same choice by doing what they can for others. Whilst this represents a variation on the Council's statement that solidarity involves serving others in whatever way one can, John Paul's words also suggest that the act of solidarity is just as significant as its actual "objective" effects. John Paul then applies "the same criterion" to "international relationships":

Surmounting every type of *imperialism* and determination to preserve their hegemony, the stronger and richer nations must have a sense of moral *responsibility* for the other nations, so that a *real international system* may be established which will rest on the foundation of the *equality* of all peoples and on the necessary respect for their legitimate differences. The economically weaker countries, or those still at subsistence level, must be enabled, with the assistance of other peoples and the international community, to make a contribution of their own to the common good with their treasures of *humanity* and *culture*. (SRS 39)

Again, the stress lies on the moral good that developed and developing nations attain by fulfilling their responsibilities to each other in whatever way they can. By helping developing nations, for example, to contribute to the common good (by treating them as equals), affluent nations act in a way which demonstrates their own inclusion of the common good among the moral goods that they pursue.

But when speaking of assisting other nations, John Paul means exactly that. This is evident from his statement that

[a]n essential condition for global *solidarity* is autonomy and free self-determination. But at the same time solidarity demands a readiness to accept the sacrifices necessary for the good of the whole world community. (SRS 45)

Both the teachings of the Council and Paul VI imply that allowing others to act is an important aspect of solidarity. The passage above not only makes this point more explicit but invests it with particular meaning. It specifies that the realization of solidarity as a good means that nations must allow each other to *decide freely* to commit themselves to the common good. To force a nation to pursue solidarity is to usurp the process of free self-determination which is intrinsic to any acquisition of moral good. The specification that nations adopting a solidarist attitude must *always* be ready to do more for the good of all is consistent with John Paul's conception of solidarity as a virtue, that is, as a moral habit which requires constant nurturing.

When John Paul turns to making specific recommendations for reform, he does not follow Paul VI's approach of linking aspects of solidarity to particular proposals. He does, nevertheless, offer practical suggestions for reordering relations between developing and affluent nations. *Sollicitudo Rei Socialis* repeats, for example, previous magisterial calls for "the *reform of the international trade system.*" It also refers to the need for "*reform of the world monetary and financial system*" which "is marked by an excessive fluctuation of exchange rates and interest rates, to the detriment of balance of payments and the debt situation of poorer countries" (SRS 43).

When it comes to "[t]he 'evil mechanisms' and 'structures of sin' of which we have spoken," John Paul states that these "can only be overcome through the exercise of the human and Christian solidarity to which the Church calls us" (SRS 40). He particularly singles out "the abandonment of the politics of blocs, the sacrifice of all forms of economic, military or political imperialism, and the transformation of mutual distrust into *collaboration.*" This is referred to as "precisely the *act proper* to solidarity among individuals and nations" (SRS 39). Evidently John Paul believes that it is only when people commit themselves to the good of all that nations will act in ways which begin to undo the structures which proceed from, and are maintained by, the human subject's sinful acts and dispositions.

7.11   An Ethic of Solidarity

Personal Reform—Structural Change

There is little question that some of *Sollicitudo Rei Socialis*'s specific recommendations for reform, such as attention to the effects of currency fluctuations, proceed from greater appreciation of the complexity of the difficulties to be overcome. When it comes, however, to explaining John Paul's insistence that the personal choice for solidarity is the key to overturning unjust structures, this may, in part, represent a response to liberationist thought. Many liberation theologians, we recall, demanded that attention be given to structural change. To this proposition, *Sollicitudo Rei Socialis*'s response is clear. Overcoming evil structures is critical. Nevertheless, meaningful change of structures must begin with, and be maintained by, the free choice of nations to commit themselves to the common good and consequently act in a collaborative manner.

Sollicitudo Rei Socialis was not, however, the first occasion that the magisterium had underlined the priority of personal change when considering how to create a more just world. *Gaudium et Spes*, we recall, presents the building up of the world as proceeding from man's building up of himself. Interestingly, it was invariably in the context of addressing points raised by liberation theologies that the magisterium underlined this priority after the Council. In 1975, for example, Paul VI's Apostolic Exhortation *Evangelii Nuntiandi* dealt extensively with the notion of liberation (EN 31–39).[52] While affirming that structural reform is important for achieving this end, Paul stated:

> the best structures and the most idealized systems soon become inhuman if the inhuman inclinations of the human heart are not made wholesome, if those who live in these structures or who rule them do not undergo a conversion of heart and of outlook. (EN 36)

---

52. EN was composed, in part, as a consequence of the failure of the 1974 Synod of Bishops, which discussed the theme of evangelization, to agree upon a final text. The *relator* of the Synod was Cardinal Karol Wojtyła. His paper was published as "Ewangelizacja współczesnego świata: Relacja teologiczna na Synodzie Biskupów 1974" [Evangelization in the Contemporary World: Theological Report at the Synod of Bishops, 1974], *Znak* 27, no. 4/5 (1975): 415–439.

Sollicitudo Rei Socialis, we recall, also uses the word "conversion" to conceptualize the change in *attitude* identified as central to overcoming structures of sin.

John Paul's first major pronouncement upon structural reform occurred during his 1979 visit to Mexico. During his Puebla address to CELAM, John Paul referred to "'re-readings' of the Gospel that are the product of theoretical speculation rather than authentic meditation on the Word of God" and of cases where "people purport to depict Jesus as a political activist . . . even as someone involved in the class struggle."[53] This may be understood as implicitly rejecting those liberation theologies which relied excessively on Marxist analytical premises.[54]

For present purposes, however, it is more significant to note that this address refers to mechanisms (a word used in the encyclical) which increase wealthy countries' prosperity at poorer nations' expense. In this connection, John Paul insists that "[t]here is no economic norm to change those mechanisms in and by itself. In international life, too, one must appeal to the principles of ethics, the exigencies of justice and the primary commandant of love. Primacy must be given to that which is moral, to that which is spiritual."[55] These words do not indicate that structural reform is pointless, but rather that structural change in itself will not penetrate to the root of the problem: man's *choice* to be unjust and disobey the commandment of love.

Libertatis Nuntius is even more precise on this matter:

> The acute need for radical reforms of the structures which conceal poverty and which themselves are forms of violence, should not let us lose sight of the fact that the sources of injustice are in the hearts of men. Therefore, it is only by making an appeal to the *moral potential* of the person and to the constant need for interior conversion, that social change will be brought about which will truly be in the service of man. (LN XI.8)[56]

It is, of course, an appeal to man's moral potential which lies at the heart of *Sollicitudo Rei Socialis*'s insistence that man's choice to commit

---

53. "Address to the Bishops of Latin America," AAS 71 (1979), I.4.

54. Note, however, that in a 1986 address to Brazilian bishops, John Paul stated that as long as it is "consistent and coherent with the gospel of the living tradition and the on-going Magisterium of the Church . . . we are convinced, we and you, that the theology of liberation is not only timely but useful and necessary." "Letter to the Brazilian Episcopal Conference," para. 5, in *Liberation Theology*, 245.

55. "Address to the Bishops," III.4.

56. See also LC 75.

himself to the common good will precipitate substantial structural change. The CDF's specification that such change requires *constant* interior conversion makes plain that the magisterium does not have in mind some sort of "fundamental option." For if "evil structures" are maintained by many personal sins, then surely their dissolution through acts of solidarity requires people *always* to act in ways which realize, among other goods, the common good. The same emphasis on lasting commitment is apparent in *Sollicitudo Rei Socialis.*

A similar reasoning about how to realize profound social change may be found in Karol Wojtyła's writings. In "Participation or Alienation," Wojtyła states that "[a]ccording to Marxist philosophy, man is alienated by his own creations: the economic and political system, property ownership and labor. . . . And so, a conclusion is drawn that it suffices to transform the world on the level of those creations, to change the economic and political system . . . and the era of alienation will end." Wojtyła observes, however, that "some contemporary Marxists rightly draw attention to the fact that various forms of alienation are not overcome in that way, and in fact, new ones arise, which in turn need to be dominated." This, in Wojtyła's view, reflects a dawning awareness on their part that what ultimately matters is not so much structural change but rather a change in man's attitude to man. Undoubtedly, he states, "[t]he transformation of the structures of the social existence of human beings in the conditions of contemporary civilization is certainly necessary." It remains, however, that "the participation of every person in the humanity of another person, of other people, shall always remain basic, and that within a universal scope."[57]

Sollicitudo Rei Socialis does not refer to alienation when discussing "structures of sin." Nor is there any direct evidence that Wojtyła wrote the words cited above in response to liberationist theories about structural change. If anything, they probably reflect Wojtyła's experience of the Marxist experiment in which radical changes in property arrangements and the political system were regarded as the way to create a new, better man and society—and the abject *failure* of such structural transformation to do so. In any event, the statements above indicate that Wojtyła was unlikely to be convinced by proposals for social reform which underrated the need for personal change. Indeed, his words imply that such strategies have been ineffective and actually produced new problems. At a minimum, then, Wojtyła's statements parallel *Sollicitudo Rei Socialis*'s

---

57. "Participation or Alienation," 72.

insistence that, in the end, the personal choice for others—what "Participation and Alienation" calls the participation of each person in the humanity of others—is fundamental: it "always remains basic" and the "scope" of this choice has universal implications. This latter point flows logically, of course, from *The Acting Person*'s previously noted insistence that the word "neighbor" reveals man's most fundamental reference point to his fellow man and is "independent of his membership of any community whatever"—which presumably includes that of nation.

Solidarity and Self-Realization

We have seen, however, that one of the most prominent developments proceeding from *Sollicitudo Rei Socialis*'s teaching about reordering relations between developed and developing nations concerns its use of the word solidarity. Though this term was given prominence by the Council and Paul VI, it was also used in pre-conciliar teaching.[58] In Catholic thought, however, solidarity is often associated with the German Jesuit economist, Heinrich Pesch. Writing mainly during the latter half of the nineteenth century, Pesch proposed "solidarism"—the strengthening of natural communities such as the family alongside encouraging the free development of cooperative, representative, and corporate associations based on rank and vocation—as an alternative to Marxism and liberalism.[59]

Sollicitudo Rei Socialis's use of solidarity bears little resemblance to Pesch's "solidarism" insofar as John Paul is primarily concerned with delineating its moral meaning for the person's fulfillment and its ethical significance for the international order. Yet it is precisely in an ethical context that Wojtyła's *The Acting Person* speaks of solidarity. Though he does not apply his conclusions to any one set of social arrangements, Wojtyła's understanding of the term concurs with that of *Sollicitudo Rei Socialis*.

A clear understanding of *The Acting Person*'s treatment of solidarity and its significance for *Sollicitudo Rei Socialis* requires clarification of

---

58. See, for example, Pius XII, Encyclical Letter *Summi Pontificatus*, AAS 31 (1939), 423. Grisez suggests that, assuming it is informed by charity, the virtue of general (or legal) justice, as Aquinas conceived it (see ST, II-II, q.58, a.5), resembles what SRS calls solidarity. See Grisez, *Living*, 342 n.39; cf. Finnis's critique of the subsequent treatment of legal justice by many Thomist scholars in J. Finnis, *Natural Law and Natural Rights* (Oxford: Oxford University Press, 1993), 184–186.
59. See R. Mulcahy, S.J., *The Economics of Heinrich Pesch* (New York: Holt, 1952), chp.1.

what Wojtyła means by "the common good." According to Wojtyła, there are two dimensions to the common good. The first is "the *goal* of common acting, when understood in a purely objective and 'material' way." For a group of laborers, the common good in "the objective sense" is completion of the excavation. But in Wojtyła's view, "it is impossible to define the common good without simultaneously taking into account the subjective moment, that is, the moment of acting in relation to the acting persons" (AP 338).[60] The "common good," then, embraces both the transitive product of acting together and the intransitive good which all those acting together may realize through contributing to the "objective" end.

When considering Wojtyła's thinking about solidarity, one immediately notices that it terminologically prefigures *Sollicitudo Rei Socialis* by referring to it as an "attitude." "The attitude of solidarity," Wojtyła claims, "is, so to speak, the natural consequence of the fact that human beings live and act together" (AP 341). Here Wojtyła seems to be following the Council's reasoning that solidarity is intrinsically linked to the fact that man is a social being by nature. But he then uses the word in ways which anticipate *Sollicitudo Rei Socialis*:

> Solidarity signifies a constant readiness to accept and realize one's share in the community. . . . In accepting the attitude of solidarity man does what he is supposed to do not only because of his membership in the group, but because he has "the benefit of the whole" in view: he does it for the "common good." The awareness of the common good leads him to look beyond his particular share in the community, though this intentional reference allows him to realize essentially his own share. (AP 341)

Though the word "virtue" is not used here, there is little question that in this instance, it is synonymous with the meaning of solidarity as an attitude. This is evident from the above extract's description of solidarity as the moral habit ("constant readiness") of doing things for the common good. It also closely parallels *Sollicitudo Rei Socialis*'s point that solidarity, as a moral attitude, expresses man's lasting commitment to including the good of others ("looking beyond his particular share") amongst the moral goods that he seeks to realize ("his own share"). As the last sentence of *The Acting Person*'s analysis of solidarity states: "It is this attitude [of solidarity] that allows man to find the fulfillment of himself by complementing others" (AP 342).

Wojtyła maintains, however, that to look beyond one's particular share

---

60. See also "The Person: Subject and Community," 300.

does not necessarily mean taking over others' share: "solidarity is to some extent a restraint from trespassing upon other people's obligations and duties, or from taking over as one's own the part that belongs to others" (AP 341). To be in solidarity with others, then, involves allowing them to self-realize moral good. This position flows naturally from Wojtyła's understanding of the common good, which, as noted, includes the subjective good that each person may realize when acting together with others. For this reason, as Wojtyła puts it, "[t]o take over a part of the duties and obligations that are not mine is intrinsically contrary to participation" (AP 342)—the process by which people realize themselves when acting together.

The same logic underlies *Sollicitudo Rei Socialis*'s point that the realization of global solidarity means that nations must be allowed to choose freely to pursue the common good. Both the encyclical and *The Acting Person* stress that solidarity involves not compromising others' capacity to choose freely moral good. To emphasize the pivotal role of choice in this process, *Sollicitudo Rei Socialis* even uses the characteristically Wojtyłan language of "free self-determination," which, as previously stated, Wojtyła defines as man's power to choose between realizing or not realizing himself.

Having emphasized that solidarity includes allowing others autonomy, *The Acting Person* adds that there are situations in which

> to keep strictly to one's own share would signify and confirm a lack of solidarity. . . . [I]n the attitude of solidarity the reference to the common good must always remain alive . . . it must dominate to the extent that it allows one to know when it is necessary to take over more than one's usual share in acting and responsibility . . . this consists in the readiness of every member of a community to "complement" by his action what is done by other members of the community. (AP 342)

Paragraph 39 of *Sollicitudo Rei Socialis*, we recall, proceeds in almost exactly the same manner. Its underlining of the importance of self-determination is followed by an insistence that commitment to solidarity involves the "readiness" (the same word used in the passage above) to do more for the good of all.

In *Sources of Renewal*, Wojtyła moves from discussing solidarity in the context of the human subject's self-realization of moral good to considering its significance for the modern world. In doing so, *Sources of Renewal* indicates that one of *Sollicitudo Rei Socialis*'s developments of teaching about solidarity may be derived from hitherto unsuspected reflection upon *Gaudium et Spes*. In defining what he calls "the moral of solidarity," Wojtyła cites the Council:

> Let everyone consider it his sacred duty to count social obligations among man's chief duties and observe them as such. For the more closely the world comes together, the more widely do men's obligations transcend particular groups and gradually extend to the whole world. This will be realized only if individuals and groups practice moral and social virtues and foster them in sacred living. (SR 286–287)[61]

Wojtyła comments that this passage

> shows how Vatican II understands the scope of human solidarity, which it considers a sacred duty. This solidarity in the broadest sense is arrived at by way of solidarity in the more limited groups to which human beings belong. This means that the moral attitude of every man, his "moral and social virtues," are the basis of solidarity on every plane including the widest. (SR 287)

Though there is no reference in these extracts to overcoming structures of sin or social evil, they parallel *Sollicitudo Rei Socialis* insofar as they suggest that a world characterized by solidarity begins with persons committing themselves to solidarity as a moral habit—as an attitude and virtue. In light of *Sources of Renewal*, then, there is good reason to suspect that this specification, as well as the encyclical's description of solidarity as a virtue and attitude, owes something to Wojtyła's reading of the section of *Gaudium et Spes* cited above.

7.12   Conclusion

In considering relations between developed and developing nations, we have seen that John Paul incorporates distinctive emphases into the teaching. In addressing the "problem-side," he underlines new difficulties and utilizes contemporary language to conceptualize a worsening situation. To this end, John Paul introduces the decidedly modern discourse of geo-politics into magisterial teaching, but grounds it in theological reflection about the character of sin in the modern world.

Some of these developments proceed from attention to decidedly

---

61. Citing GS 30.

negative changes in the world since 1967. On the other hand, there is a case for viewing *Sollicitudo Rei Socialis*'s geo-political analysis as reflecting the incorporation of a "second world" element into magisterial teaching. Other developments, however, owe much to the magisterium's response to liberationist propositions, especially the teaching contained in CELAM documents and the CDF Instructions of 1984 and 1986. It is as part of this response that Wojtyłan thought may have influenced one aspect of magisterial development. This concerns *Sollicitudo Rei Socialis*'s stipulation that because man alone is the subject of moral acts, then, from a moral-anthropological viewpoint, personal sin is at the root of problematic structures and perpetuates their existence.

Like the Council and Paul VI, Pope John Paul views the principle of solidarity as the key to reforming relations between developing and developed nations. However, *Sollicitudo Rei Socialis* also uses this word to conceptualize the way in which individuals and nations may acquire moral good by including the common good amongst the higher values they pursue. This understanding of solidarity permits John Paul to underline two guidelines that should govern relations between nations: that nations must be permitted to choose freely to pursue the common good; but once nations have committed themselves to the good of others, they must be ready to undergo sacrifices for others. The encyclical also specifies that the acquisition of the attitude/virtue of solidarity is central to undermining the structures of sin disordering relations between developed and developing nations.

Most of *Sollicitudo Rei Socialis*'s developments of teaching about solidarity have been shown to proceed from the extension and integration of teachings contained in *Gaudium et Spes* and *Populorum Progressio* as well as those post-conciliar magisterial texts which consider the question of how man overcomes unjust structures. Nevertheless, Wojtyłan ideas have also been influential, especially in relation to *Sollicitudo Rei Socialis*'s use of the term solidarity. This appears to reflect the application of Wojtyłan ethical-anthropological thought about how man may realize moral good when acting with others, to the issue of how affluent and developing nations should reorder the character of their relationship.

In both sub-issues considered in this chapter, John Paul insists that it is man's *choices* for, and *acts* of, good or evil which are of prime importance. This is a remarkable position to maintain in the face of a problem which defines a profound cleavage in the modern world and seems almost impervious to all the good will in the world. The same claim, however, appears in each of the three case studies that we have considered. Turning now to summarizing the conclusions of this study, we see that this emphasis is an important feature of John Paul's overall development of Catholic social teaching, and that it reflects, in part, Wojtyłan influences upon this development.

8

A CRITICAL ENGAGEMENT WITH MODERNITY

8.1 Introduction

In *Religion and the Rise of Capitalism*, R. H. Tawney succinctly summarizes the continuing challenge for Christian social thinking:

> Granted that I should love my neighbor as myself, the questions which, under modern conditions of large-scale organizations, remain for solution are: "Who precisely *is* my neighbor?" and, "How exactly am I to make my love for him effective in practice?" . . . Traditional social doctrines had no specific to offer, and were merely repeated, when, in order to be effective, they should have been thought out again from the beginning and formulated in new and living terms.[1]

The tradition of Catholic social teaching which began with Leo XIII cannot be accused of simply repeating traditional principles. Emerging shortly after the papacy's loss of its last temporal possessions, the teaching initiated by *Rerum Novarum* represents possibly the most comprehensive effort of a Christian church to provide people with principles for reflection, criteria for judgment, and directives for actions in the face of changing social, economic, and political conditions.

The key to the Church's rethinking of its teaching amidst evolving circumstances is the concept of development. Of course, if, as the Second

---

1. R. H. Tawney, *Religion and the Rise of Capitalism* (New York: New American Library, 1958), 156.

Vatican Council claims, history is indeed speeding up, then one might expect that developments in Catholic social teaching would be more overt than indicated by this study. This, however, is to underestimate Roman Catholicism's depth as a depository of knowledge. Writing about the Catholic Church, Schall maintains:

> Nothing quite like it exists in terms of a living organism, as it were that can reflect upon itself and on what it taught, say one hundred years ago, or a thousand years ago, as if such reflections all belong to the same coherent discourse going on today, in any today. The Church can quote Augustine or Origen or Aquinas or Ignatius of Loyola as if each were equally present in current dialogue. In one sense, this record serves as a kind of independent or parallel commentary on the events of each era.[2]

Roman Catholicism may thus be understood as possessing a living memory going back 2,000 years and even beyond to the writers of Genesis. There is consequently little about man and social life that the Church has not encountered in some way before. The roots of Pope John Paul's analysis of consumerism, for instance, may be found in St. Paul's view that although man knows what is good, he is capable of succumbing to instinctual urges. "Old" truths, then, proclaimed by the Church can be retrieved from its vast intellectual heritage and used to deepen man's understanding of contemporary problems and the meaning of unfolding historical changes.

It remains, however, that the Church's provision of guidance to man through its social teaching in the midst of modern conditions is not easy. The Council itself portrayed the modern world as full of contradictions:

> In no other age has mankind enjoyed such an abundance of wealth, resources and economic well-being; and yet a huge proportion of the people of the world are plagued by hunger and extreme need. . . . At no time have men had such a keen sense of freedom, only to be faced by new forms of slavery in living and thinking. . . . If there is a growing exchange of ideas, there is still widespread disagreement about the meaning of words expressing our key concepts. There is lastly a painstaking search for a better material world, without a parallel spiritual advancement.
>
> Small wonder then that many of our contemporaries are prevented by this complex situation from recognizing permanent values and duly applying them to recent discoveries.[3] (GS 4)

---

2. Schall, "The Teaching of *Centesimus Annus*," 23.
3. Even the phrase "the world" is plagued with ambivalence in scripture and subsequent

In light of such conditions, it is always difficult to discern how man may continue to act in accordance with revealed truth and, as a consequence, build up a just social order in the modern world. Nevertheless, the Council formally committed the Church to engaging with this world, and John Paul II's social teaching represents continuation of this dialogue.

One of our aims has been to arrive at some general conclusions about the character of ensuing developments in Catholic social teaching. The other has involved assessing something about which many have speculated, but few given systematic consideration: the influence of Wojtyłan thought upon these developments. Here we outline the results of these inquiries. It begins by outlining the nature of John Paul's development of the teaching. The task of summarizing the Wojtyłan influence is necessarily preceded by reviewing what have been identified as the main sources of development. Having specified the character and extent of the Wojtyłan impact, we look beyond our immediate conclusions to consider their broad implications for Catholic social thought, the study of development in Catholic social teaching, and the stance of Catholic social teaching vis-à-vis contemporary secular thought about the nature of freedom.

8.2 The Nature of Development

One thing demonstrated by preceding chapters is that identifying developments in Catholic social teaching is a complex and lengthy exercise. Statements that initially appear to have developed the teaching, for example, often amount to the reiteration or more precise articulation of previous claims—something for which the Church is often criticized.[4]

The following summation of the nature of developments in Catholic social teaching does not, of course, comprehensively embrace every single

---

Christian literature. See C. Butler, O.S.B., *The Theology of Vatican II* (London: Darton, Longman, and Todd, 1981), 187.

4. See, for example, J. Nash, "Questioning the Efficacy of One Hundred Years of Catholic Social Teaching," *Social Thought* 17, no. 2 (1991): 52–64. Others, however, such as Finnis, insist that when it comes to public policy, bishops ought not to make "the kind of assessment of complex, contingent facts that is necessary to reach a deliberative judgement about, say, a social welfare policy or a strategy of nuclear deterrence." They are called, rather, "to teach in season and out all the moral principles and norms which any such policy must meet if it is to be morally acceptable to Catholics or anyone of good will." Cited in A. Fisher, O.P., "An Ethic of Life for the Public Square," *The Tablet*, 9 August 1997, 1026.

development identified in the three case studies. To categorize all developments in such terms would be misleading and reductionist. Rather, it is proposed as a synopsis of the general character of developments in the social teaching articulated by the Roman magisterium since 1978, based on the analysis conducted in preceding chapters. For clarity's sake, this is divided into two sections: the first concerns the basic emphases characterizing development; the second focuses upon the nature of development vis-à-vis the social teaching's engagement with the modern world.

Man as Subject—Man as Person

The general character of John Paul's development of Catholic social teaching owes a great deal to *Laborem Exercens*'s moral-anthropology of man: that man is a subject of acts, the conscious subject of moral acts, and the free and creative subject of work-acts. However, this subject is also a person, the *imago Dei*, a creature who possesses the spiritual properties of reason and free will. It is these attributes of personhood which endow the human subject's work-acts with their creative character and moral-spiritual significance.

Through these work-acts, man as a person and subject is capable of realizing himself as that which he is meant to be. On one level, man is charged with actualizing the dominion over the world with which he has been endowed. This occurs through the objective-transitive dimension of the creative subject's work-acts. Man is, however, also called upon to actualize dominion over himself by freely choosing to undertake the difficult task of acquiring moral good through the same work-acts. Hence, this subjective-intransitive dimension of work is more important than work's objective effects.

By placing this understanding of man and work at the heart of Catholic social teaching, John Paul is able to reshape the magisterium's position on many matters in two broad ways.

- It permits John Paul to integrate particular anthropological emphases into the teaching so as to deepen understanding of why the social order, however it is organized, must adhere to certain principles. Entrepreneurial acts, for example, are conceptualized as work-acts that proceed from the creative subject. Thus, if a government denies people the right of economic initiative, such a policy amounts to defiance of the truth that man is by nature the creative subject. Moreover, by characterizing entrepreneurship as an *act* of work proceeding from the creative subject, John Paul heightens appreciation of the profound inner significance of such acts for man. Not only do they represent a continuation of God's creative Act, but work-acts of economic initiative also allow man to realize himself in the sense that they actualize his free choice of virtues. On similar grounds, the pope is able to stress that, despite the enormous material and technological progress generated by work, socio-economic arrangements must reflect the truth that man's realization of moral good and self-dominion through work's subjective dimension is *always* the most important work of all—even, presumably, if it means less material prosperity. No property or enterprise arrangement is immune from this consideration. Nor are modern forms of political economy. Even John Paul's treatment of international relations is affected by his moral-anthropological emphases. As observed, the concept of solidarity is developed in a way which brings to the fore the notion that if nations are to realize the common good as a moral good, they must be allowed to choose freely to pursue the good of others.

- John Paul is able to rethink the essence of social disorder in terms of the defiance of anthropological truths about man. Worker exploitation, for instance, is defined as the treatment of man as an instrument of production rather than as the creative human subject capable of self-realization through work. Likewise, economic systems such as rigid capitalism and state-collectivism are presented as trivializing each person's status as the subject of work with an initiative of their own. In effect, the pope's anthropological emphasis allows the teaching to stress that if man mistakenly understands himself to be essentially a material creature with no transcendental vocation, then there is a reasonable possibility that he will view himself, his work, and other people primarily in economistic and consumeristic terms. In all of these instances, the end result is, according to John Paul, alienation. For apart from becoming cognitively disorientated, man gradually becomes estranged from his own nature as the *imago Dei* and creative subject.

A Critical Engagement

What, then, may be said about John Paul's development of the social teaching vis- à -vis the magisterium's engagement with the modern world? In 1996, Judt described John Paul as a pope devoted to *Reconquista*, to breaking with his predecessor's Roman acquiescence in modernity, secularism and compromise. . . . This is a man whose central contention about the modern world, as expounded in his many writings, is that it has undertaken for 300 years a war against God and Christian values, a conflict in which he has now sought to engage himself and his Church to the full.[5]

Much of this assessment is questionable. To claim that Paul VI "acquiesced in modernity" is a somewhat dubious proposition: few would describe *Humanae Vitae* as compromising with the modern world. Nor do any of the three case studies considered in this study indicate that John Paul views the modern world in quite the way suggested by Judt's dramatic but rather simplistic representation.

John Paul refers, for example, to the growing prevalence of entrepreneurship as a source of wealth in the modern world as a "new" expression of an "old" Christian truth—that "besides the earth, man's principal resource is man himself" (CA 32). This is a clear instance of reading a sign of "modern times" and identifying it as positive. The pope also speaks quite directly about the differing formations assumed by modern capitalism. Whilst criticizing the affluent society for its conceptualization of man as *homo oeconomicus*, he praises the post-war social market experiments. He is even willing to recommend "capitalism" as a model for post-Communist states, if it means certain things. This hardly suggests that John Paul views the modern world in terms analogous to Pius IX.

Then there is the fact that John Paul uses certain modern ideas to develop magisterial teaching at different points. Whilst detailing the fundamental inadequacies of its Marxist interpretation, John Paul believes that the concept of alienation conveys a real sense of man's experience of estrangement from his own nature. Similarly, the idea of man as a conscious being is utilized to emphasize the human subject's awareness of the moral significance of his work-acts. We also observe John Paul engaging with contemporary ideas about worker and union struggle and then outlining how people may struggle for justice—even in conflictual situations—in a way which is Christian rather than Marxist in its inspiration and ends. Nor does the pope shy away from incorporating a geo-political dimension into the teaching to conceptualize some of the complex dynamics shaping relations between the developed and

---

5. Judt, "Holy Warrior," 9.

developing worlds. In each of these examples, John Paul develops the social teaching via a dialogue with the modern world: first, he uses some of its language and insights to help deepen aspects of magisterial social teaching; secondly, he "speaks" to the world in terms with which it is familiar. It is therefore a way of dialogue faithful to that proposed by the Council.

At the same time, certain apprehensions about the modern world also characterize John Paul's teaching. His attention to the apparent prevalence of consumerism in the West and the deepening chasm between developed and developing nations are two instances of this. So too is his concern about the potential for the spread of laissez-faire ideas throughout post-Communist and third world nations.

On a broader level, however, the primary negative tendency in the modern world highlighted by John Paul's teaching is what he evidently regards as its propensity to conceptualize man in materialist terms—in other words, the prevalence of a faulty anthropology of man. Exemplifying this are his statements about certain modern philosophies, the origins of which are traced to the eighteenth century and the Enlightenment. Primitive liberalism's mistake, according to John Paul, was that it essentially ignored the fact that man is the creative subject of work and effectively reduced the worker to the status of an object. *Laborem Exercens* later adds that Marxism arose, in part, as a reaction against liberalism's materialistic-economistic view of man. Yet it too was flawed because in Marxist dialectical materialist thought, man "continues to be understood and treated, in dependence on what is material, as a kind of 'resultant' of the economic or production relations prevailing at a given period" (LE 13).

In other words, two of the major philosophical forces commonly associated with modernity are understood by John Paul to be based upon the same false view of human nature. He does not, however, see the problems associated with these forces as relying upon the ideological articulation of materialist conceptions of man. John Paul insists that such problems will arise whenever man thinks "in the categories of economism" (LE 13). In this light, the decidedly non-ideological contemporary phenomenon of the "civilization of consumption" may be viewed as resulting from the same error of defining man in materialist-economistic terms.

Finally, it should be noted that John Paul's development of teaching challenges any tendency to shift primary responsibility for modern social problems away from man. *Laborem Exercens*, for example, denies that worker-employer conflict is primarily a consequence of economic production structures. It arises, in the first instance, from man's choice to deny the personhood of others. Similarly, while *Sollicitudo Rei Socialis* affirms that structures can have detrimental effects, it maintains that this is because man allows them to do so, or uses them irresponsibly: since man alone is the subject of moral acts, he ultimately remains the cause of all evil, be it personal or social. Taken together, these statements amount to a refutation of that view given its classic expression in Rousseau's claim that man is naturally good and has only become bad because of institutions.[6]

Though *Gaudium et Spes* also traces problematic social environments to man's personal sins, John Paul is far more forceful on this point. One cannot help wondering if he believes that many in the modern world do not fully appreciate the significance of this fact about the causes of social good and evil. As we have seen, John Paul even insists that the key to justice among nations is not, in the first instance, structural reform. Instead, the replacement of structures of sin with an ethic of solidarity must begin with people freely choosing to include the common good among the higher values that they pursue in their everyday life. Likewise, *Centesimus Annus* specifies that man must look to his power of free choice and learn to use it responsibly if the consumerism which the magisterium associates with Western capitalist systems is to be resisted. Put another way, if people want to change negative aspects of the modern world, they must first make difficult choices about themselves and act accordingly. A similar sentiment pervades Ratzinger's claim that in many ways it is easier to demonstrate for the rights of others than to practice in everyday life the discipline of freedom.[7]

8.3   The Sources of Development

Commenting upon change in papal and conciliar teaching, Hehir observes that "how the church speaks to a social question is due in part to its conception of who the audience is."[8] This certainly holds true for John Paul II's social teaching. Though his audience is, strictly speaking, all

---

6. M. Cranston, *Jean-Jacques: The Early Life and Work of Jean-Jacques Rousseau, 1712-1754* (London: Penguin, 1983), 160–161.
7. See J. Ratzinger, "Consumer Materialism and Christian Hope," *Briefing* 18, no. 3 (1988): 46.
8. Hehir, "Continuity," 132.

people of good will, each of the case studies suggest that some developments in teaching emanate, in part, from the pope's effort to address particular audiences responsible for and/or affected by historical and intellectual changes.

Although *Laborem Exercens* makes no mention of Poland, chapter 5 illustrates that several developments identified in this encyclical may be legitimately understood as proceeding from reflection upon Solidarity's travails throughout 1981. Certainly, John Paul's teachings about the degree to which unions may involve themselves in politics build upon statements of the Council and Paul VI. Nevertheless, several points of development in this teaching were especially pertinent to Solidarity's problems throughout 1981, particularly John Paul's statements about the appropriate form and ends of union struggle.

Sollicitudo Rei Socialis, on the other hand, addresses quite different audiences. Its teaching about the civilization of consumption appears particularly directed at Western capitalist societies. The encyclical's geo-political analysis, however, may be legitimately regarded as attempting to show both "West" and "East" how their pursuit of political, military, and ideological goals negatively affects developing nations' autonomy and development. It may also be construed as a response to those liberationist analyses which conceptualized the problematic character of relations between the developed and developing worlds without sufficient reference to the impact of superpower rivalry on the situation. Likewise, John Paul's statements concerning the structures of sin may be regarded as a rejoinder to certain theses often associated with liberation theology.

In *Centesimus Annus*'s case, there is little question that it has been shaped by consideration of the consequences of a profound historical event: communism's collapse. On one level, this takes the form of attempting to ensure that as they embrace the market, post-Communist and developing nations understand its benefits and limits, and correctly comprehend the state's role in a market economy. In this context, John Paul states that while the free economy has undoubted economic and moral benefits, laissez-faire models remain, from a Catholic viewpoint, as unacceptable now as they were before.

Despite the influence of this attention to the "external," one is nevertheless struck by the extent to which developments proceeding from John Paul's teaching have resulted from reflection—both acknowledged and unacknowledged—upon previous magisterial teaching. In thematic terms, *Gaudium et Spes* is obviously crucial in this regard, especially its statements concerning the nature and ends of human activity. Here we find the roots of John Paul's focus upon Genesis's first chapter, the creative character of human work, the two dimensions of work-acts, and much of his anthropological emphasis. Other less prominent but nonetheless important thematic sources are *Populorum Progressio*'s teaching on integral human development, and the CDF Instructions of 1984 and 1986. It is in the CDF texts, for example, that we find a systematic outline of the relationship between personal sin and problematic structures which prefigures much of *Sollicitudo Rei Socialis*'s teaching.

When it comes to John Paul's development of teaching on specific matters, each case study shows that this involves the extension and clarification of positions articulated by *Gaudium et Spes*, Paul VI's social documents, the CDF Instructions and, somewhat less obviously, particular texts produced by CELAM. *Gaudium et Spes*'s teachings about participation in the enterprise, for example, provide John Paul with most of the basic guidelines underlying his proposals for the reorganization of work groups. Similarly, the pope's teachings about trade unions and consumerism build upon statements articulated in *Octogesima Adveniens*. Even John Paul's treatment of entrepreneurship and economic initiative may be regarded as owing much to the integration of ideas expressed in different magisterial texts, including *Gaudium et Spes, Populorum Progressio, Pacem in Terris*, and *Quadragesimo Anno*.

8.4   The Wojtyłan Dimension

Developments in Catholic social teaching during John Paul's pontificate, then, can essentially be understood as proceeding from a combination of the internal and external factors summarized above. This, of course, makes any effort to discern where Wojtyłan emphases and concepts have influenced such developments far from easy. One cannot overstate the effect of the self-denying ordinance which restrains popes and their literary collaborators from imposing a particular theological or philosophical system upon magisterial teaching. Indeed, the whole process of development, as it is understood by the magisterium, would seem to militate against a pope leaving a distinctly pre-pontifical imprint on the teaching.

But although these factors create obstacles to discerning the impact of Wojtyłan notions, the difficulties are not insurmountable. Comparative analysis of magisterial texts and Karol Wojtyła's writings does allow one to make an assessment of the extent to which Wojtyłan thought has influenced development.

In certain instances, this influence may be described as almost systematic. This is most obviously true in the case of *Laborem Exercens*. Both its anthropology of man as the conscious subject whose work is an *actus personae* as well as the encyclical's explanation of the subjective-intransitive and objective-transitive effects of work-acts, have been shaped by ideas expressed in *Love and Responsibility, The Acting Person,* several related Wojtyłan articles, as well as poems composed in the late 1950s. *Laborem Exercens* may be legitimately regarded as bringing together various concepts spread throughout these texts so as to rethink man's nature as a person and the free and creative subject of work. Even its treatment of the origin, nature, and ends of human dominion have been affected by Wojtyłan ideas, especially those expressed in *Sign of Contradiction*'s meditation on Genesis.

With magisterial teaching on work being invested with these Wojtyłan ethical-anthropological emphases, they proceed to shape John Paul's statements about various questions. In the case of worker exploitation, the pope follows the Council's lead in stating that the essence of exploitation involves man being treated as a thing rather than as a person. Yet the Wojtyłan aspects of *Laborem Exercens*'s statements about work permit John Paul to define more precisely the nature of that exploitation: the prioritization of work's objective dimension over the process of self-realization that occurs through work. This error is even given a Wojtyłan name—economism. The same criteria are used to uncover in a new way the error of state-collectivism and early capitalism. They also affect *Laborem Exercens'* teaching about how such error might be avoided: that is, ensuring that economic systems and the organization of work reflect the truth that man is the creative subject as well as the priority of work in the subjective sense.

When one turns to *Sollicitudo Rei Socialis* and *Centesimus Annus*, our three case studies demonstrate that one could not describe the Wojtyłan influence upon these encyclicals as being as systematic as in *Laborem Exercens*'s case. Nonetheless, many specific points of development identified in these encyclicals seem to owe something to this effect. One example is *Centesimus Annus*'s teaching about the alienation which man can experience in work relationships and consumer societies. Others include *Sollicitudo Rei Socialis*'s depiction of the civilization of consumption and its reflection upon Genesis, which, in blending biblical and theological motifs with recognizably natural law themes, parallels thoughts articulated in *Sign of Contradiction*. Moreover, like *Laborem*

Exercens, *Centesimus Annus* contains echoes of *Love and Responsibility*'s Kantian-personalist language. Other prominent cases of Wojtyłan notions influencing specific magisterial developments include *The Acting Person*'s analysis of the attitudes of opposition and solidarity, as well as the ideas articulated in Wojtyła's poems, plays, and articles about how man should struggle against injustice.

There are several reasons why many Wojtyłan ideas and emphases have lent themselves so easily to influencing magisterial development. The first is that for all his interest in phenomenology, Kant, and Scheler, Wojtyła's thought was pervaded by Thomist and personalist themes. There is little doubt that modern Catholic social teaching owes much to these two sources.

Secondly, by the 1970s, Wojtyła had begun to elaborate upon the wider implications of his ethical-anthropological conclusions about man. Examples of this include Wojtyła's disputation of Marxist conceptions of work, his critique of the view that structural change was the key to ending alienation, and his attention to the consequences of reversing the priority of the intransitive over the transitive. In short, by the time Wojtyła became pope in 1978, he had already embarked upon the process of applying his ideas to social-philosophical issues. Magisterial social teaching provided him with a new medium for continuing to do so.

Another major reason why John Paul was able to develop aspects of the social teaching in particularly Wojtyłan directions is that many of Wojtyła's ideas owed a great deal to reflection upon *Gaudium et Spes*. Not only do we have Wojtyła's own statement to this effect, but our analysis of the relevant texts has provided strong confirming evidence. Indeed, *The Acting Person* may be understood as blending *Love and Responsibility*'s moral-anthropology of man as a person and a subject of moral acts, with the Pastoral Constitution's teachings about the meaning of human work-activity.

But while it is true, as de Lubac states, that Wojtyła was a man of the Council, he was, without question, also a man ready *for* the Council. The direction of his pre-conciliar thought would have made Wojtyła very sympathetic to some of *Gaudium et Spes*'s central themes. His 1958 poems on work are particularly revealing in this respect. Their terse images anticipate the Council's teaching concerning human activity's inner and outer effects, the greater importance of the former, man's capacity to go beyond himself through work, and the relationship between human work and God's creative Act. These poems also underline Wojtyła's willingness to consider such ideas in the very modern setting of industrial labor. This, of course, raises the question of the extent to which the outlook on the modern world expressed in Wojtyła's writings has influenced John Paul's development of teaching.

Throughout these texts, there prevails an attitude towards the modern world which foreshadows important aspects of the viewpoint permeating John Paul's encyclicals. Wojtyła was, for example, quite willing to enlist modern ideas and terminology to develop his own thought. Examples of this include his integration of Kantian language as well as the concepts of consciousness and alienation into his ethical-anthropology of man. As observed, each of these have influenced, to varying degrees, several developments in John Paul's social teaching.

Nevertheless, Wojtyła's writings also betray a wariness about certain features of the modern world. *Love and Responsibility* repeated Scheler's charge that modern man did not feel obliged to pursue virtue. *The Acting Person* expressed the fear that amidst so much contemporary progress, man was losing sight of the central importance of understanding his own nature. *Sign of Contradiction* was especially concerned about what Wojtyła viewed as the spread of philosophical and practical materialism, the purely "horizontal" meaning which the modern world tended to give to progress, and the widespread detachment of reason from the discernment of metaphysical truth.

Here one should not discount the possibility that Wojtyła's experience of living in a Marxist-Leninist system may have inclined him to a somewhat more critical view of the modern world than, for example, Paul VI. Wojtyła's major everyday experience of modernity was not Western democracy, but rather the forced modernization carried out by a coercive party-state bureaucracy. The Polish-Jewish sociologist, Zygmunt Bauman, explains why those who have experienced real existing communism are less likely to be naïve about modernity than people living in democracies:

Communism was modernity's most devout, vigorous, gallant champion. . . Indeed, it was under communist, not capitalist, auspices that the audacious dream of modernity, freed from obstacles by the merciless and seemingly omnipotent state, was pushed to its radical limits: grand designs, unlimited social engineering, huge and bulky technology, total transformation of nature. Deserts were irrigated (but they turned into salinated bogs); marshlands were drained (but they turned into deserts) . . . millions were lifted from "the idiocy of rural life" (but they got poisoned by the effluvia of rationally designed industry, if they did not perish first on the way).[9]

---

9. Z. Bauman, *Intimations of Post-Modernity* (London: Routledge, 1992), 179.

Living in a situation where attempts at structural transformation failed again and again was only likely to confirm Wojtyła's belief that, in the final analysis, the best way to cope with an alienated social order was to strive for personal self-realization.

Many of the concerns about the modern world expressed in Wojtyła's writings appear to have influenced John Paul's encyclicals. The latter's attention to materialism, consumerist alienation, and their stress upon the importance of pursuing virtue are examples of this. So too is *Laborem Exercens*'s insistence that for all the immense material progress generated by human work throughout history, people should not lose sight of the fact that the most important work remains man's formation of himself. However, these magisterial texts do not go so far as to label, as *Sign of Contradiction* does, the twentieth century as the era of the concentration camp. Indeed, a basic theme of John Paul's encyclicals is that by acting correctly, people *can* overcome social disorder. In this respect, these documents are, as Weigel states, "an extraordinary statement of faith: faith in freedom; faith in man's capacity to order his public life properly; above all, faith in God, who created man with intelligence and free will."[10]

It should not, however, be forgotten that a similar point is made in *Sign of Contradiction*. Using the example of Maximilian Kolbe, Wojtyła claims that choices for moral good and truth *can* prevail, even in as barbaric a place such as Auschwitz, where decidedly modern technology and organizational methods—the fruits of human labor—were employed to realize as efficiently as possible the mass obliteration of man.

One may say, then, that it is characteristic of Wojtyła's thought, both as philosopher and pontiff, to meet the challenge of the modern world directly and confidently. His pre-pontifical writings and his social teachings neither wholly endorse nor wholly condemn the modern world. The prevailing message is that people must search the ambiguity of modern life in order to sift out what is good for man and what is not. For Karol Wojtyła/John Paul II, what ultimately matters is that man is able to choose freely to realize dominion over himself by, as *Sign of Contradiction* says, living in truth, or, as *Sollicitudo Rei Socialis* puts it, by freely conforming to the same divine truth which confers upon man his dignity as *imago Dei*. Only then will man attain true freedom. Appropriating the modern language of liberation, Wojtyła underlined this linkage between freedom and truth when addressing the Synod of Bishops in 1974:

---

10. G. Weigel, "Prologue," in *A New Worldly Order*, 20.

economic and social liberation is crucial today . . . but this liberation cannot be separated from that higher liberation which is the absolute liberation in God who is Truth. . . . Therefore the vertical and horizontal dimensions of liberation should not be opposed to each other. What unites them is obedience to the Truth.[11]

8.5 Implications

The conclusions of this book have many implications. The significance of particular developments could be considered. One might ask, for instance, what John Paul's incorporation of a geo-political analysis into magisterial teaching suggests about the Catholic Church's view of international affairs. Hehir contends that it symbolizes the culmination of the Church's gradual move away from a position of de facto support for the Western alliance towards one of detachment from all superpowers.[12] On a less global scale, attention could be given to the ramifications of John Paul's teaching about unions. Hebblethwaite, for example, claims that *Laborem Exercens* calls for a serious rethinking on the part of Catholics as to whether unions should have any formal links with political parties at all.[13]

Here three broad implications arising from the central concerns of this study are briefly contemplated. The first involves the study of development in the social teaching. The significance of John Paul's focus upon the social teaching's moral-anthropological dimension for contemporary Catholic social thought is then to be examined. Finally, consideration is given to the question of what this emphasis suggests about the position of Catholic social teaching vis-à-vis that of secular thought about freedom in a post-Communist era.

The Study of Development

In each of the three case studies, we observed that an explanation of magisterial development involves careful assessment of the likely sources of development. In this regard, this study has demonstrated the validity of Coleman's claim that development may be studied in terms of viewing any one exposition of the social teaching as part of an interconnected tradition. Above all, it illustrates that by taking into account both external

---

11. "Ewangelizacja współczesnego świata," 417.
12. See Hehir, "Papal Foreign Policy," 28–40.
13. See Hebblethwaite, "Labor Encyclical," 71–73.

factors and previous teaching, one may make judgments about the varying degrees of influence exerted by different factors, be they specific situations in part of the world, broader evolutions within Catholic social thought, or efforts to refine past teaching in light of new circumstances. We have seen, however, that a certain degree of inference is involved in this process. Consequently, exact correlations are not always possible.

Our study of development does, however, raise questions about those analyses which attempt to attribute development to one main factor and/or fail to place an encyclical sufficiently within the context of previous teaching. As an example, let us consider Baum's commentary upon *Laborem Exercens*. Baum, we recall, suggests that this encyclical's teachings about work proceed largely from a dialogue with Marxism which is implicit to the text. In chapter 5, we noted that there are some grounds for claiming that something of this nature has contributed to *Laborem Exercens*. Nevertheless, we also observed that if there is a dialogue, then it is probably more accurately characterized as a disputation of any materialist anthropology of man and his work, of which the Marxist version is perhaps the most sophisticated. Here one may submit that Baum might have arrived at a similar conclusion if he had accurately ascertained Karol Wojtyła's place in the Polish Catholic-Marxist dialogue and examined some of Wojtyła's writings. Wojtyła's 1977 article on human praxis, for example, makes clear his view that Marx's focus on the material rendered him incapable of appreciating that work's most creative effect upon man occurs not so much through the products produced through human work, but rather via the work-act's intransitive moral effect within man.

In more general terms, Baum's attempt to explain this encyclical's central propositions without detailed reference to previous teaching about human work-activity raises serious doubts about the soundness of his conclusions. To study, as Baum does, *Laborem Exercens* without substantial reference to *Gaudium et Spes* is to ignore a critical source of this encyclical's theological inspiration, anthropological emphasis, and conceptual framework. As chapter 4 illustrates, in light of *Gaudium et Spes*'s statements about human activity, *Laborem Exercens* appears much less "radical" than Baum claims it to be.

In short, this book illustrates that any study of development *must* involve careful examination of the precise form of words and arrangements of concepts contained in previous teaching on any one issue. Only then can reasoned judgments be made as to when a document is using a certain concept in a new way, expanding upon a particular idea, or attempting to take into account new conditions. When this occurs, it soon becomes apparent that *Sollicitudo Rei Socialis*'s teaching about the structures of sin, for instance, forms part of an ongoing process of magisterial reflection about the relationship between man and his structures. Such an approach is almost certain to result in less "exciting" conclusions about developments in Catholic social teaching. They will, however, be more sustainable.

The Emphases of Catholic Social Thought

For all its detailed consideration of politically contentious matters such as the role of unions or the market's limits, John Paul's development of social teaching underlines a central point for anyone who wishes to study and/or develop Catholic social thought in a way faithful to authoritative teaching. To paraphrase Mary Ann Glendon, all such matters are discussed only to place these aspects of human life in a proper perspective. That perspective—applicable to economics, politics, law and all other disciplines relating to man—is rooted in a view of the human person which aspires to be *correct*.[14] This point of view is profoundly anthropological in its orientation, inasmuch as it stresses that everything must be considered in terms of what man really is: a fallible spiritual-material creature called to an other-worldly destiny; a chooser; a knower; and the subject of moral acts, alone and in association with others.

In this sense, John Paul's teaching may be understood as constituting a call for Catholic social thinkers to "return to the person" and ground their thoughts in a correct anthropology of man. This indirectly calls into question the direction of much contemporary Catholic social thought. In 1984, Ratzinger suggested that a tendency to overemphasize the significance of "the structural" was becoming increasingly characteristic of Catholic thinking:

> some theologians have made their own the schema of an enlightenment à la Rousseau, with the dogma that lies at the base of modern culture—capitalist or marxist—that of the man good by nature who is corrupted only by false education and by social structures in need of reform.[15]

---

14. See M. A. Glendon, "A Challenge to the Human Sciences," in *A New Worldly Order*, 80.
15. Ratzinger, *The Ratzinger Report*, 79.

Ernest Fortin's discussion of contemporary Catholic thought about social sin expresses similar concerns. In Fortin's view, to accord priority to social sin over personal sin means effectively adopting Rousseau's theory that as

> society and its accidental structures are the primary cause of the corruption of human beings and the evils attendant upon it, they must be changed. Social reform takes precedence over personal reform; it constitutes the first and perhaps the only moral imperative. Better institutions will give us better human beings and not vice-versa. Under such circumstances, the premodern emphasis on education and moral character as the true causes of the happiness of the individual and the community could be safely laid aside. The only true evil is social evil, just as the only sin is social sin.[16]

Examples of Catholic social thought which seem to reflect such tendencies are not difficult to find. One case is the analysis of *Sollicitudo Rei Socialis* by Phillip Land, S.J., and Peter Henriot, S.J. Prefacing their remarks by way of commentary on the first draft of the American Catholic bishops' pastoral letter on women's concerns, they argue that while the bishops acknowledge the sinfulness of certain attitudes and actions prejudicial to women, they fail completely to provide any structural analysis. Had the bishops done so, Land and Henriot submit, "they would discover that the sinfulness in the attitudes and actions stems from structures of dominant and dominative male patriarchy."[17] They then suggest that John Paul avoids the bishops' mistake. In explaining world injustice, Land and Henriot maintain that the Pope "goes to the heart of the matter. It is structures—'sinful structures'—that are behind the injustice in the relationships of interdependence/dependency that bind the poor nations of the South to the rich nations of the North."[18]

This is a rather misleading interpretation of John Paul's teaching. As noted in chapter 6, *Sollicitudo Rei Socialis*, while acknowledging that structures may influence people, specifies that structures *cannot* be sinful in themselves, because they are *not* the subject of moral acts. Secondly, because man is a person and the conscious subject of moral acts—a being who makes free choices about himself—he is ultimately responsible for

---

16. E. Fortin, "Natural Law and Social Justice," *American Journal of Jurisprudence* 30, no. 1 (1985): 14–15.

17. P. Land, S.J., and P. Henriot, S.J., "Towards a New Methodology in Catholic Social Teaching," in *The Logic of Solidarity*, 71.

18. Land and Henriot, "Towards a New Methodology," 72.

his sinful attitudes and acts, *not* structures. In this respect, one may say that Henriot and Land overlook the anthropology of man as the conscious subject of moral acts which is spelt out in *Laborem Exercens* and applied to the issue of structures in *Sollicitudo Rei Socialis*. Henriot and Land's analysis also implies that changing structures is the key to realizing a more just social order. John Paul, however, insists that what ultimately matters is inner conversion: *metanoia*. This is reiterated in his discourse introducing *Centesimus Annus* to the world:

> A great commitment on the political, economic, social and cultural level is necessary to build a society that is more just and worthy of the person. But this is not enough! A decisive commitment must be made in the very heart of man, in the intimacy of his conscience, where he makes his personal decisions. Only on this level can the human person affect a true, deep and positive change in himself, and that is the undeniable premise of contributing to change and the improvement of all society.[19]

True Freedom

The stress in the above citation upon the significance of the person's free choices about himself raises the matter of the implications of John Paul's moral-anthropological emphases for the position of Catholic social teaching vis-à-vis contemporary secular thought concerning the nature of free choice and, indeed, the very meaning of freedom itself. In the century of the totalitarian state, it is hardly surprising that freedom has often been understood primarily in terms of freedom from state oppression. In a post-Communist era, however, it is perhaps easier to see that the meaning and realization of freedom is actually a more complex matter. Indeed, even in the later years of Communist rule, dissidents such as Václav Havel were positing that one could, in fact, be free, even amidst the bureaucratic grayness and institutionalized lies of Communist Czechoslovakia.[20]

During the general audience in which he introduced *Centesimus Annus*, John Paul stated that while the Marxist system was finished, "the liberation of so many peoples . . . should not, however, be transformed into an inappropriate sense of satisfaction or unjustified triumphalism."[21] He then added:

---

19. "Confronting the Challenges," 3.
20. See Havel, "The Power of the Powerless," *Open Letters*, 125–215.
21. "Confronting the Challenges," 3.

> In contrast to the over-bureaucratic and centralized command economy, the free and socially inspired economy presupposes truly free subjects who assume precise responsibilities upon themselves, loyally respect their duties to their co-workers, and constantly take the common good into account.[22]

In these words, the pope indicates that while people are no longer burdened by a flawed system, they must *become* truly free themselves if they want a free society. To be "free from" is not enough. True freedom, the pope specifies, involves assuming responsibility, fulfilling duties, and pursuing the common good. Freedom, then, is something that each human subject must acquire. During the Council debates on religious liberty in 1965, Karol Wojtyła articulated a very similar position. "It is not sufficient," he stated, "to say 'I am free'. It is necessary to say rather that 'I am responsible'. . . . Responsibility is the necessary culmination and fulfillment of freedom."[23]

Reflecting upon post-Communist Polish society in 1991, Tischner claimed that, for many people, the realization of freedom in this sense was proving to be difficult:

> Totalitarian rule consists in subordination and creates subordinates. After its fall, old habits do not disappear. You can see inscriptions on city walls in Poland saying "Commies—come back!!" Their authors are people of whom the liberalization of the economy and politics demand something they are incapable of—a personal responsibility for their own actions. Communism's material ravages are small compared with the devastation of the internal, spiritual world of the individual.[24]

Put another way, the decidedly unfree system of communism presupposed and effected a suppression of personal responsibility. Thus, from John Paul's perspective, it stands to reason that if people are to be truly free, they must recognize that man is, by virtue of being a person and the subject of moral acts, responsible for himself. *Centesimus Annus* even

---

22. "Confronting the Challenges," 4.
23. ASCV, IV–2 (1977), 22 September 1965, 292.
24. Tischner, "A View from the Ruins," 165–166. Addressing the Czech parliament in 1998, Havel expressed a similar opinion: "along with Communism, the structure of daily values held in place by the system for decades collapsed overnight. . . . The time of certainties, as false as these certainties were, gave way to freedom. . . . With it, completely new demands were placed on individual responsibility, and many found this responsibility unbearable." V. Havel, "The State of the Republic," *New York Review of Books* 45, no. 4 (1998): 42.

goes so far as to suggest that socialism was predicated upon denial of this moral-anthropological truth about man:

> The fundamental error of socialism is *anthropological* in nature. Socialism considers the individual person simply as an element, a molecule within the social organism, so that the good of the individual is completely subordinated to the functioning of the socio-economic mechanism. Socialism likewise maintains that the good of the individual can be realized without reference to *his free choice, to the unique and exclusive responsibility which he exercises in the face of good or evil.* Man is thus reduced to a series of social relationships, and the concept of the person as *the autonomous subject of moral decision* disappears, the very subject whose decisions build the social order. (CA 13) [italics added]

Though obviously a scathing assessment of socialism, the moral-anthropology of man from which John Paul's critique proceeds may also prove disconcerting to some of a decidedly non-socialist bent. The extract above refers to the folly of building a socio-economic system which denies that man, as a person and subject, possesses the unique capacity of free choice. It also indicates, however, that this does not mean that free choice itself is man's moral reference point—that there is no factor but the choosing itself that settles which alternative is chosen. Free choice is exercised "in the face of" good and evil. Hence, it is *not* about doing whatever one wills or "feels like," but doing what one *ought to do* in light of the truth. That is why, in the extract above, free choice is defined as a responsibility. Reference to truth, then, links the subject's natural capacity for freedom with the acquisition of responsibility—or, as *Laborem Exercens* understands it, self-dominion.

Throughout *Centesimus Annus*, this linkage between freedom and truth is made many times.[25] In more than one commentator's view, it brings us to the heart of the conflict between Catholic social teaching and certain versions of liberalism.[26] The disquiet felt by many who identify with the latter is captured in the closing sentences of Friedman's article on *Centesimus Annus*:

> I must confess that one high-minded sentiment, passed off as if it were a self-evident proposition, sent shivers down my back: *"Obedience to the*

---

25. See CA 4, 17, 41, 44, 46.
26. See, for example, M. Zięba, O.P., "Two or Even Three Liberalisms," *Dialogue and Humanism* 4, no. 5 (1994): 89.

truth about God and man is the first condition of freedom." Whose "truth"?
Decided by whom?[27]

These words suggest that Friedman is skeptical of the very idea of
metaphysical truth as well as wary of anyone claiming that they know *the*
truth. John Paul, on the other hand, regards discernment of truth as the
very purpose of the human intellect,[28] and *free obedience* to the truth about
God and man as both the prerequisite to man's attainment of true freedom
as well as the foundation of a fully human and fully free society. Indeed, if
one places Friedman's statement alongside that of John Paul's
understanding of freedom, it would seem that Tischner may have been
remarkably prescient in 1990, when he stated that "[f]ollowing the
confrontation of Christianity with Communism, Christianity now faces the
confrontation with Liberalism."[29]

Throughout our study, we have seen that John Paul's social teaching
stresses that freedom is more than being—to use the title of Friedman's
book—"free to choose." Rather, freedom is that moment of transcendence
which man may realize—even in the most marginalized circumstances—
by freely choosing to actualize that which is truly good for man: virtue.
The person who constantly acts in this way is free in the fullest sense of
the word. This amounts to a re-statement of the Judeo-Christian
understanding of the bond between truth and freedom captured in the
Deuteronomic verse: "I set before you life or death, blessing or curse.
Choose life, then, so that you and your descendants may live" (Dt 30:19).

It is also a view of freedom which prevails throughout Karol Wojtyła's
writings. *The Acting Person* does not define free self-realization as simply
free choice. Man's self-realization involves him constantly ordering his
freely willed actions to the truth about good and evil. As a vision of
freedom, it is aptly summarized in the following extract from one of
Wojtyła's 1976 articles:

> Freedom has been given to man by his Creator not in order to commit what
> is evil (cf. Gal.5:13), but to do good. God bestowed upon man

---

27. Friedman, "Goods in Conflict," 77.
28. See, for example, CA 46: "The Christian upholds freedom and serves it, constantly
offering to others *the truth he has known*. While paying heed to every fragment of truth
which he encounters in the life experience and in the culture of individuals and nations, he
will not fail to affirm in dialogue with others all that *his faith and the correct use of his
reason* have enabled him to understand." Italics added.
29. J. Tischner, "Homo Sovieticus – 1," *Tygodnik Powszechny*, 7 April 1990, 2.

understanding and conscience to show him what is good and what ought to be done, what is wrong and what ought to be avoided. . . . Freedom has been given to man in order to love, to love true good: to love God above all, to love man as his neighbor and brother (cf. Dt.6:5; Lv.19:18; Mk.12:30-33). Those who obey this truth . . . achieve thus, as the Council puts it, a state of "royal freedom," for they follow "that King whom to serve is to reign."

Freedom is therefore offered to man and given to him as a task. He must not only possess it, but also conquer it. He must recognize the work of his life in a good use, in an increasingly good use of his liberty. This is the truly essential, the fundamental work on which the value and the sense of his whole life depend.[30]

Man's achievement of freedom, then, involves the never-ending and difficult work of conquering himself by fulfilling the responsibilities of love of God and neighbor which are his according to the divine law. The response of Karol Wojtyła/John Paul II to liberals like Friedman is that man is certainly free to choose—but to choose what he ought. To those who focus upon freedom from exploitation and want, John Paul affirms that man should be free from oppression and deprivation, but specifies that this does not absolve him from the fundamental work of attaining true freedom in the form of moral good. If a person like Kolbe can do so in the most horrendous of circumstances, then, from the pope's perspective, there is every reason to expect that others, in far more bearable situations, can do the same.

8.6 Conclusion

This book began by citing Juliusz Słowacki's 1849 prediction that one day, in the midst of revolutionary discord, a Slav would become pope. Rather than fleeing the forces of "the world," this pope would stand and give fight—not with weapons of destruction, but with his heart and mind. It could not be said that Karol Wojtyła was elected pope in such circumstances. Nor has he, as John Paul II, approached the modern world in terms analogous to Pius IX's *Syllabus*. Instead, he has continued the critical engagement with this world which began with *Rerum Novarum* and gave rise to modern Catholic social teaching.

In developing this teaching, John Paul has paid attention to what is

---

30. "Eucharystia a ludzki głod wolności" [The Eucharist and Man's Hunger for Freedom], *Notificationes e Curia Metropolitana Cracoviensi* 11/12 (1976): 270.

"going on" in the modern world. This has ranged from assessing the meaning and implications of particular events to the use of decidedly contemporary language. Nevertheless, the pope has also insisted that no matter how much history appears to be undergoing a period of *acceleratio*, that which is good for man, the *bonum hominis*, does not change. It is man and not the future which bears the burden and dignity of morality. In the end, what matters is that each and every free and creative human subject is able to realize himself. His teaching, then, challenges those who, according to Neuhaus, wish that John Paul "would give a little on his ideas about the person and about freedom, since these, they say, may have to be bent somewhat in order to achieve a just society."[31] From John Paul's standpoint, unless the human person is free to realize himself, there can be no just society.

Like the Council, John Paul celebrates man's building up of the modern world as a confirmation and continuation of divine truths and commands articulated in the first chapter of the first biblical text. But his view of history is not that of the Enlightenment: that is, one of an "automatic" linear forward movement achieved almost by passage of time and without enormous personal effort. The work of establishing of a more just world must begin with man undertaking the toil of building up himself. Indeed, man's most profound contribution to establishing "the Kingdom" is to realize "kingship" over himself. It is a view which has been much influenced by Karol Wojtyła's contemplation of the phenomenon of man over the fifty-eight years preceding his election as pope.

In a broader sense, John Paul's development of teaching, indeed the whole tradition of Catholic social teaching, testifies to Christianity's continuing civilizational capacities. One does not have to be a believer to recognize that, at a minimum, Catholic social teaching outlines some very basic principles, which, if adhered to, are likely to help prevent the social order from becoming nasty, short, and brutish—an order in which worker exploitation would prevail, alienated consumer societies constitute the norm, and relations between the developed and developing worlds reflect a state of injustice. More generally, it militates against tendencies on man's part to use his work, as Wojtyła might have put it, to turn the modern world into something resembling one vast concentration camp. An English journalist expressed similar sentiments after reading *Centesimus Annus*:

---

31. R. Neuhaus, "The Mind of the Most Powerful Man in the World," *Worldview* 24, no. 9 (1981): 13.

Others might read all sorts of internecine Church nuances into it, or mock the Vatican's publicists, who are selling this encyclical as hard as they can. Not a Catholic myself, I prefer to take the Pope's words at face value. Religious intolerance can be murderous, as we all know from contemporary events in the Middle East, but the absence of all religion, as envisaged by the late Mr. John Lennon, is a terrifying prospect. It would return humanity to the jungle, armed to the teeth. We all need the Pope, and his encyclicals. If there were no such thing it would be necessary to invent him.[32]

32. J. Rogaly, "The Papacy and Political Economy," *Financial Times*, 3 May 1991, 15.

BIBLIOGRAPHY

For ease of reference, this has been divided into the following sections and subsections.

Primary Sources
1. Official Church Texts
2. Books by Karol Wojtyła
3. Articles by Karol Wojtyła
4. Statements by Karol Wojtyła during the Second Vatican Council
Secondary Sources
1. Books
2. Articles
3. Doctoral Dissertations

PRIMARY SOURCES

1. Official Church Texts

Acta Apostolicae Sedis. Città del Vaticano: Libreria Editrice Vaticana.
Acta Synodalia Sacrosancti Concilii Oecumenici Vaticani II. Città del Vaticano: Libreria Editrice Vaticana.
Catechism of the Catholic Church. London: Catholic Truth Society, 1994.
Congregation of the Doctrine of the Faith. *Libertatis Nuntius.* London: Catholic Truth Society, 1984.
———. *Libertatis Conscientia.* London: Catholic Truth Society, 1986.
Constitutiones Decreta Declarationes, Sacrosanctum Oecumenicum Concilium Vaticanum II. Roma: Libreria Editrice Vaticana, 1966.
Denzinger-Schönmetzer collection of Church documents in Jesuit Fathers

of St. Mary's College. *The Church Teaches: Documents of the Church in English Translation*. Rockford: Tan Books and Publishers, 1973.

Hennelly, S.J., A., ed. *Liberation Theology: A Documentary History* Maryknoll: Orbis, 1990.

John XXIII. *Mater et Magistra*. London: Catholic Truth Society, 1961.

——. *Pacem in Terris*. London: Catholic Truth Society, 1963.

John Paul II. *Centesimus Annus*. London: Catholic Truth Society, 1991.

——. *Laborem Exercens*. London: Catholic Truth Society, 1991.

——. *Redemptor Hominis*. London: Catholic Truth Society, 1991.

——. *Sollicitudo Rei Socialis*. London: Catholic Truth Society, 1988.

——. *Veritatis Splendor*. London: Catholic Truth Society, 1993.

Leo XIII. *Rerum Novarum*. London: Catholic Truth Society, 1931.

Paul VI. *Ecclesiam Suam*. London: Catholic Truth Society, 1964.

——. *Evangelii Nuntiandi*. London: Catholic Truth Society, 1976.

——. *Octogesima Adveniens*. London: Catholic Truth Society, 1971.

——. *Populorum Progressio*. London: Catholic Truth Society, 1967.

Pius XI. *Quadragesimo Anno*. London: Catholic Truth Society, 1931.

Second Vatican Council. *Dei Verbum*. London: Catholic Truth Society, 1966.

——. *Dignitatis Humanae*. London: Catholic Truth Society, 1966.

——. *Gaudium et Spes*. London: Catholic Truth Society, 1966.

——. *Lumen Gentium*. London: Catholic Truth Society, 1966.

Synod of Bishops. *Iustitia in Mundo*. London: Catholic Truth Society, 1972.

2.   Books by Karol Wojtyła

The Acting Person, tr. A. Potocki. Dordrecht: Reidel, 1979. Originally published as *Osoba i Czyn*. Kraków: Polskie Towarzystwo Teologiczne, 1969.

The Collected Plays and Writings on Theater, tr. B. Taborski. Berkeley: University of California Press, 1987. For original dates of dramatic publications, see "Editorial Note and Sources": ix–x.

Faith According to St. John of the Cross, tr. J. Aumann, O.P. San Francisco: Ignatius Press, 1981. A translation of "Doctrina de fide apud s. Joannem a Cruce." Diss. ad laureaum. Pont. Univ. S. Thomae Aquinat. Romae 1948. Ms. 1948/59 of the Archive of the Theology Faculty, Pontifical University of St. Thomas, Rome.

Love and Responsibility, tr. H. Willets. New York: Farrar, Straus, Giroux, 1981. Originally published as *Miłość i odpowiedzialność. Studium etyczne* [Love and Responsibility: An Ethical Study]. Kraków: Znak, 1960.

Ocena możliwości zbudowania etyki chrześcijańskiej przy założeniach systemu Maksa Schelera [The Possibility of Constructing a Christian Ethic on the Basis of the System of Max Scheler]. Lublin: TNKUL, 1959. Published in Italian as *Max Scheler*. Roma: Logos, 1980.

The Place Within: The Poetry of John Paul II, tr. J. Peterkiewicz. London: Hutchinson, 1995.

Sign of Contradiction. New York: Geoffrey Chapman, 1979. Originally published as *Znak, któremu sprzeciwiać się będą*. Poznań: Pallotinum, 1976.

Sources of Renewal: Study on the Implementation of the Second Vatican Council, tr. S. Falla. London: Collins, 1980. Originally published as *U podstaw odnowy: Studium o realizacji Vaticanum II*. Kraków: Polskie Towarzystwo Teologiczne, 1972.

3. Articles by Karol Wojtyła

"Apostolstwo świeckich" [The Apostolate of the Laity]. *Ateneum Kapłańskie* 71, no. 5 (1968): 274–280.

"Chrześcijanin a kultura" [The Christian and Culture]. *Znak* 16, no. 10 (1964): 1153–1157.

"Consilia et vota episcopi K. Wojtyła." In *Acta et Documenta Concilio Vaticano II Apparando, Series I, Antepreparatoria*, Vol. II, Part II. Roma: Libreria Editrice Vaticana, 1960: 741–748.

"Człowiek jest osobą: Stosunek Kościoła do świata współczesnego" [Man Is a Person: The Relation of the Church to the Contemporary World]. *Tygodnik Powszechny* 18, no. 52 (1964): 2.

"Czym powinien być teologią moralną?" [What Should Moral Theology Be?]. *Ateneum Kapłańskie* 58, no. 1/3 (1959): 97–104.

"The Degrees of Being from the Viewpoint of the Phenomenology of Action." *Analecta Husserliana* 11 (1981): 125–130.

"Dramat słowa i gestu" [The Drama of Word and Gesture]. *Tygodnik Powszechny* 11, no. 14 (1957): 5.

"Etyka a teologia moralna" [Ethics and Moral Theology]. *Znak* 19, no. 9 (1967): 1077–1082.

"Etyka niezależna w świetle idei sprawiedliwości" [Independent Ethics in Light of the Idea of Justice]. *Tygodnik Powszechny* 12, no. 6 (1958): 7.

"Eucharystia a ludzki głod wolności" [The Eucharist and Man's Hunger for Freedom]. *Notificationes e Curia Metropolitana Cracoviensi* 11/12

(1976): 270–275.

"Ewangeliczna zasada naśladowania: Nauka źródeł Objawienia a system filozoficzny Maxa Schelera" [The Gospel on the Principle of Imitation: Revelation and the Philosophical System of Max Scheler]. *Ateneum Kapłańskie* 55, no. 1 (1957): 57–67.

"Ewangelizacja w świecie współczesnym" [Evangelization in the Contemporary World]. *Tygodnik Powszechny* 28, no. 51/52 (1974): 1, 10–11.

"Ewangelizacja współczesnego świata: Relacja teologiczna na Synodzie Biskupów 1974" [Evangelization in the Contemporary World: Theological Report at the Synod of Bishops, 1974]. *Znak* 27, no. 4/5 (1975): 415–439.

"O godności osoby ludzkiej: Przemówienie w Radio Watykańskim, 19 X 1964" [The Dignity of the Human Person: Speech on Vatican Radio, 19 October 1964]. *Notificationes e Curia Metropolitana Cracoviensi* 12 (1964): 287–289.

"Humanizm a cel człowieka" [Humanism and Man's Purpose]. *Tygodnik Powszechny* 11, no. 31 (1957): 7.

"O humaniźmie św. Jana od Krzyża" [The Humanism of St. John of the Cross]. *Znak* 6, no. 1 (1951): 6–20.

"Idea i pokora" [Ideals and Humility]. *Tygodnik Powszechny* 11, no. 41 (1957): 7.

"Instynkt, miłość, małżeństwo" [Instinct, Love, and Matrimony]. *Tygodnik Powszechny* 8, no. 42 (1952): 1–2, 11.

"The Intentional Act and the Human Act, that is, Act and Experience." *Analecta Husserliana* 5 (1976): 269–280.

"Kamień węgielny etyki społecznej" [The Cornerstone of the Social Ethic]. *Tygodnik Powszechny* 12, no. 1 (1958): 7.

"O kierowniczej lub służebnej roli rozumu w etyce. Na tle poglądów Tomasza z Akwinu, Hume'a i Kanta" [The Directing or Subservient Role of Reason in Ethics discussed in relation to Thomas Aquinas, Hume and Kant]. *Roczniki Filozoficzne* 6, no. 2 (1958): 13–33.

"Kościół wobec współczesnego świata: Przemówienie w Radio Watykańskim, 28 IX 1964" [The Church and the Contemporary World: Speech on Vatican Radio, 28 September 1964]. *Notificationes e Curia Metropolitana Cracoviensi* 12 (1964): 282–284.

"Logika wewnętrzna Vaticanum II" [The Internal Logic of Vatican II]. *Wrocławskie Wiadomości Kościelne* 21, no. 7 (1966): 159–163.

"O metafizycznej i fenomenologicznej podstawie normy moralnej W oparciu o koncepcję św. Tomasza z Akwinu oraz Maksa Schelera"

[The Metaphysical and Phenomenological Basis of the Moral Norm Based on the Conceptions of St. Thomas Aquinas As Well As Max Scheler]. *Roczniki Teologiczno-Kanoniczne* 6, no. 1/2 (1959): 99–124.

"Miłość i odpowiedzialność" [Love and Responsibility]. *Ateneum Kapłańskie* 59, no. 2 (1959): 163–170.

"Mission de France." *Tygodnik Powszechny* 5, no. 9 (1949): 1–2.

"Moralność a etyka" [Morality and Ethics]. *Tygodnik Powszechny* 11, no. 9 (1957): 3.

"Myśli o małżeństwie" [Thoughts on Marriage]. *Znak* 9, no. 9 (1957): 597–605.

"Myśli o uczestnictwie" [Thoughts on Participation]. *Znak* 23, no. 2/3 (1971): 209–225.

"Natura i doskonałość" [Nature and Perfection]. *Tygodnik Powszechny* 11, no. 13 (1957): 11.

"Natura ludzką jako podstawa formacji etycznej" [Human Nature As the Basis of Ethical Formation]. *Znak* 11, no. 6 (1959): 693–697.

"Notatki na marginesie konstytucji *Gaudium et Spes*" [Notes on the Margin of the Constitution *Gaudium et Spes*]. *Ateneum Kapłańskie* 74, no. 1 (1970): 3–6.

"Osoba i czyn na tle dynamizmu człowieka" [The Person and the Act from the Viewpoint of the Dynamism of Man]. In *O Bogu i o człowieku: problemy filozoficzne* [On God and Man: Philosophical Problems], edited by B. Bejze. Warszawa: Polskie Towarzystwo Teologiczne, 1968: 204–226.

"Osoba i czyn: Refleksywne funcjonowanie świadomości i jej emocjonalizacja" [The Person and the Act: The Reflexive Functioning of Consciousness and Its Emotionalization]. *Studia Theologica Varsaviensia* 6, no. 1 (1968): 101–119.

"Osoba i czyn w aspekcie świadomości" [The Person and the Act in the Aspect of Consciousness]. In *Pastori et Magistro*, edited by A. Krupa. Lublin: TNKUL, 1966.

"Osoba ludzką a prawo naturalne" [The Human Person and Natural Law]. *Roczniki Filozoficzne* 18, no. 2 (1970): 53–59.

"Ostatnie słowo należy do miłości" [The Last Word Belongs to Love]. *Przewodnik Katolicki* 11 (1970): 89.

"Participation or Alienation." *Analecta Husserliana* 6 (1977): 61–73.

"The Person: Subject and Community." *Review of Metaphysics* 33 (1979): 273–301. Originally published as "Osoba: podmiot i wspólnota" [The Person: Subject and Community]. *Roczniki Filozoficzne* 24, no. 2 (1976): 5–39.

"The Personal Structure of Self-Determination." In *Tomasso d'Aquino nel suo VIII centenario*. Roma/Napoli: Congresso Internazionale, 1974: 187–195.

"Personalizm tomistyczny: Dyskusja" [Thomistic Personalism: A Discussion]. *Znak* 13, no. 5 (1961): 664–675.

"Perspektywy człowieka: Integralny rozwój a eschatologia" [The Perspectives of Man: Integral Development and Eschatology]. *Colliquium Salutis* 7 (1975): 133–145.

"O pochodzeniu norm moralnych" [The Origin of Moral Norms]. *Tygodnik Powszechny* 11, no. 11 (1957): 11.

"W poczuciu odpowiedzialności" [Awareness of Responsibility]. *Kierunki* 11, no. 20 (1966): 3.

"W poszukiwaniu podstaw perfekcjoryzmu w etyce" [In Search of the Basis of Perfectionism in Ethics]. *Roczniki Filozoficzne* 5, no. 4 (1955/1957): 303–317.

"Prawo natury" [The Natural Law]. *Tygodnik Powszechny* 11, no. 28 (1957): 7.

"Problem bezinteresowności" [The Problem of Disinterestedness]. *Tygodnik Powszechny* 11, no. 34 (1957): 7.

"Problem doświadczenia w etyce" [The Problem of Experience in Ethics]. *Roczniki Filozoficzne* 17, no. 2 (1969): 5–24.

"Problem etyki naukowej" [The Problem of a Scientific Ethic]. *Tygodnik Powszechny* 11, no. 10 (1957): 3.

"Problem oderwania przeżycia od aktu w etyce na tle poglądów Kanta i Schelera" [The Problem of the Separation of Experience from the Act in Kant and Scheler's Ethics]. *Roczniki Filozoficzne* 5, no. 3 (1955/1957): 113–140.

"Problem prawdy i miłosierdzia" [The Problem of Truth and Charity]. *Tygodnik Powszechny* 11, no. 33 (1957): 11.

"Problem teorii moralności" [The Problem of Moral Theory]. In *W nurcie zagadnień posoborowych* [In the Current of Postconciliar Considerations] Vol. 3, edited by B. Bejze. Warszawa: Polskie Towarzystwo Teologiczne, 1969: 217–249.

"Problem walki" [The Problem of Struggle]. *Tygodnik Powszechny* 12, no. 3 (1958): 7.

"Il problema del costituirsi della cultura attraverso la 'praxis' umana" [The Problem of the Constitution of Culture through Human "Praxis"]. *Rivista de Filosofia Neo-Scolastica* 69, no. 3 (1977): 513–524. Also published as "Problem konstytuowania się kultury proprzez ludzką praxis." *Ethos* 2, no. 8 (1989): 39–49.

"Problematyka dojrzewania człowieka: Aspekt antropologiczno-teologiczny" [The Problem of Human Development: The Anthropological-Theological Aspect]. *Nasza Rodzina* 9 (1977): 2–15.

"Program wykładów nauk etyce społecznych w seminariach duchownych i instytutach teölogicznych w Polsce" [The Program of Teaching Social Ethics in Seminaries and Theological Institutes in Poland]. *Roczniki Teologiczno-Kanoniczne* 8, no. 3 (1961): 65–66.

"Przemówienie radiowe: Náswietlenie deklaracji o wolności religijnej Radio Watykańskie 20 X 1965" [Radio Address: Elucidation on the Declaration on Religious Liberty Vatican Radio, 20 October 1965]. *Notificationes e Curia Metropolitana Cracoviensi* 11/12 (1965): 269–271.

"Przemówienie w Radio Watykańskim przed uroczystością beatyfikacyjną O. Maksymiliana Marii Kolbego" [Address on Vatican Radio for the Imminent Beatification of Fr. Maximilian Maria Kolbe]. *Notificationes e Curia Metropolitana Cracoviensi* 10/12 (1971): 242–244.

"Quaestio de Fide apud S. Joannem a Cruce." *Collectanea Theologica* 21, no. 4 (1950): 418–468.

"Realizm w etyce" [Realism in Ethics]. *Tygodnik Powszechny* 11, no. 12 (1957): 7.

"Refleksje na marginesie Synodu–1974" [Reflections on the Margins of the Synod–1974]. *Notificationes e Curia Metropolitana Cracoviensi* 9/10 (1974): 224–236.

"Rodzicielstwo a 'communio personarum'" [Parenthood and the "Communio Personarum"]. *Ateneum Kapłańskie* 84, no. 1 (1975): 17–31.

"Rodzina jako 'communio personarum'" [The Family as a "Communio Personarum"]. *Ateneum Kapłańskie* 83, no. 3 (1974): 347–361.

"Rozważania o Królestwie" [Considerations about the Kingdom of God]. *Tygodnik Powszechny* 14, no. 44 (1960): 1–2.

"Słowo końcowe dyskusji nad *Osobą i czynem*" [Closing Remarks at a Discussion about *The Acting Person*]. *Analecta Cracoviensia* 5/6 (1973/1974): 243–263.

"Sobór a praca teologów" [The Council and the Work of Theologians]. *Tygodnik Powszechny* 19, no. 9 (1965): 1.

"Sobór od wewnątrz: List do redakcji *Tygodnika Powszechnego*" [The Council from the Inside: A Letter to the Editor of *Tygodnik Powszechny*]. *Tygodnik Powszechny* 19, no. 16 (1965): 1, 3.

"Sprawiedliwość a miłość" [Justice and Love]. *Tygodnik Powszechny* 12, no. 2 (1958): 7.

"Stosunek do przyjemności" [The Attitude towards Pleasure]. *Tygodnik Powszechny* 11, no. 38 (1957): 7.

"Stworzenie a odkupienie" [Creation and Redemption]. *Notificationes e Curia Metropolitana Cracoviensi* 3/4 (1966): 59–62.

"Subjectivity and the Irreducible in Man." *Analecta Husserliana* 7 (1978): 107–114.

"Świadomość Kościoła wedle Vaticanum II" [The Consciousness of the Church according to Vatican II]. In *W nurcie zagadnień posoborowych* [In the Current of Post-Conciliar Considerations], Vol. 5, *Jan XXIII i jego dzieło* [John XXIII and His Works], edited by B. Bejze. Warszawa: Polskie Towarzystwo Teologiczne, 1972: 255–309.

"Synod Biskupów: zebranie nadzwyczajne Rzym, 1969" [World Synod of Bishops: Special Meeting in Rome]. *Analecta Cracoviensia* 2 (1970): 131–156.

"O Synodzie Biskupów" [The Synod of Bishops]. *Tygodnik Powszechny* 26, no. 10 (1972): 1, 5.

"System etyczny Maksa Schelera jako środek do opracowania etyki chrześcijańskiej" [The Ethical System of Max Scheler as an Instrument for Elaborating a Christian Ethic]. *Polonia sacra* 6, no. 2/4 (1953/1954): 143–161.

"Tajemnica i człowiek" [Mystery and Man]. *Tygodnik Powszechny* 7, no. 51/52 (1951): 1–2.

"The Task of Christian Philosophy Today." *Proceedings of the American Catholic Philosophical Association* 53 (1979): 3–4.

"Teologia i teologowie w Kościele posoborowym" [Theology and Theologians in the Post-Conciliar Church]. In *Teologia i antropologia* [Theology and Anthropology], edited by Kongres Teologów Polskich [Congress of Polish Theologians]. Kraków: Polskie Towarzystwo Teologiczne, 1972: 27–42.

"Teoria e prassi nella filosofia della persona umana" [Theory and Practice in the Philosophy of the Human Person]. *Sapienza* 29, no. 4 (1976): 377–384.

"The Transcendence of the Person in Action and Man's Self-Teleology." *Analecta Husserliana* 9 (1979): 203–219.

"Uwagi o życiu wewnętrznym młodej inteligencji" [Reflections on the Spiritual Life of the Young Intelligentsia]. *Znak* 13, no. 6 (1961): 761–769.

"Vaticanum II a praca teologów" [Vatican II and the Work of Theologians]. *Collectanea Theologica* 36, no. 1/4 (1966): 8–14.

"La verità sull'uomo." *L'Osservatore Romano*, 2 aprile 1976, 2.

"La visione antropologica della *Humanae Vitae.*" *Lateranum* 44, no. 1 (1978): 125–145.

"Wartości" [Values]. *Tygodnik Powszechny* 11, no. 39 (1957): 11.

"Właściwa interpretacja nauki o szczęściu" [The Proper Interpretation of the Teaching on Happiness]. *Tygodnik Powszechny* 11, no. 36 (1957): 11.

"Wymowa Oświęcimia" [The Eloquence of Auschwitz]. *Notificationes e Curia Metropolitana Cracoviensi* 3/4 (1965): 81–83.

"Wypowiedź na Synodzie w dniu 15 IX 1969" [Remarks at the Synod, 15 September 1969]. *Tygodnik Powszechny* 23, no. 43 (1969): 5.

"Wypowiedź wstępna w czasie dyskusji nad *Osobą i czynem* w katolickim Uniwersytecie Lubelskim dnia 16 XII 1970" [Introductory Remarks at a Discussion of *The Acting Person* at the Catholic University of Lublin, 16 December 1970]. *Analecta Cracoviensia* 5/6 (1973/1974): 53–55.

"Zagadnienie wiary w dziełach św. Jana od Krzyża" [The Problem of Faith in the Work of John of the Cross]. *Ateneum Kapłańskie* 52, no. 1 (1950): 24–26, and *Ateneum Kapłańskie* 52, no. 2 (1950): 103–105.

"Zagadnienie woli w analizie aktu etycznego" [The Problem of the Will in the Analysis of the Ethical Act]. *Roczniki Filozoficzne* 5, no. 1 (1955/1957): 111–135.

"Znaczenie kardynała Stefana Wyszyńskiego dla współczesnego Kościoła" [The Importance of Cardinal Stefan Wyszyński for the Church of Today]. *Zeszyty Naukowe Katolickiego Uniwersytetu Lubelskiego* 14, no. 3 (1971): 19–37.

"Znaczenie Konstytucji pastoralnej dla teologów" [The Importance of the Pastoral Constitition for Theologians]. *Collectanea Theologica* 38, no. 1 (1968): 5–18.

"Znaczenie powinności" [The Importance of Obligation]. *Tygodnik Powszechny* 11, no. 16 (1957): 11.

"Znak naszej epoki" [Sign of Our Times]. *Tygodnik Powszechny* 25, no. 42 (1971): 1.

4. Statements by Karol Wojtyła during the Second Vatican Council

"Animadversiones scripto exhibitae quoad cap.IV schematis de Ecclesia in mundo temporis." ASCV, III–7 1975: 380–382 [Amendments to schema De Ecclesia in mundo; on behalf of Polish Episcopate].

"Animadversiones scripto exhibitae quoad schema de Ecclesia in mundo huius temporis, cap.I–III." ASCV, III–5 1975: 680–683 [Amendments to schema De Ecclesia in mundo; on behalf of Polish Episcopate].

"Animadversiones scripto exhibitae quoad schema de Ecclesia in mundo huius temporis Parten II, cap.II." ASCV, IV–3 1977: 349–350 [Church in the Modern World].

"Animadversiones scripto exhibitae quoad schema de Ecclesia in mundo huius temporis Parten II in genere et cap.I." ASCV, IV–3 1977: 242–243 [Church in the Modern World].

"Animadversiones scripto exhibitae quoad schema declarationis de libertate religiosia." ASCV, IV–2 1977: 292–293 [Religious Liberty].

"De Ecclesia in mundo huius temporis." ASCV, III–5 1975: 298–300 [Church in the Modern World].

"Oratio de Ecclesia in mundo huius temporis Pars I." ASCV, IV–2 1977: 660–663 [Church in the Modern World].

For a complete bibliography of Karol Wojtyła's works, see Gramatowski, W., and Z. Wilińska. *Karol Wojtyła w świetle publikacji/Karol Wojtyła negli scritti: Bibliografia* [Karol Wojtyła in the Light of His Writings: A Bibliography]. Città del Vaticano: Libreria Editrice Vaticana, 1980. The bibliography lists Wojtyła's pre-papal writings by year, providing the original Polish title and source together with an Italian translation of the title. It also lists articles about Karol Wojtyła written prior to his papal election.

SECONDARY SOURCES

1. Books

Acta Pii IX, Bk. 1, Vol. III. Graz: Piper, 1971.

After 1991: Capitalism and Ethics. A Colloquium in the Vatican. Vatican City: Libreria Editrice Vaticana, 1992.

Alberigo, G. and J. Jossua, eds. *La réception de Vatican II*. Paris: Cerf, 1985.

Antonazzi, G. *L'enciclica 'Rerum Novarum', testo autentico e redazioni preparatorie dei documenti originali*, 2nd ed. Roma: Edizioni di storia e letteratura, 1992.

Aretin, K. von. *The Papacy and the Modern World*, tr. R. Hill. New York: Weidenfeld and Nicolson, 1970.

Assmann, H. *Practical Theology of Liberation*. London: Search Press, 1975.

Avila, C. *Ownership: Early Christian Teaching*. Maryknoll: Orbis, 1983.

Bartell, C.S.C., E. *'Laborem Exercens': A Third World Perspective*. Notre Dame: University of Notre Dame Press, 1982.

Barth, K. *Ad Limina Apostolorum: An Appraisal of Vatican II*. Edinburgh: T. and T. Clark, 1967.

———. *Church Dogmatics*, tr. A. MacKay et al., Bk. 3, Vol. IV. Edinburgh: T. and T. Clark, 1961.

Baum, G. *The Priority of Labor: A Commentary on 'Laborem Exercens'*. New York: Paulist Press, 1982.

Baum, G. and R. Ellsberg, eds. *The Logic of Solidarity: Commentaries on Pope John Paul's Encyclical 'On Social Concern'*. New York: Orbis, 1989.

Bauman, Z. *Intimations of Post-Modernity*. London: Routledge, 1992.

Beigel, G. *Faith and Social Justice in the Teaching of John Paul II*. New York: Peter Lang Publishing, 1997.

Biffi, F. *The Social Gospel of Pope John Paul II: A Guide to the Encyclicals on Human Work and the Authentic Development of Peoples*. Rome: Pontifical Lateran University, 1989.

Bigongiari, D., ed. *The Political Ideas of St. Thomas Aquinas*. New York: Hafner Press, 1981.

Blazynski, G. *John Paul II: A Man from Kraków*. London: Sphere, 1979.

Block, W., and I. Hexham, eds. *Religion, Economics and Social Thought*. Vancouver: Fraser Institute, 1986.

Budde, M. *The Two Churches: Catholicism and Capitalism in the World System*. London/Durham: Duke University Press, 1992.

Butler, O.S.B., C. *The Theology of Vatican II*, rev. ed. London: Darton, Longman, and Todd, 1981.

Buttiglione, R., ed. *La filosofia di Karol Wojtyła*. Bologna: CSEO, 1983.

———. *Karol Wojtyła: The Thought of the Man Who Became Pope John Paul II*, tr. P. Guietti and F. Murphy. Cambridge: Eerdmans, 1997.

Calvez, S.J., J.-Y. *L'église devant le libéralisme économique*. Paris: Cerf, 1994.

———. *Necessite du travail: Disparition d'une valeur ou redefinition?* Paris: Cerf, 1997.

———. *The Social Thought of John XXIII: 'Mater et Magistra'*, tr. G. McKenzie. London: Burn and Oates, 1965.

Calvez, S.J., J.-Y., and J. Perrin, S.J. *The Church and Social Justice: The Social Teachings of the Popes from Leo XIII to Pius XII 1878-1958*, tr.

J. Kirwan. London: Burn and Oates, 1961.

Camp, R. *The Papal Ideology of Social Reform: A Study in Historical Development, 1870-1967*. Leiden: E.J. Brill, 1969.

Capovilla, L. *Giovanni XXIII, Quindicic Letture*. Roma, 1978.

Caprile, S.J., G. *Il Concilio Vaticano II*, 5 vols. Roma: Civiltà Cattolica, 1965– .

Cardinale, H. *The Holy See and the International Order*. Geralds Cross: Colin Smythe, 1976.

Caron, J. *Implications for Management: 'Laborem Exercens'*. Notre Dame: University of Notre Dame Press, 1982.

Carrier, H. *The Social Doctrine of the Church Re-Visited*. Vatican City, 1990.

Catholic Bishops' Conference of England and Wales. *The Common Good*. London: Catholic Truth Society, 1996.

Center of Concern. *Reflections on the Papal Encyclical 'Centesimus Annus'*. Washington, D.C.: Center of Concern, 1991.

Chadwick, O. *The Popes and European Revolution*. Oxford: Oxford University Press, 1981.

Charles, S.J., R. *Christian Social Witness and Teaching: The Catholic Tradition—From 'Genesis' to 'Centesimus Annus'*, 2 vols. Leominster: Gracewing, 1998.

———. *The Social Teaching of Vatican II: Its Origins and Development. Catholic Social Ethics—An Historical and Comparative*. Oxford/San Francisco: Plater Press/Ignatius Press, 1982.

Chenu, O.P., M.-D. *La 'doctrine sociale' de l'église comme idéologie*. Paris: Cerf, 1979.

———. *Pour une théologie du travail*. Paris: Editions du Seuil, 1955.

Coleman, S.J., J., ed. *One Hundred Years of Catholic Social Thought: Celebration and Challenge*. Maryknoll: Orbis, 1991.

Coman, P. *Catholics and the Welfare State*. London: Longman, 1977.

Congar, O.P., Y.-M. *Report from Rome*. London: Geoffrey Chapman, 1963.

Congar, O.P., Y.-M., and M. Peuchmaurd, O.P., eds. *L'église dans le monde de ce temps*, 2 vols. Paris: Cerf, 1967.

Copleston, S.J., F. *A History of Philosophy*. New York: Image Books, 1985.

———. Bk. 1, Vol. II, *Augustine to Scotus*.

———. Bk. 2, Vol. VI, *Wolf to Kant*.

———. Bk. 3, Vol. VII, *Fichte to Nietzsche*.

Coste, R. *L'église et les droits de l'homme*. Paris: Aubier, 1982.

Cox, H. *The Silencing of Leonardo Boff: The Vatican and the Future of World Christianity.* Oak Park: Meyer Stone Books, 1988.

Cranston, M. *Jean-Jacques: The Early Life and Work of Jean-Jacques Rousseau, 1712-1754.* London: Penguin, 1983.

Curran, C., and R. McCormick, S.J., eds. *Readings in Moral Theology,* Vol. 5, *Official Catholic Social Teaching.* New York: Paulist Press, 1986.

Djilas, M. *The New Class.* London: Unwin Books, 1966.

Doran, K. *Solidarity: A Synthesis of Personalism and Communalism in the Thought of Karol Wojtyła/John Paul II.* New York: Peter Lang Publishing, 1996.

Dorr, D. *Option for the Poor: A Hundred Years of Vatican Social Teaching,* rev. ed. Dublin: Gill and Macmillan, 1992.

Droulers, P. *Cattolicesimo sociale nei secoli xix e xx: Saggi di storia e sociologia.* Roma: Politica e storia, 1982.

Duncan, C.Ss.R., B. *The Church's Social Teaching: From 'Rerum Novarum' to 1931.* North Blackburn: Collins Dove, 1991.

Duska, R., ed. *'Rerum Novarum': A Symposium Celebrating One Hundred Years of Catholic Social Thought.* New York: Mellen, 1991.

Dwyer, J., ed. *The New Dictionary of Catholic Social Thought.* Collegeville: Liturgical Press, 1994.

———. *Questions of Special Urgency: The Church in the Modern World Two Decades after Vatican II.* Washington, D.C.: Georgetown University Press, 1986.

Dybciak, K. *La grande testimonianiza.* Bologna: CSEO, 1981.

———. *Karol Wojtyła a literatura* [Karol Wojtyła and Literature]. Tarnów: Polskie Nagraria, 1991.

Esposito, C., ed. *Karol Wojtyła e il pensiero europeo contemporaneo.* Bologna: CSEO, 1984.

Evans, E. *The German Center Party, 1870-1933: A Study in Political Catholicism.* Carbondale: Southern Illinois University Press, 1974.

Fanfani, A. *Catholicism, Protestantism and Capitalism.* Notre Dame: University of Notre Dame Press, 1984.

Fappani, A., and F. Molinari. *Giovanni Battista Montini Giovane, Documenti inediti e testimonianze.* Torino: Marietti, 1979.

Filibeck, G. *Les droits de l'homme dans l'enseignement de l'église: De Jean XXIII à Jean Paul II.* Città del Vaticano: Libreria Editrice Vaticana, 1992.

Filipiak, M., and A. Szostek, eds. *Karol Wojtyła w Katolickim Uniwersytecie Lubelskim* [Karol Wojtyła in the Catholic University of

Lublin]. Lublin: TNKUL, 1987.

Finnis, J. *Aquinas: Moral, Political, and Legal Theory*. Oxford: Oxford University Press, 1998.

——. *Natural Law and Natural Rights*. Oxford: Oxford University Press, 1993.

Freedman, R. *Marx on Economics*. London: Penguin, 1960.

Fremantle, A., ed. *The Papal Encyclicals in Their Historical Context*, rev. ed. New York: Herder and Herder, 1963.

Fromm, E., ed. *Socialist Humanism*. London: Penguin, 1967.

Frossard, A. *N'ayez pas peur: dialogues avec Jean-Paul II*. Paris: R. Laffont, 1982.

Fukuyama, F. *The End of History and the Last Man*. London: Penguin, 1992.

Furlong, P., and D. Curtis, eds. *The Church Faces the Modern World: 'Rerum Novarum' and Its Impact*. London: Earlsgate Press, 1994.

Gaillardetz, R. *Teaching with Authority: A Theology of the Magisterium in the Church*. Collegeville: Liturgical Press, 1997.

Galbraith, J. *The Affluent Society*. London: Penguin, 1991.

Garton Ash, T. *The Polish Revolution: Solidarity*, rev. ed. London: Granta, 1991.

——. *The Uses of Adversity: Essays on the Fate of Central Europe*, 2nd ed. London: Granta, 1991.

Gasperi, A. de. *I tempi e gli uomini che prepararono la 'Rerum Novarum'*, 2nd ed. Milano: Vita e Pensiero, 1931.

Gawronski, J. *Il Mondo di Giovanni Paolo II*. Milano: Vita e Pensiero, 1994.

Giełżyński, W. *Edward Abramowski, zwiastun solidarności* [Edward Abramowski, Harbinger of Solidarity]. London: Polonia, 1986.

Gilby, O.P., T., ed. *St. Thomas Aquinas, Summa Theologiae*. London: Blackfriars, 1963.

González, J. *Faith and Wealth: A History of Early Christian Ideas on the Origin, Significance and Use of Money*. New York: Harper and Row, 1990.

Grémillion, J. *The Gospel of Peace and Justice: Catholic Social Teaching Since John XXIII*. New York: Orbis, 1976.

Grisez, G. *The Way of the Lord Jesus*, Vol. 2, *Living a Christian Life*. Quincy: Franciscan Press, 1993.

Grygiel, S., et al. *Karol Wojtyła. Filosofo, Teologo, Poeta*. Città del Vaticano: Libreria Editrice Vaticana, 1984.

Gudorf, C. *Catholic Social Teaching on Liberation Themes*. Washington,

D.C.: Georgetown University Press, 1981.

Gutiérrez, G. *A Theology of Liberation: History, Politics and Salvation*, tr. C. Inda and J. Eagleson. Maryknoll: Orbis, 1973.

Habiger, O.S.B., M. *Papal Teaching on Private Property, 1891-1981.* Lanham: University Press of America, 1990.

Hales, E. *Pio Nono: A Study in European Politics and Religion in the Nineteenth Century*, 2nd ed. London: Eyre and Spottiswoode, 1956.

Hanson, E. *The Catholic Church in World Politics*. Princeton: Princeton University Press, 1987.

Havel, V. *Open Letters: Selected Prose 1965-1990*, tr. P. Wilson. London: Faber and Faber, 1991.

Hayek, F. von. *The Constitution of Liberty*. Chicago: University of Chicago Press, 1960.

Hebblethwaite, P. *John XXIII: Pope of the Council*. London: Geoffrey Chapman, 1984.

———. *Paul VI: The First Modern Pope*. London: HarperCollins, 1993.

———. *Pope John Paul II and the Church*. Kansas City: National Catholic Reporter, 1995.

Heckel, R. *The Human Person and Social Structures*. Rome: Pontifical Commission Iustitia et Pax, 1980.

Heidegger, M. *Basic Writings*. New York: Harper and Row, 1977.

Hellman, J. *Emmanuel Mounier and the New Catholic Left, 1930-1950*. Toronto: University of Toronto Press, 1981.

Hobgood, M. *Catholic Social Teaching and Economic Theory: Paradigms in Conflict*. Philadelphia: Temple University Press, 1991.

Höffner, J. *Economic Systems and Economic Ethics: Guidelines in Catholic Social Teaching*, 3rd ed. Kölin: Vereinigung zur Förderung der Christlichen Sozialwissenschaften, 1988.

———. *Fundamentals of Christian Sociology*. Cork: Mercier Press, 1962.

Hollenbach, S.J., D. *Claims in Conflict: Retrieving and Renewing the Catholic Human Rights Tradition*. New York: Paulist Press, 1979.

Hollenbach, S.J., D., and R. Douglass, eds. *Catholicism and Liberalism: Contributions to American Public Philosophy*. Cambridge: Cambridge University Press, 1994.

Holmes, D. *The Papacy in the Modern World*. London: Burn and Oates, 1981.

Houck, J., and O. Williams, C.S.C., eds. *Catholic Social Thought and the New World Order: Building on One Hundred Years*. Notre Dame: University of Notre Dame Press, 1993.

——. *Co-creation and Capitalism: John Paul II's 'Laborem Exercens'*. Lanham: University Press of America, 1983.

——. *The Making of an Economic Vision: John Paul II's 'On Social Concern'*. Washington, D.C.: University Press of America, 1991.

John Paul II. *Crossing the Threshold of Hope*. London: Cape, 1994.

——. *Original Unity of Man and Woman: Catechesis on the Book of Genesis*. Boston: Daughters of St. Paul, 1981.

Johnson, P. *Pope John Paul II and the Catholic Restoration*. London: Weidenfeld and Nicholson, 1981.

Johnston, G., and W. Roth, eds. *The Church in the Modern World*. Toronto: University of Toronto Press, 1967.

Kavanaugh, J. *Following Christ in a Consumer Society: The Spirituality of Cultural Resistance*. Maryknoll: Orbis, 1981.

Keane, J., ed. *Civil Society and the State: New European Perspectives*. London: Verso, 1988.

Kirwan, J. *Christianising the Social Order: A Commentary on 'Mater et Magistra'*. Oxford: Catholic Social Guild, 1962.

Kirzner, I. *Discovery and the Capitalist Process*. Chicago: University Of Chicago Press, 1985.

Krąpiec, O.P., M. *I-Man: An Outline of Philosophical Anthropology*, tr. A. Woźnicki. New Britain: Mariel Publications, 1983.

Kwitny, J. *Man of the Century: The Life and Times of Pope John Paul II*. London: Little, Brown and Company, 1997.

Laba, R. *The Roots of Solidarity: A Political Sociology of Poland's Working-Class Democratization*. Princeton: Princeton University Press, 1991.

Latourelle, S.J., R. *Theology of Revelation*. Cork: Mercier Press, 1968.

Lawler, P., ed. *Papal Economics*. Washington, D.C.: Heritage Foundation, 1982.

Lawler, R. *The Christian Personalism of Pope John Paul II*. Chicago: Franciscan Herald Press, 1982.

Leonardi, R., and D. Wertman. *Italian Christian Democracy: The Politics of Dominance*. London: Macmillan, 1989.

Leslie, R., ed. *The History of Poland Since 1863*. Cambridge: Cambridge University Press, 1980.

Levine, D., ed. *Religion and Political Conflict in Latin America*. Chapel Hill: University of North Carolina Press, 1988.

Linden, I. *Back to Basics: Revisiting Catholic Social Teaching*. London: Catholic Institute for International Relations, 1994.

Lipski, J. *KOR: A History of the Workers' Defense Committee in Poland,*

1976-1981, tr. O. Amsterdamska and G. Moore. Berkeley: University of California Press, 1984.

Lobkowitz, N. *Marxism, Communism, and Western Society*, Vol. 1. New York: Herder and Herder, 1972.

Lubac, S.J., H. de. *The Drama of Atheistic Humanism*. London: Sheed and Ward, 1949.

Magister, S. *La Politica Vaticana e l'Italia, 1943-1978*. Roma: Riuniti, 1979.

Maliński, M. *Pope John Paul II: The Life of Karol Wojtyła*. London: Burn and Oates, 1979.

Malley, F. *Le Père Lebret: l'économie au service des hommes*. Paris: Éditions Spes, 1968.

Manz, J. *Vatican II: Renewal or Reform*. St. Louis: Concordia Publishing House, 1966.

Maritain, J. *Existence and the Existent*, tr. J. Fitzgerald. London: Geoffrey Bles, 1956.

——. *The Person and the Common Good*, tr. J. Fitzgerald. London: Geoffrey Bles, 1947.

——. *The Rights of Man and Natural Law*, tr. D. Anson. New York: Gordian Press, 1971.

Mattai, G. *Il Lavoro: le encicliche sociali dalla 'Rerum Novarum' alla 'Laborem Exercens'*. Padova: Edizioni Augustinus, 1981.

Mayeur, J.-M. *Catholicisime social et democratie chrétienne: Principes romains, experiences françaises*. Paris: Cerf, 1986.

Mazowiecki, T. *Rozdroża i wartości* [Crossroads and Values]. Warszawa: Więź, 1970.

McDermott, S.J., J., ed. *The Thought of Pope John Paul II: A Collection of Essays and Studies*. Rome: Editrice Pontificia Gregoriana, 1993.

McDermott, T., ed. and tr. *Aquinas: Selected Philosophical Writings*. Oxford/New York: Oxford University Press, 1993.

McGovern, S.J., A. *Marxism: An American Christian Perspective*. Maryknoll: Orbis, 1980.

McHugh, F., and S. Natal, eds. *Things Old and New: Catholic Social Teaching Revisited*. Lanham: University Press of America, 1993.

Messner, J. *Social Ethics: Natural Law in the Western World*, tr. J. Doherty. St. Louis: B. Herder Book Company, 1965.

Metz, J.B. *Zur Theologie der Welt*. Mainz: Matthais-Grünwald Verlag, 1968.

Michel, P. *Politics and Religion in Eastern Europe: Catholicism in Hungary, Poland and Czechoslovakia*, tr. A. Braley. Cambridge:

Polity, 1991.

Michnik, A. *The Church and the Left*, tr. D. Ost. Chicago: University of Chicago Press, 1993.

———. *Letters from Prison and Other Essays*, tr. D. Ost. Berkeley: University of California Press, 1986.

Misner, P. *Social Catholicism in Europe: From the Onset of Industrialization to the First World War*. London: Darton, Longman and Todd, 1991.

Molony, J. *The Emergence of Political Catholicism in Italy: Partito Popolare, 1919-1926*. Totowa: Rowman and Littlefield, 1977.

Monticone, R. *The Catholic Church in Communist Poland*. New York: Columbia University Press, 1986.

Montini, G.B. *Discorsi e scritti sul Concilio, 1959-1963*. Brescia: Instituto Paulo VI, 1983.

Moody, J., ed. *Church and Society: Catholic Social and Political Thought and Movements, 1789-1950*. New York: Arts Inc., 1952.

Mueller, F. *The Church and the Social Question*. Washington, D.C.: AEI Press, 1984.

Mulcahy, S.J., R. *The Economics of Heinrich Pesch*. New York: Holt, 1952.

Murphy, F. *The Papacy Today*. New York: Weidenfeld and Nicholson, 1981.

Myers, K., ed. *Aspiring to Freedom: Commentaries on John Paul II's Encyclical 'The Social Concerns of the Church'*. Grand Rapids: Eerdmans, 1988.

Naughton, M. *The Good Stewards: Practical Applications of the Papal Social Vision of Work*. Lanham: University Press of America, 1992.

Nell-Breuning, S.J., O. von. *Reorganization of Social Economy: The Social Encyclical Developed and Explained*. New York: Bruce, 1936.

Newman, J. *An Essay on the Development of Christian Doctrine*. Westminster: Christian Classics, 1968.

Novak, M. *The Catholic Ethic and the Spirit of Capitalism*. New York: Free Press, 1993.

———. *Free Persons and the Common Good*. Lanham: Madison Books, 1989.

———. *Freedom with Justice: Catholic Social Thought and Liberal Institutions*, 2nd ed. New Brunswick: Transaction, 1989.

———. *The Spirit of Democratic Capitalism*, 2nd ed. Lanham: Madison Books, 1991.

———. *This Hemisphere of Liberty: A Philosophy of the Americas*.

Washington, D.C.: AEI Press, 1992.

——. *Will It Liberate? Questions about Liberation Theology.* Mahwah: Paulist Press, 1986.

OECD. *Facing the Future.* Paris: OECD, 1979.

Oram, J. *The People's Pope.* Sydney: Bay Books, 1979.

Paolo VI e il rapporto Chiesa-Mondo al Concilio. Brescia: Instituto Paulo VI, 1991.

Pontifical Commission Iustitia et Pax. *At the Service of the Human Community: An Ethical Approach to the International Debt Question.* Vatican City: Libreria Editrice Vaticana, 1986.

——. *From 'Rerum Novarum' to 'Laborem Exercens': Towards the Year 2000.* Vatican City: Libreria Editrice Vaticana, 1982.

——. *International Economics: Interdependence and Dialogue.* Vatican City: Libreria Editrice Vaticana, 1984.

Pontifical Council Iustitia et Pax. *Human Rights and the Church: Historical and Theological Reflections.* Vatican City: Libreria Editrice Vaticana, 1990.

Precan, V., ed. *Krestane a Charta 77* [Christians and Charter 77]. Munich: Opus Bonum, 1980.

Raina, P. *Poland 1981: Towards Social Renewal.* London: Allen and Unwin, 1985.

Ratzinger, J., and V. Messori. *The Ratzinger Report: An Exclusive Interview on the State of the Church.* San Francisco: Ignatius Press, 1985.

Reese, S.J., T. *Inside the Vatican: The Politics and Organization of the Catholic Church.* Cambridge/London: Harvard University Press, 1996.

Rhodes, A. *The Vatican in the Age of the Cold War, 1945-1980.* Norwich: Michael Russell, 1992.

——. *The Vatican in the Age of the Dictators, 1922-1945.* London: Hodder and Stoughton, 1973.

Ricoeur, P. *The Symbolism of Evil,* tr. E. Buchanan. Boston: Beacon Press, 1967.

Riedmatten, O.P., H. de., et al. *L'église dans le monde de ce temps.* Paris: Éditions St. Paul, 1966.

Schaff, A. *Markism i jednostka* ludza [Marxism and the Human Individual]. Warszawa: PWN, 1965.

Schall, S.J., J. *The Church, the State and Society in the Thought of John Paul II.* Chicago: Franciscan Press, 1982.

——, ed. *Liberation Theology.* San Francisco: Ignatius Press, 1982.

Scheler, M. *Formalism in Ethics and Non-Formal Ethics of Values,* tr. M.

Frings and R. Funk. Evanston: Northwestern University Press, 1973.

Schmitz, K. *At the Center of the Human Drama: The Philosophical Anthropology of Karol Wojtyła/Pope John Paul II*. Washington, D.C.: Catholic University of America Press, 1994.

Schner, G. *The Church Renewed: The Documents of Vatican II Reconsidered*. Lanham: University Press of America, 1986.

Schotte, J. *Reflections on 'Laborem Exercens'*. Vatican City: Libreria Editrice Vaticana, 1982.

Schuck, M. *That They May Be One: The Social Teaching of the Papal Encyclicals, 1740-1989*. Washington, D.C.: Georgetown University Press, 1991.

Segundo, S.J., J. *Theology of the Church: A Response to Cardinal Ratzinger and a Warning to the Whole Church*. London: Chapman, 1985.

Skilling, H.G. *Samizdat and an Independent Society in Central and Eastern Europe*. London: Macmillan, 1989.

Słowaki, J. *Dzieła* [Works], Vol. 1. Wrocław: Polski Nagraria, 1959.

Stacpoole, O.S.B., A., ed. *Vatican II: By Those Who Were There*. London: Geoffrey Chapman, 1986.

Staude, J. *Max Scheler: An Intellectual Portrait*. New York: Free Press, 1967.

Stone, N., and E. Stouhal, eds. *Czechoslovakia: Crossroads and Crises*. London: Basingstoke, 1989.

Strauss, L. *Persecution and the Art of Writing*. Chicago: University Of Chicago Press, 1952.

Szajkowski, B. *Next to God . . . Poland: Politics and Religion in Contemporary Poland*. London: Pinter, 1983.

Szulc, T. *Pope John Paul II: The Biography*. New York: Scribner, 1995.

Tawney, R. H. *Religion and the Rise of Capitalism: A Historical Study*. New York: New American Library, 1958.

Tischner, J. *Marxism and Christianity in Poland: The Quarrel and the Dialogue*, tr. M. Zaleski and B. Fiore, S.J. Washington, D.C.: Georgetown University Press, 1987.

———. *The Spirit of Solidarity*, tr. M. Zaleski and B. Fiore, S.J. San Francisco: Harper and Row, 1984.

Troeltsch, E. *The Social Teaching of the Christian Churches*, Vol. 1. tr. Olive Wyon. Louisville: Westminster/John Knox Press, 1954.

Turowicz, J. *Chrześcijanin we współczesnym świecie* [The Christian in the Modern World]. Kraków: Znak, 1963. Introduction by Archbishop K. Wojtyła.

Tygodnik Solidarność, 29 special issue, 16 October 1981.

Vidler, A. *A Century of Social Catholicism, 1820-1920*. London: SPCK, 1964.

Viner, J. *Religious Thought and Economic Society: Four Chapters of an Unfinished Work*. Durham: Duke University Press, 1978.

Vorgrimler, H. ed. *Commentary on the Documents of Vatican II*, 5 vols. New York: Herder and Herder, 1969.

Wallace, L. *Leo XIII and the Rise of Socialism*. Durham: Duke University Press, 1966.

Walsh, M. and B. Davies, O.P., eds. *Proclaiming Justice and Peace: Documents from John XXIII to John Paul II*. London: CAFOD, 1991.

Weber, M. *The Protestant Ethic and the Spirit of Capitalism*, tr. T. Parsons. New York: Charles Scribner's Sons, 1958.

Weigel, G., ed. *A Century of Catholic Social Thought: Essays on 'Rerum Novarum' and Nine Other Key Documents*. Washington, D.C.: Ethics and Public Policy Center, 1991.

——. *The Final Revolution: The Resistance Church and the Collapse of Communism*. Oxford: Oxford University Press, 1992.

——. ed. *A New Worldly Order: John Paul II and Human Freedom—A 'Centesimus Annus' Reader*. Washington, D.C.: Ethics and Public Policy Center, 1992.

——. *Soul of the World: Notes on the Future of Public Catholicism*. Leominster: Gracewing, 1996.

Welty, E. *Handbook of Christian Social Ethics*. London: Herder, 1960.

Whale, J., ed. *The Pope from Poland: An Assessment*. London: Fount, 1980.

Williams, G.H. *The Contours of Church and State in the Thought of John Paul II*. Waco: Baylor University Press, 1983.

——. *The Mind of John Paul II: Origins of His Thought and Action*. New York: Seabury Press, 1981.

Windass, S., ed. and tr. *The Chronicle of the Worker-Priests*. London: Merlin Press, 1966.

Wójtowicz, A. *Osoba i Transcendencja: Karol Wojtyły antropologia wiary i Kościoła* [The Person and Transcendence: Karol Wojtyła's Anthropology of Faith and Church].Wrocław: Wydawn. Uniwersytetu Wrocławskiego, 1993.

Woźnicki, A. *A Christian Humanism: Karol Wojtyła's Existentialist Personalism*. New Britain: Mariel Publications, 1980.

——. *The Dignity of Man As Person: Essays on the Christian Humanism of John Paul II*. San Francisco: Society of Christ Publications, 1987.

Wyszyński, S. *Duch pracy ludzkiej* [The Spirit of Human Work]. Włocławek: Nakl. Katolickiego Osroda Wydawniczego 'Veritas', 1946.

Zmijewski, N. *The Catholic-Marxist Ideological Dialogue in Poland, 1945-1980.* Sydney: Dartmouth, 1991.

2. Articles

d'Apollonia, L. "Nations riches et nations pauvres." *Relations* 21, no. 3 (1961): 230–237.

Armstrong, J. "A Protestant Looks at *Centesimus Annus.*" *Journal of Business Ethics* 12, no. 12 (1993): 933–944.

Aumann, O.P., J. "Led by the Spirit: Cardinal Karol Wojtyła." *Angelicum* 56, no. 2/3 (1979): 329–347.

Bandas, R. "The Word 'Socialization' in *Mater et Magistra.*" *Priest* 17 (1961): 839–841.

Barta, R. "Work: In Search of New Meaning." *Chicago Studies* 23 (1984): 155–168.

Bauer, P. "An Economist Replies: Ecclesiastical Economics is Envy Exalted." *This World* 1 (1982): 65–74.

Baum, G. "The Anti-Cold War Encyclical." *The Ecumenist* 26, no. 2 (1989): 65–74.

———. "Capitalism *Ex Cathedra.*" *Health Progress* 73 (1991): 44–48.

———. "Class Struggle and the Magisterium: A New Note." *Theological Studies* 45, no. 4 (1984): 690–701.

———. "The Impact of Marxism on the Thought of John Paul II." *Thought* 62, no. 244 (1987): 26–38.

———. "John Paul II's Encyclical on Labor." *The Ecumenist* 19, no. 4 (1981): 3–10.

———. "A Pope from the Second World." *The Ecumenist* 18, no. 1 (1980): 22–27.

———. "The Pope's Progressive Labor Policy." *Social Policy* 13, no. 2 (1982): 12–13.

Bayer, R. "Christian Personalism and Democratic Capitalism." *Horizons* 21 (1994): 313–331.

Bednarski, O.P., F. "Les implications axiologiques et normatives de l'analyse de l'expérience moral d'après le card. Karol Wojtyła." *Angelicum* 56, no. 2/3 (1979): 245–272.

Bedoyere, Q. de la. "Man and His Work." *The Tablet* 235 (1981): 1192–1194.

Benda, V. "The Curse of Social Equality." *Rozmluvy* 3 (1984): 36–39.

Benestad, J. "The Political Vision of John Paul II: Justice through Faith and Culture." *Communio* 8 (1981): 3–13.

Biffi, F. "All'astratto homo oeconomicus la dottrina sociale cristiana oppone l'uomo concreto e storico." *Sociologia* 26, no. 2/3 (1992): 199–206.

Bloch, A. "Phenomenology and the Pope: An Incredible Misreading" (Letter to the Editor). *New York Times*, 24 December 1978, E10.

Boff, C. "The Social Teaching of the Church and the Theology of Liberation: Opposing Social Practices?" In *Christian Ethics: Uniformity, Universality, Pluralism*, edited by J. Pohier and D. Mieth. Edinburgh: T. and T. Clark, 1981.

Borowik, Z. "A Vision of the Church's Social Teaching in the Encyclical *Sollicitudo Rei Socialis*." *Christian Life in Poland* 10 (1988): 10–20.

Bowe, P. "*Centesimus Annus*." *Doctrine and Life* 41 (1991): 312–318, 324–331.

———. "*Sollicitudo Rei Socialis*: A Commentary on the Encyclical." *Doctrine and Life* 38 (1988): 227–233.

Briefs, G. "Catholic Social Doctrine, *laissez-faire* Liberalism, and Social Market Economy." *Review of Social Economy* 41, no. 3 (1983): 246–258.

Bromke, A. "The Znak Group in Poland." *East Europe* 11, no. 1/2 (1962): 10–19.

Buckley, W. "What Is the Pope Saying?" *National Review*, 18 March 1988: 17–18.

Burgalassi, S. "Dall'Homo oeconomicus alla centralità dell'uomo: *Centesimus Annus*." *Sociologia* 26, no. 2/3 (1992): 105–151.

Buttiglione, R. "Behind *Centesimus Annus*." *Crisis* 9, no. 7 (1991): 20–24.

———. "Christian Economics 101." *Crisis* 10, no. 7 (1992): 14–16.

———. "The Post-Modern Pope." *New Perspectives Quarterly* 4, no. 2 (1987): 54–59.

Byron, S.J., W. "The 1993 Pope John XXIII Lecture: The Future of Catholic Social Thought." *Catholic University Law Review* 42, no. 3 (1993): 557–569.

———. "Solidarity: Path to Development and Peace." *America* 158, no. 17 (1988): 445–447.

Calvez, S.J., J.-Y. "Théologie politique et doctrine sociale de l'église: les courants de la pensée sociale catholique en Allemagne au lendemain du Concile Vatican II." *Revue d'Allemagne* 25, no. 1 (1993): 53–62.

"Il card. Wojtyła all Cattolica di Milano." *L'Osservatore Romano*, 1 aprile

1977, 2.

"Cardinal Wyszyński Speaks to Solidarity Representatives." *Daily Report of the Foreign Broadcasting Information Service: Eastern Europe (Poland)*, 8 December 1980, G22.

Čarnogursky, J. "United Nations Symposium on *Centesimus Annus.*" *L'Osservatore Romano* (English Weekly Edition) 47 (1991), 9.

Casaroli, A. "Paolo VI e il dialogo." *Il Regno*, 11 November 1984: 594–595.

Charenteny, P. de. "Jean-Paul II et la libération integrale de l'homme: *Centesimus Annus.*" *Le Monde-Diplomatique* 38 (1991): 10–11.

Christiansen, D. "Social Justice and Consumerism in the Thought of Pope John Paul II." *Social Thought* 13, no. 2/3 (1987): 60–73.

Clark, C. "The Development of Peoples: Some Implications of the Papal Encyclical." *The Tablet*, 15 April 1967, 400–401; 13 May 1967, 536–537; 27 May 1967, 590; 3 June 1967, 619.

Composta, D. "La persona umana e la proprieta privata." *Divinitas* 23 (1979): 62–87.

Concetti, O.P., G. "The Preparation of *Rerum Novarum.*" *L'Osservatore Romano*, reprinted in *Social Survey* 41, no. 4 (1992): 114–118.

Cormie, L. "Charting the Agenda of the Church: Vatican Social Teaching in a Changing Capitalist World System." *Social Compass* 37, no. 2 (1990): 255–267.

Corrie, B. "The Papal Social Encyclical: *Centesimus Annus* of Pope John Paul II." *Challenge* 35, no. 1 (1992): 63–64.

Coste, R. "Le Travail et l'homme: L'encyclique *Laborem Exercens.*" *Esprit et vie*, 21 January 1982: 30–41.

Cottier, O.P., G. "The Church's Social Teaching as a Non-Ideology." *Communio* 8 (1981): 118–130.

Cousineau, J. "Une Civilisation chrétienne du travail." *Relations* 21, no. 3 (1961): 237–239.

Cox, H. "The Political Theology of Pope John Paul II." *Michigan Quarterly Review* 19, no. 2 (1980): 140–155.

Crosby, J. "Karol Wojtyła on the Objectivity and the Subjectivity of Moral Obligation." In *Christian Humanism: International Perspectives*, edited by R. Francis. 171–186. New York: Paulist, 1995.

——. "The Teaching of John Paul II on the Christian Meaning of Suffering." *Christian Bioethics* 2, no. 2 (1996): 154–171.

Czemarnik, A., and M. Boniecka. "A Marxist's View on the Philosophy of Peace Advanced by John Paul II." *Dialectics and Humanism* 14, no. 1 (1987): 209–217.

Darricau, R. "La Poesie de Karol Wojtyła." *Revue française d'histoire du livre* 32, no. 3 (1981): 397–417.

Dauphin-Meunier, A. "Morale chrétienne et redistribution des revenus." *Revue Internationale de Sociologie/International Review of Sociology* 7, no. 2 (1971): 756–778.

Dietrich, D. "Post-Modern Catholic Thought: Correlation between Theology and Praxis." *History of European Ideas* 20, no. 4/6 (1995): 673–679.

Dinan, S. "The Phenomenological Anthropology of Karol Wojtyła." *New Scholasticism* 55, no. 3 (1981): 317–330.

"Doktorat honoris causa księdza kardynała Karola Wojtyły (Uniwersytetu im. Jana Gutenberga w Moguncji)" [Honorary Doctorate for Cardinal Karol Wojtyła]. *Notificationes e Curia Metropolitana Cracoviensi* 9/10 (1977): 237–239.

Dorr, D. "The New Encyclical." *The Furrow* 32, no. 12 (1981): 700–712.

Dougherty, J. "The Thomistic Element in the Social Philosophy of John Paul II." *Proceedings of the American Catholic Philosophical Association* 58 (1986): 156–165.

"Drafted in French." *The Tablet*, 1 April 1967, 359.

Drane, J. "The Political Philosophical Roots of John Paul II." *America* 140, no. 20 (1979): 426–429.

Dulles, S.J., A. "The Pope and Bishops: Who Leads and How?" *The Tablet*, 28 June 1997: 836–837.

Duncan, R. "On Reading *Laborem Exercens*." *Homiletic and Pastoral Review* 86 (1986): 11–19.

Dustin, D., and C. Pire. "Politics According to John Paul II." *Revue théologique de Louvain* 26, no. 2 (1995): 243–244.

Duval, L.-E. "The Relevance of *Populorum Progressio* Today." *L'Osservatore Romano* (English Weekly Edition) 16 (1977): 4–5.

Elsbernd, M. "Whatever Happened to *Octogesima Adveniens*?" *Theological Studies* 56, no. 1 (1995): 39–60.

Elson, J. "Lives of the Pope: Roman Pontiff and Polish Priest, Philosopher and Autocrat, Sovereign, Servant, Aging Idealist." *Time*, 26 December 1994 – 2 January 1995: 36–43.

"Episcopate Meets, Urges Calm, Stabilisation." *Daily Report of the Foreign Broadcasting Information Service: Eastern Europe (Poland)*, 15 December 1980, G19.

"The Episcopate on the Pope's Encyclical." *Daily Report of the Foreign Broadcasting Information Service: Eastern Europe (Poland)*, 16 September 1981, G5.

Etchegaray, R. "Presentation at the Press Conference for the Publication of *Centesimus Annus*." *L'Osservatore Romano* (English Weekly Edition) 18 (1991): 1, 4.

——. "Presentation at the Press Conference for the Publication of *Sollicitudo Rei Socialis*." *L'Osservatore Romano* (English Weekly Edition) 9 (1988), 4.

Evans, E. "The Vatican's Foreign Policy after the Collapse of Soviet Communism." *World Affairs* 155, no. 1 (1992): 27–30.

Evans, M. "How 'Catholic' is Liberal Catholicism?" *Priests and People* 3, no. 7 (1989): 47–54.

Faley, R. "Pope as Prophet: The New Social Encyclical." *America* 158, no. 17 (1988): 447–451.

Faulhaber, R. "The Church and Culture: John Paul II's *On Human Work*." *Listening* 18, no. 1 (1983): 103–118.

Fedoryka, D. "The 'Third Way' of *Centesimus Annus*: Is It Elusive or Merely an Illusion?" *Social Justice Review* 83, no. 11/12 (1992): 151–164.

Finnis, J. "Catholic Social Teaching Since *Populorum Progressio* – 1." *Social Survey* 27, no. 7 (1978): 213–220.

——. "Catholic Social Teaching Since *Populorum Progressio* – 2." *Social Survey* 27, no. 8 (1978): 250–254.

——. "Faith and Morals: A Note." *The Month* 21 (1988): 563–567.

——. "The Fundamental Themes of *Laborem Exercens*." In *Catholic Social Thought and the Teaching of John Paul II: Proceedings of the Fifth Convention (1982) of the Fellowship of Catholic Scholars*, edited by P. Williams. 20–31. Chicago: Northeast Books, 1983.

——. "Goods Are Meant for Everyone." *L'Osservatore Romano* (English Weekly Edition) 12 (1988), 11.

——. "Letters to the Editor." *The Tablet*, 14 December 1991, 1544–1545; 4 January 1992, 14; 18 January 1992, 70–71; 1 February 1992, 140; 8 February 1992, 170.

Fisher, O.P., A. "An Ethic of Life for the Public Square." *The Tablet*, 9 August 1997: 1025–1027.

Fonseca, A. "Reflections on the Encyclical Letter *Sollicitudo Rei Socialis*." *Gregorianum* 70, no. 1 (1989): 5–24.

Fortin, E. "From *Rerum Novarum* to *Centesimus Annus*: Continuity or Discontinuity." *Faith and Reason* 17 (1991): 411–420.

——. "Markets Have Their Limits: Two Cheers for Capitalism." *Crisis* 10, no. 11 (1992): 20–25.

——. "Natural Law and Social Justice." *American Journal of*

Jurisprudence 30, no. 1 (1985): 1–20.

——. "'Sacred and Inviolable': *Rerum Novarum* and Natural Rights." *Theological Studies* 53, no. 2 (1992): 203–233.

Forycki, R. "Antropologia w ujęciu Kard. Karola Wojtyły (na podstawie książki *Osoba i czyn*)" [Anthropology in the Thought of Cardinal Karol Wojtyła (Based on the book *The Acting Person*)]. *Analecta Cracoviensia* 5/6 (1973/1974): 117–124.

Fouilloux, E. "Vatican II et ses papes." *Vingtième Siècle* 13 (1987): 120–124.

Gałkowski, O.P., J. "Natura, osoba, wolność" [Nature, Person, Freedom]. *Analecta Cracoviensia* 5/6 (1973/1974): 177–182.

——. "The Place of Thomism in the Anthropology of Karol Wojtyła." *Angelicum* 65, no. 2 (1988): 181–194.

Garelli, F. "Cent'ani dopo: il ruolo della Chiesa nelle trasformazioni sociali." *Quaderni di Sociologia* 36, no. 1 (1992): 97–104.

Gawronski, J. "Io, il Papa tra l'Ovest e l'Est." *La Stampa*, 2 November 1993: 1–2.

Gendreau, B. "The Integral Humanism of Maritain and the Personalism of John Paul II." In *J. Maritain: A Philosopher*, edited by J.-L. Allard. 128–135. Ottawa: University of Ottawa Press, 1986.

Gini, A. "Meaningful Work and the Rights of the Worker: A Commentary on *Rerum Novarum* and *Laborem Exercens*." *Thought* 67, no. 266 (1992): 225–239.

Ginsburg, H. "The Teachings of John Paul II on Work and the Rights of Workers." *Social Thought* 13, no. 2/3 (1987): 46–59.

Gledhill, R. "Pope Gives Warning against Unbridled Capitalism: Encyclical Charts Fall of Marxism." *The Times*, 3 May 1991: 11, 19.

Gogacz, M. "Hermeneutyka *Osoby i czynu*" [The Hermeneutics of *The Acting Person*]. *Analecta Cracoviensia* 5/6 (1973/1974): 125–138.

Grémillion, J. "L'enciclica e la Commissione Giustizia e Pace." *L'Osservatore Romano*, 23 aprile 1967: 1–2.

——. "The Fifth Anniversary of *Populorum Progressio*." *L'Osservatore Romano* (English Weekly Edition) 15, 1972: 3–4.

Grygiel, S. "Hermeneutyka czynu oraz nowy model świadomości" [The Hermeneutics of Action and the New Model of Consciousness]. *Analecta Cracoviensia* 5/6 (1973/1974): 139–151.

Gutiérrez, G. "El Evangelio del Trabajo." In *Sobre el Trabajo Humano*, edited by C.E.P. 53–57. Lima: C.E.P., 1982.

Habiger, O.S.B., M. "Reflections on *Centesimus Annus*." *Social Justice Review* 82, no. 2 (1991): 139–142.

——. "Situating *Sollicitudo Rei Socialis* in Catholic Social Teaching." *Social Justice Review* 79, no. 2 (1988): 138–144.

Hauerwas, S. "In Praise of *Centesimus Annus.*" *Theology* 95, no. 768 (1992): 416–432.

Havel, V. "The State of the Republic." *New York Review of Books* 45, no. 17 (1998): 42–46.

Hebblethwaite, P. "Husserl, Scheler and Wojtyła: A Tale of Three Philosophers." *Heythrop Journal* 27, no. 4 (1986): 441–445.

——. Karol Jekyll and Hyde-Wojtyła Debate Capitalism." *National Catholic Reporter*, 10 May 1991: 4–6.

——. "Labor Encyclical: Worker, Not Capital, Key to Moral Order." *National Catholic Reporter*, 25 September 1981: 3–4.

——. "Liberation and John Paul II: The Vatican's Perception of Latin America." *Index on Censorship* 12, no. 5 (1983): 9–12.

——. "Pope John Paul II As Philosopher and Poet." *Heythrop Journal* 21, no. 2 (1980): 123–136.

——. "The Popes and Politics: Shifting Patterns in Catholic Social Doctrine." *Daedalus* 11, no. 1 (1982): 85–99.

——. "*Sollicitudo Rei Socialis.*" *National Catholic Reporter*, 26 February 1988, 7.

Heckel, R. "Continuity and Renewal." *L'Osservatore Romano* (English Weekly Edition) 40 (1981): 4–5.

——. "*Populorum Progressio* Today." *L'Osservatore Romano* (English Weekly Edition) 17 (1977), 9.

Hehir, J.B. "Church-State and Church-World." *Proceedings of the Catholic Theological Society of America* 41 (1986): 54–74.

——. "Papal Foreign Policy." *Foreign Policy* 78 (1990): 26–48.

——. "Taking on the Super-Rivals: Reactions to the Pope's Latest Encyclical." *Commonweal* 115 (1988): 169–170.

——. "Vatican II and the Signs of the Times: Catholic Teaching on Church, State and Society." In *Religion and Politics in the American Milieu*, edited by L. Griffin. 183–194. Notre Dame: University of Notre Dame Press, 1986.

Hellman, J. "John Paul II and the Personalist Movement." *Cross Currents* 30, no. 4 (1980/1981): 409–419.

——. "The Prophets of Solidarity." *America* 147, no. 14 (1982): 266–269.

Higgins, G. "The Condition of Labor Today in the Light of One Hundred Years of Catholic Social Teaching." *Social Thought* 17, no. 2 (1991): 39–51.

Hiscocks, R. "Some Liberal Marxists and Left-Wing Catholics in

Contemporary Poland." *Canadian Journal of Economics and Political Science* 30, no. 1 (1964): 12–21.

Hittinger, R. "The Pope and the Liberal State." *First Things* 28 (1992): 33–41.

——. "The Problem of the State in *Centesimus Annus.*" *Fordham International Law Journal* 15, no. 4 (1991/1992): 952–996.

Hollenbach, S.J., D. "Christian Social Ethics after the Cold War." *Theological Studies* 53, no. 1 (1992): 74–100.

Hoy, T. "Gustavo Gutiérrez: Latin American Liberation Theology." *International Journal of Social Economics* 13, no. 9 (1986): 3–16.

Huerga, O.P., A. "Karol Wojtyła: Commentador de San Juan de la Cruz." *Angelicum* 56, no. 2/3 (1979): 348–366.

Hug, S.J., J. "*Centesimus Annus*: Rescuing the Challenge, Probing the Vision." *Center Focus* 102 (1991): 1–9.

Huntington, S. "Religion and the Third Wave." *The National Interest* 24 (1991): 29–42.

Hurley, M. "*Centesimus Annus.*" *America* 165, no. 12 (1991): 291–292.

Illanes, J. "Trabajo, historia y persona: Elementos para una teología del trabajo en la *Laborem Exercens.*" *Scripta theologica* 15, no. 1 (1983): 205–232.

Jarlot, G. "L'Église et le développement, l'encyclique *Populorum Progressio.*" *Etudes*, mai (1967): 674–688.

Jaworski, M. "Koncepja antropologii filozoficznej w ujęciu Kardynała Wojtyły" [The Conception of Philosophical Anthropology in the Thought of Cardinal Wojtyła]. *Analecta Cracoviensia* 5/6 (1973/1974): 91–106.

——. "Sartre, l'uomo e Papa Wojtyła." *CSEO documentazione* 143 (1979): 2–15.

Jeannet, T. "The Dialogue Continues: *On Human Work* and Marxism." *Logos* 5, no. 1 (1984): 41–66.

Joblin, S.J., J. "La Doctrine sociale de l'église est-elle universelle?" *Gregorianum* 74, no. 4 (1993): 659–687.

John Paul II. "Confronting the Challenges of Our Time." *L'Osservatore Romano* (English Weekly Edition) 18 (1991): 3–4.

——. "Homily at Mass for Youth (Belo Horizonte, Brazil)." *L'Osservatore Romano* (English Weekly Edition) 27 (1980): 1.

——. "Speech to Scholars at the Catholic University of Lublin." *L'Osservatore Romano* (English Weekly Edition) 27 (1987): 2.

Johnson, T. "Capitalism after Communism: John Paul Sets Foundation for Meaningful Dialogue." *America* 165, no. 12 (1991): 290–291.

Judt, T. "Holy Warrior." *New York Review of Books* 43, no. 17 (1996): 8–14.

Kaczyński, O.P., E. "Il 'Momento della verità' nella riflessione di Karol Wojtyła." *Angelicum* 56, no. 2/3 (1979): 273–296.

——. "Prawda o dobru w koncepcji moralności Kard. K. Wojtyły" [The Truth about Good in the Moral Conception of Card. K. Wojtyła]. *Roczniki Filozoficzne* 28, no. 2 (1980): 47–71.

Kalinowski, G. "Autour de *The Acting Person*." *Revue Thomiste* 82, no. 4 (1982): 626–633.

——. "Edith Stein et Karol Wojtyła sur la personne." *Revue philosophique de Louvain* 82, no. 4 (1984): 545–561.

——. "Karol Wojtyła face à Max Scheler ou l'origine de *Osoba i Czyn*." *Revue Thomiste* 80, no. 3 (1980): 456–465.

——. "Metafizyka i fenomenologia osoby ludzkiej. Pytania wywolane przez *Osobą i czyn*" [The Metaphysics and Phenomenology of the Human Person: Questions Evoked by *The Acting Person*]. *Analecta Cracoviensia* 5/6 (1973/1974): 63–71.

——. "La Pensée philosophique de Karol Wojtyła et la faculté de philosophie de l'Université Catholique de Lublin." *Aletheia* 4 (1988): 198–216.

——. "La Réforme du thomisme et de la phénoménologie chez Karol Wojtyła selon Rocco Buttiglione." *Archives de philosophie* 49, no. 1 (1986): 127–146.

Kalvoda, J. "Karol Wojtyła, Marxism, and the Marxist-Leninists." *Nationalities Papers* 10, no. 2 (1982): 203–219.

Kennedy, E. "America's Activist Bishops: Examining Capitalism." *New York Times Magazine*, 12 November 1984: 14–30.

Kiliroor, M. "Social Doctrine in *Sollicitudo Rei Socialis*." *The Month* 21 (1988): 711–714.

Kim, A. "The Vatican, Marxism and Liberation Theology." *Cross Currents* 34, no. 4 (1984/1985): 439–455.

Kirwan, J. "How the Pope Planned for Revolutions." *Priests and People* 5, no. 5 (1991): 169–172.

Kitchel, J.-C. "The Value of Human Suffering: Pope John Paul II and Karol Wojtyła." *Proceedings of the American Catholic Philosophical Association* 58 (1986): 185–193.

Kłósak, K. "Theoria doświadczenia człowieku w ujęciu Kard. Karola Wojtyły" [The Theory of Human Experience in the Thought of Cardinal Karol Wojtyła]. *Analecta Cracoviensia* 5/6 (1973/1974): 81–84.

Klose, A. "Geistige Grundlagen der Sozialpartnerschaft im katholischen Sozialdenken" [The Intellectual Foundations of Social Partnership in Catholic Social Thought]. *Wiener Beiträge zur Geschichte der Neuzeit* 12/13 (1985/1986): 53–68.

Köchler, H. "The Dialectical Conception of Self-Determination: Reflections on the Systematic Approach of Cardinal Karol Wojtyła." *Analecta Husserliana* 6 (1977): 75–80.

———. "The Phenomenology of Karol Wojtyła: On the Problem of the Phenomenological Foundation of Anthropology." *Philosophy and Phenomenological Research* 42, no. 3 (1981/1982): 326–334.

Kołakowski, L. "Jezus Chrystus—prorok i reformator" [Jesus Christ: Prophet and Reformer]. *Argumenty* 51/52 (1965): 19–26.

Kondziela, J. "The Democracy of Workers in the Light of John Paul II's Encyclical *Laborem Exercens*." *Dialectics and Humanism* 14, no. 1 (1987): 49–55.

Kowalczyk, S. "Personalisme polonais contemporain." *Divus Thomas* 88, no. 1/3 (1985): 58–76.

———. "Personalist and Universalistic Aspects of the Idea of Development in the Encyclical *Sollicitudo Rei Socialis*." *Dialogue and Humanism* 4, no. 2/3 (1994): 93–105.

———. "Tomistyczno-fenomenologiczny personalizm Kard. Karola Wojtyły" [The Thomistic-Phenomenological Personalism of Cardinal Karol Wojtyła]. *Ateneum Kapłańskie* 77, no. 2 (1985): 84–95.

Krąpiec, O.P., M. "Książki kardynała Karola Wojtyły monografią osoby jako podmiotu moralności" [Cardinal Karol Wojtyła's Works: A Monograph on the Person as the Subject of Morality]. *Analecta Cracoviensia* 5/6 (1973/1974): 57–61.

Krucina, J. "Koncepcja wyzwolenia w nauczaniu Jana Pawła II" [The Conception of Liberation in the Teaching of John Paul II]. *Colloquium Salutis* 14 (1982): 105–120.

Kuczyński, J. "John Paul II's Manifesto on Labor and Vision of a Universal Society." *Dialogue and Humanism* 4, no. 2/3 (1994): 107–117.

———. "To Elevate the World: The Potential of John Paul II's Pontificate." *Dialectics and Humanism* 6, no. 1 (1979): 5–27.

Kung, G. "Man As an Active Agent: On the New Pope's Work As a Philosopher." *Universitas* 21, no. 2 (1979): 105–117.

Lacoste, J.-Y. "Vérité et liberté: Sur la philosophie de la personne chez Karol Wojtyła." *Revue Thomiste* 81, no. 3 (1981): 586–614.

Ladriere, P. "La Révolution française dans la doctrine politique des papes de la fin du XVIIIe a la moitie du XXe siècle." *Archives de Sciences Sociales des Religions* 33 (1988): 87–112.

Laje, E. "El sentido de 'Socializacion' en *Laborem Exercens.*" *Stromata* 38, no. 1 (1982): 117–126.

Lavigne, J.-C. "Une Encyclique peut en cacher une autre: de *Populorum Progressio* a *Sollicitudo Rei Socialis.*" *Economie et Humanisme* 302, juillet-août (1988): 47–52.

Lawler, R. "Experience As the Foundation of Karol Wojtyła's Personalist Ethics." *Proceedings of the American Catholic Philosophical Association* 58 (1986): 148–155.

Leech, K. "Some Recent Trends in Catholic Social Theology." *Theology* 88, no. 725 (1985): 365–374.

Lefébure, O.P., M. "Private Property According to St. Thomas and Recent Papal Encyclicals." In *St. Thomas Aquinas, Summa Theologiae*, Vol. 38, *Injustice*. 275–283. Edinburgh: University of Edinburgh Press, 1975.

Legutko, R. "Pokusa totalnego liberalizmu" [The Temptation of Total Laissez-faire]. *Znak* 37, no. 8 (1985): 1077–1094.

Lenches, E. "*Centesimus Annus*: Towards a New Capitalism?" *International Journal of Social Economics* 20, no. 2 (1993): 27–50.

Lepargneur, F.-H. "*Mater et Magistra* et les pays sous-developpés: pour une doctrine efficace sur l'etat." *Informations Catholiques internationales* 15 (1961): 3–4, 32.

Lévinas, E. "Note sul pensiero filosofico del Cardinale Wojtyła." *Communio* 7 (1980): 99–105.

Liszka, J. "The Philosophical Thought of Cardinal Karol Wojtyła." *Polish Review* 24, no. 2 (1979): 27–34.

Loades, A. "On *Centesimus Annus.*" *Theology* 95 (1992): 405–432.

Lobato, O.P., A. "La persona en el pensamiento de Karol Wojtyła." *Angelicum* 56, no. 2/3 (1979): 166–210.

Lubian, W. "To Penetrate the Deepest Layers of Morality: Karol Wojtyła's Ethics." *Christian Life in Poland* 1 (1987): 39–46.

Lustig, B. A. "Property and Justice in the Modern Encyclical Literature." *Harvard Theological Review* 83, no. 4 (1990): 415–446.

Lynn, T. "Of Politics, Catholics and the Social Doctrine." *Social Justice Review* 84, no. 1 (1993): 18–21.

Maheu, R. "L'UNESCO et l'encyclique *Populorum Progressio.*" *La Documentation Catholique* 64 (1967): 1021–1028.

Mahoney, R. "Perspectives for Viewing the Social Concerns Encyclical." *Origins* 18 (1988): 69–72.

Majka, J. "Praca w rozwoju osobowości człowieka na podstawie encykliki *Laborem Exercens*" [Labor in the Development of Man's Personality according to the Encyclical *Laborem Exercens*]. *Chrześcijanin w świecie* 14, no. 6 (1982): 1–8.

——. "Społeczne wymiary grzechu" [The Social Dimension of Sin]. *Colloquium Salutis* 10 (1978): 33–46.

Marczewski, A. "Man in the Face of Fundamental Questions: Encounters with Karol Wojtyła's Dramaturgy." *Dialectics and Humanism* 10, no. 1 (1983): 111–118.

Margiotta Broglio, F. "Il papato degli ultimi cinquant'anni. Dalla 'nuova cristianita' di Pio XII alla geopolitica di Karol Wojtyła." *Rivista di Studi Politici Internazionali* 56, no. 1 (1989): 47–56.

Marzani, C. "The Vatican As a Left Ally?" *Monthly Review* 34, no. 1 (1982): 1–42.

Masiello, R. "A Note on Transcendence in *The Acting Person*." *Doctor Communis* 35, no. 4 (1982): 327–335.

Mavrodes, G. "Property." *Personalist* 53, no. 3 (1972): 245–262.

McCormick, P. "That They May Converse: Voices of Catholic Social Thought." *Cross Currents* 42, no. 4 (1992): 521–527.

McGovern, S.J., A. "Marxism, Liberation Theology and John Paul II." *Logos* 5, no. 1 (1984): 5–24.

——. "Pope John Paul II on Human Work." *Telos* 57/58 (1983/1984): 215–218.

McGovern, S.J., A., J. Kelly, J. Varacalli, and J. Casanova. "A Symposium on the Catholic Ethic and the Spirit of Socio-Economic Justice." *International Journal of Politics, Culture and Society* 6, no. 2 (1992): 299–329.

McGregor, B. "Commentary on *Evangelii Nuntiandi*." *Doctrine and Life* 27 (1977): 70–71.

McHugh, F. "A Century of Catholic Social Teaching." *Priests and People* 5, no. 5 (1991): 173–178.

McKee, A. "The Market Principle and Roman Catholic Thought." *Kyklos* 17 (1964): 65–68.

Mertens, C. "La Participation des travaillieurs à la vie de l'enterprise." *Relations* 21, no. 3 (1961): 239–241.

Min, A. "John Paul II: Anthropology of Concrete Totality." *Proceedings of the American Catholic Philosophical Association* 56 (1984): 120–129.

Misner, P. "The Predecessors of *Rerum Novarum* within Catholicism." *Review of Social Economy* 49, no. 4 (1991): 444–464.

Modras, R. "A Man of Contradictions: The Early Writings of Karol Wojtyła." In *The Church in Anguish: Has the Vatican Betrayed Vatican II?* edited by H. Küng and L. Swidler. 39–51. San Francisco: Harper and Row, 1987.

———. "The Thomistic Personalism of Pope John Paul II." *The Modern Schoolman* 59, no. 2 (1982): 117–127.

Montini, G.B. "Le Magistère pastoral de S.S. Pie XII." *La Documentation Catholique* 57 (1957): 1147–1148.

Mounier, E. "L'Ordre regne-t-il a Varsovie?" *Esprit* 6 (1946): 970–1003.

Mueller, F. "Catholic Social Doctrine between Scylla and Charybdis? Some Comments on Two Books." *Review of Social Economy* 44, no. 1 (1986): 40–56.

———. "Labor before Capital: Comment on the Encyclical *Laborem Exercens.*" *Review of Social Economy* 42, no. 1 (1984): 69–71.

———. "Random Comments on the Economics of *Rerum Novarum.*" *Review of Social Economy* 49, no. 4 (1991): 502–513.

———. "Three Stages of Encyclical Social Philosophy: *Rerum Novarum, Quadragesimo Anno* and *Mater et Magistra.*" *Social Justice Review* 54, no. 2 (1961): 184–188.

Murphy, C. "Action for Justice as Constitutive of the Preaching of the Gospel: What Did the 1971 Synod Mean?" *Theological Studies* 44, no. 2 (1983): 299–311.

Murphy, J. " 'Marxism, Liberation Theology and John Paul II': A Critical Assessment." *Logos* 5, no. 1 (1984): 25–28.

Muscari, P. "On Human Nature: A Look at the Subject from Karol Wojtyła's work *The Acting Person.*" *Journal of Mind and Behavior* 9, no. 1 (1988): 13–28.

Mysłek, W. "Zwrot w katolickiej interpretacji pracy" [Change in the Catholic Interpretation of Work]. *Studia filozoficzne* 4 (1977): 121–128.

Nash, J. "Questioning the Efficacy of One Hundred Years of Catholic Social Teaching: The Intrinsic Connection between Faith and Justice." *Social Thought* 17, no. 2 (1991): 52–64.

Naughton, M. "The Virtuous Manager and *Centesimus Annus.*" *Social Justice Review* 85, no. 2 (1994): 150–152.

Nell-Breuning, S.J., O. von. "Politische theologie papst Johannes Pauls II" [Pope John Paul II's Political Theology]. *Stimmen der Zeit* 198 (1980): 675–686.

Neuhaus, R. "John Paul's 'Second Thoughts' on Capitalism." *First Things* 41 (1994): 65–67.

———. "The Mind of the Most Powerful Man in the World." *Worldview* 24, no. 9 (1981): 11–16.

———. "The Pope Affirms the New Capitalism." *Wall Street Journal*, 3 May 1991: 1, 2.

Nitsch, T. "Social Catholicism, Marxism and Liberation Theology: From Antithesis to Coexistence, Coalescence and Synthesis." *International Journal of Social Economics* 13, no. 9 (1986): 52–74.

Northcott, M. "Preston and Hauerwas on *Centesimus Annus*: Reflections on the Incommensurability of the Liberal and Post-Liberal Mind." *Theology* 96, no. 769 (1993): 27–35.

Nota, J. "Max Scheler and Karol Wojtyła." *Proceedings of the American Catholic Philosophical Association* 58 (1986): 135–147.

Novak, M. "The Creative Person." *Journal of Business Ethics* 12, no. 12 (1993): 975–979.

———. "The Economic System: The Evangelical Basis of a Social Market Economy." *Review of Politics* 43, no. 3 (1981): 355–380.

Nowacki, O.P., H. "Karol Wojtyła e la teologia nella Chiesa postconciliare." *Angelicum* 56, no. 2/3 (1979): 387–408.

Nowaczyk, M. "Karol Wojtyła's Social Thought." *Dialectics and Humanism* 6, no. 4 (1979): 79–92.

Nuesse, J. "Before *Rerum Novarum*: A Moral Theologian's View of Catholic Social Movements in 1891." *Social Thought* 17, no. 2 (1991): 5–17.

O'Connor, D. "An Economic Evaluation of John Paul II's Encyclical *On Social Concerns*." *Social Justice Review* 79, no. 1 (1988): 131–137.

Olejnik, S. "Karol Wojtyła, theologien éminent, contemporain, polonais." *Collectanea theologica* 50, special issue (1980): 11–33.

O'Malley, S.J., J. "Developments, Reforms and Two Great Reformations: Towards a Historical Assessment of Vatican II." *Theological Studies* 44, no. 2 (1983): 373–406.

Ombres, O.P., R. "The Roman Curia Reorganised." *Priests and People* 3, no. 7 (1989): 59–65.

Pappin, J. "*The Acting Person*: John Paul II." *Thomist* 45, no. 3 (1981): 472–480.

———. "Karol Wojtyła and Jean-Paul Sartre on the Intentionality of Consciousness." *Proceedings of the American Catholic Philosophical Association* 58 (1986): 130–139.

Paulus, N. "Uses and Misuses of the Term 'Social Justice' in the Roman Catholic Tradition." *Journal of Religious Ethics* 15, no. 3 (1987): 261–282.

Pell, G. "*Rerum Novarum*: One Hundred Years Later." A modified version of a paper originally presented at the first *Boston Conversazione* held at 'The Castle', Boston University, 4 February 1991.

Phillips, R. "Communitarianism, the Vatican, and the New Global Order." *Ethics and International Affairs* 5 (1991): 135–147.

Pinto de Oliveira, C. "L'Esprit agit dans l'histoire. La totalisation hegelienne de l'histoire confrontée avec les perspectives du Concile de Vatican II." In *Hegel et la théologie contemporaine: L'absolu dans l'historie*, edited by L. Rumpf. Neufchâtel/Paris: Aubier, 1977.

Piwowarczynk, J. "Ku Katolickiej Polsce." *Tygodnik Powszechny* 1, no. 1 (1945), 1.

Piwowarski, W. "Social Motives in the Teaching of John Paul II." *Christian Life in Poland* 5 (1989): 44–53.

Półtawski, A. "Człowiek a świadomość w związku z książką Kard. Karola Wojtyły *Osoba i Czyn*" [Man and Consciousness in Cardinal Karol Wojtyła's Book *The Acting Person*]. *Analecta Cracoviensia* 5/6 (1973/1974): 159–175.

——. "The Epistemological Basis of Karol Wojtyła's Philosophy." *Proceedings of the American Catholic Philosophical Association* 60 (1988): 79–91.

——. "Freedom and Dignity in the Work of Karol Wojtyła." *Aletheia* 4 (1988): 235–241.

——. "Phenomenological Personalism: Edith Stein and Karol Wojtyła." *Kwartalnik Filozoficzne* 23, no. 1 (1995): 33–44.

Pontifical Commission Iustitia et Pax, "*Populorum Progressio* à l'heure du nouvel ordre international." *La Documentation Catholique* 74 (1977): 473–475.

Pontifical Council for Social Communications. "Ethics in Advertising." *L'Osservatore Romano* (English Weekly Edition) 14 (1997), Special Insert.

Porta, P. "Il papa e il mercato." *Rivista Internazionale di Scienze Economiche e Commerciali* 38, no. 8 (1991): 657–662.

Poulat, E., and C. Bouteloupt. "Un Nouveau Fonds d'archives: les papiers du père Lebret." *Revue d'Histoire Ecclésiastique* 78, no. 2 (1983): 468–472.

Poupard, P. "A Message That Illumines the Conscience of the World: *Populorum Progressio*—Ten Years Later." *L'Osservatore Romano* (English Weekly Edition) 17 (1977), 9.

Preston, R. "*Centesimus Annus*: An Appraisal." *Theology* 95, no. 768 (1992): 405–416.

——. "Pope John Paul II on Work." *Theology* 86, no. 709 (1983): 19–24.

——. "Twenty Years after *Populorum Progressio*: An Appraisal of Pope John Paul's Commemorative Encyclical." *Theology* 92, no. 750 (1989): 519–525.

Pryor, F. "The Roman Catholic Church and the Economic System: A Review Essay." *Journal of Comparative Economics* 17, no. 1 (1993): 129–150.

Ratzinger, J. "Consumer Materialism and Christian Hope." *Briefing* 18, no. 3 (1988): 43–50.

——. "Freedom and Liberation: The Anthropological Vision of the Instruction *Libertatis Conscientia.*" *Communio* 14 (1987): 64–69.

"Redakcyjny." *Tygodnik Powszechny* 4, no. 25 (1948): 5.

Reed, D. "Critical Theory and the Catholic Church's Ambivalence about Capitalism." *International Journal of Social Economics* 22, no. 2 (1995): 19–39.

Reimers, A. "The Thomistic Personalism of Karol Wojtyła." In *Atti del IX Congresso tomistico internazionnale*, Vol. 6, edited by A. Piolanti. 364-369. Città del Vaticano: Libreria Editrice Vaticana, 1992.

Riedmatten, O.P., H. de. "For an Evangelical Reading of *Populorum Progressio.*" *L'Osservatore Romano* (English Weekly Edition) 17 (1977), 8.

Rimoldi, A. "Bibliografia sull'episcopato Milanese del Card. G.B. Montini, 1955-1963." In *G.B. Montini arcivescovo*. 347–356. Milano: Nuove Edizioni Duomo, 1983.

Rogaly, J. "The Papacy and Political Economy." *Financial Times*, 3 May 1991, 15.

Ryan, L. "The Modern Popes as Social Reformers." *The Furrow* 42, no. 2 (1991): 86–90.

Safire, W. "Structures of Sin." *New York Times*, 22 February 1988, A–19.

Salleron, L. "Jean-Paul II explique par Karol Wojtyła." *La Pensée Catholique* 192, mai-juin (1981): 62–69.

Schall, S.J., J. "The Call Contained in the Being of Things: The Import of John Paul II's *Centesimus Annus.*" *Vital Speeches* 58 (1992): 213–217.

——. "The Teaching of *Centesimus Annus.*" *Gregorianium* 74, no. 1 (1993): 17–43.

——. "To Defend and to Teach: The Intellectual Legacy of Paul VI." *Lay Witness* 15, no. 11 (1993): 1–7.

——. "The Unexpected Encyclical: On the Extraordinary Uniqueness of *Centesimus Annus.*" *Social Justice Review* 82, no. 2 (1991): 143–147.

Schotte, J. "The Social Teaching of the Church: *Laborem Exercens*, a New

Challenge." *Review of Social Economy* 40, no. 3 (1982): 354–359.

Schroeder, W. "Oswald von Nell-Breuning: der Jesuit, der Katholizismus und die Arbeiterbewegung" [Oswald von Nell-Breuning: The Jesuit, Catholicism and the Labor Movement]. *Internationale Wissenschaftliche Korrespondenz zur Geschichte der Deutschen Arbeiterbewegung* 26, no. 1 (1990): 34–49.

Schroeffer, J. "Continuity of the Conciliar and Pontifical Magisterium: From *Gaudium et Spes* to *Populorum Progressio.*" *L'Osservatore Romano* (English Weekly Edition) 17 (1977): 6–7.

Seifert, J. "Karol Cardinal Wojtyła (Pope John Paul II) As Philosopher and the Cracow/Lublin School of Philosophy." *Aletheia* 2 (1981): 130–199.

——. "Truth, Freedom, and Love in Wojtyła's Philosophical Anthropology and Ethics." In *Philosophy and Culture*, Vol. 4, edited by V. Cauchy. 317–329. Montreal: University of Montreal Press, 1988.

Seligman, D. "Unfair to Capitalism." *Fortune*, November, 1981: 60–65.

Selling, J. "The Theological Presumptions of *Centesimus Annus.*" *Louvain Studies* 17 (1991): 35–44.

"Seminar on Pope John Paul's Encyclical *Sollicitudo Rei Socialis.*" *L'Osservatore Romano* (English Weekly Edition) 45 (1988), Supplement.

Serretti, M. "La cons123ienza in Karol Wojtyła." *Sapienza* 36, no. 2 (1983): 187–203.

——. "Etica e antropologica filosofia. Considerazioni su Maritain e Wojtyła." *Sapienza* 38, no. 1 (1985): 15–31.

Sethi, S., and P. Steidmeiser. "Religion's Moral Compass and a Just Economic Order: Reflections on Pope John Paul II's Encyclical *Centesimus Annus.*" *Journal of Business Ethics* 12, no. 12 (1993): 901–917.

Sieger Derr, T. "The Economic Thought of the World Council of Churches." *This World* 1 (1982): 20–33.

Siemek, M. "Poland: Philosophy and Society." *Studies in Soviet Thought* 42, no. 3 (1991): 221–234.

Sienkiewicz, M. "Wojtyła's 'Our God's Brother'." *Theatre en Pologne—Theatre in Poland* 23, no. 4 (1981): 3–11.

Skok, C. "The Social Economics of *Gaudium et Spes.*" *International Journal of Social Economics* 13, no. 9 (1986): 25–44.

Ślipko, T. "Le Développement de la pensée éthique du Cardinal Karol Wojtyła." *Collectanea Theologica* 50, special issue (1980): 61–87.

Sorgia, O.P., R. "Approccio con l'opera prima di K. Wojtyła." *Angelicum* 57, no. 3 (1980): 401–423.

Spader, P. "The Primacy of the Heart: Scheler's Challenge to Phenomenology." *Philosophy Today* 29 (1985): 223–229.

Spiazzi, R. "Gospel of Work and the Dignity of Man." *L'Osservatore Romano* (English Weekly Edition) 41 (1981): 9–10.

Stępień, A. "Fenomenologia tomizujaca w książce *Osoba i czyn*" [Phenomenology Made Thomistic in *The Acting Person*]. *Analecta Cracoviensia* 5/6 (1973/1974): 153–157.

Stomma, S. "Maksymalne i minimale tendencjé społeczne w Polsce." *Znak* 1, no. 1 (1945), 12.

Styczeń, T. "Metoda antropologii filozoficznej w *Osobie i Czynie* Kardynała Karola Wojtyły" [The Method of Philosophical Anthropology Used in Cardinal Karol Wojtyła's *The Acting Person*]. *Analecta Cracoviensia* 5/6 (1973/1974): 113–115.

———. "O metodzie antropolgii filozoficznej. Na marginesie *Osoby i czynu*" [The Philosophical Anthropological Method: On the Margins of *The Acting Person*]. *Roczniki Filozoficzne* 21, no. 2 (1973): 105–114.

———. "Reply to Kalinowski: By Way of an Addendum to the Addenda." *Aletheia* 4 (1988): 217–225.

Sullivan, B. "*Laborem Exercens*: A Theological and Philosophical Foundation for Business Ethics." *Listening* 20, no. 1 (1985): 128–146.

Suro, R. "Papal Encyclical Says Superpowers Hurt Third World." *New York Times*, 20 February 1988, 1.

Świeżawski, S. "Karol Wojtyła at the Catholic University of Lublin." In *Person and Community: Selected Essays*, edited and translated by T. Sandok, O.S.M. iii–xiv. New York: Peter Lang Publishing, 1993.

Szostek, A. "Karol Wojtyła's View of the Human Person in the Light of the Experience of Morality." *Proceedings of the American Catholic Philosophical Association* 58 (1986): 50–64.

Szulc, T. "Politics and the Polish Pope." *New Republic*, 28 October 1978: 19–21.

Tanalski, D. "John Paul II vis-à-vis Atheism and Materialism." *Dialectics and Humanism* 14, no. 1 (1987): 99–108.

Tischner, J. "The Drama of Politics and Ethics." *Polish Review* 36, no. 1 (1991): 1–9.

———. "Homo Sovieticus – 1." *Tygodnik Powszechny*, 7 April 1990, 2.

———. "Homo Sovieticus – 2." *Tygodnik Powszechny*, 24 June 1990, 4.

———. "The Horizons for Polish Labor." *Dialectics and Humanism* 9, no. 1 (1982): 117–126.

———. "Metodologiczna strona dzieła *Osoba i Czyn*" [The Methodological Side of *The Acting Person*]. *Analecta Cracoviensia* 5/6 (1973/1974):

85–89.

Torre, J. de la. "John Paul II's Stubborn Humanism." *Homiletic and Pastoral Review* 92 (1992): 56–59.

Traffas, J. "The Spirit of Community and the Spirituality of Work: A Note on *Laborem Exercens.*" *Communio* 10 (1983): 407–411.

Tucker, J. "Papal Economics 101: The Catholic Ethic and the Spirit of Capitalism." *Crisis* 9, no. 6 (1991): 16–21.

Turner, F. "John Paul II's Social Analysis." *The Month* 24 (1991): 344–349.

Turowicz, J. "Kościoł i polityka" [The Church and Politics]. *Tygodnik Powszechny*, 24 March 1985: 1–2.

Tymieniecka, A.-T. "The Origins of the Philosophy of John Paul II." *Proceedings of the American Catholic Philosophical Association* 53 (1979): 16–27.

——. "A Page of History or from *Osoba i Czyn* to *The Acting Person.*" *Phenomenology Information Bulletin* 3 (1979): 3–52.

Utz, A. "*Centesimus Annus* Gives Us a Profoundly Ethical View of Social and Economic Politics." *L'Osservatore Romano* (English Weekly Edition) 26 (1991): 8, 10.

Vallin, P. "*Laborem Exercens.*" *Etudes*, novembre, 1981: 546–550.

Volf, M. "On Human Work: An Evaluation of the Key Ideas of the Encyclical *Laborem Exercens.*" *Scottish Journal of Theology* 37 (1984): 65–79.

Walgrave, J. "Doctrine, Development of." In *New Catholic Encyclopedia*, Vol. IV. 940–944. New York: McGraw-Hill, 1967.

Walicki, A. "Polish Romantic Messianism in Comparative Perspective." *Slavonic Studies* 22, no. 1 (1978): 1–15.

Walsh, W., and J. Langan, S.J. "Patristic Social Consciousness: The Church and the Poor." In *The Faith That Does Justice*, edited by J. Haughey. 175–199. New York: Paulist, 1977.

Ward, B. "Looking Back at *Populorum Progressio*: An Address to the Roman Curia, 18 April 1977." *Catholic Mind* 76 (1978): 9–25.

Waterman, A. "The Intellectual Context of *Rerum Novarum.*" *Review of Social Economy* 49, no. 4 (1991): 465–482.

——. "John Locke's Theory of Property and Christian Social Thought." *Review of Social Economy* 40, no. 2 (1982): 97–115.

Wilder, O.P., A. "Community of Persons in the Thought of Karol Wojtyła." *Angelicum* 56, no. 2/3 (1979): 211–244.

Wilhelmsen, E. "Faith according to St. John of the Cross." *Thomist* 50, no. 2, (1986): 300–306.

Williams, G.H. "The Ecumenical Intentions of John Paul II." *Harvard Theological Review* 72, no. 2 (1982): 141–176.

———. "The Ecumenism of John Paul II." *Journal of Ecumenical Studies* 19, no. 4 (1982): 681–719.

———. "An Intellectual Portrait of Pope John Paul II." *Worldview* 22, no. 1/2 (1979): 21–26.

———. "John Paul II's Concepts of Church, State and Society." *Journal of Church and State* 24, no. 3 (1982): 463–496.

———. "John Paul II's Relations with Non-Catholic States and Current Political Movements." *Journal of Church and State* 25, no. 1 (1983): 13–55.

———. "Karol Wojtyła and Marxism." In *Christianity Under Stress*, Vol. 2, *Catholicism and Politics in Communist Societies*, edited by P. Ramet. 356–381. Durham/London: Duke University Press, 1990.

———. "The Philosophical Thought of Pope John Paul II." *Catholic Mind* 77 (1979): 13–21.

———. "The Place and Prospects of a Polish Prelate as Pope: Provisional Reflections on the Papacy of John Paul II." *Polish Review* 24, no. 2 (1979): 7–26.

Williams, C.S.C., O. "Catholic Social Teaching: A Communitarian Democratic Capitalism for the New World Order." *Journal of Business Ethics* 12, no. 12 (1993): 919–932.

Wojciechowski, O.P., K. "Jedność duchowo-cielesna człowieka w książce *Osoba i czyn*" [The Spiritual-Physical Unity of Man in *The Acting Person*]. *Analecta Cracoviensia* 5/6 (1973/1974): 191–199.

———. "Rinnovamento conciliare: Karol Wojtyła e la formazione degli atteggiamenti cristiani." *Angelicum* 56, no. 2/3 (1979): 367–386.

Wolicka, E. "Participation in Community: Wojtyła's Social Anthropology." *Communio* 8 (1981): 108–118.

Woźnicki, A. "The Christian Humanism and Adequate Personalism of Karol Wojtyła." In *Faith, Philosophy and Theology*, edited by J. Ratzinger et al. 213–220. Slough, St. Paul, 1985.

———. "The Christian Humanism of Cardinal Karol Wojtyła." *Proceedings of the American Catholic Philosophical Association* 53 (1979): 28–35.

———. "Ecumenical Consciousness according to Karol Wojtyła." *Center Journal* 3, no. 2 (1984): 111–125.

———. "Lublinism: A New Version of Thomism." *Proceedings of the American Catholic Philosophical Association* 58 (1986): 27–37.

———. "Revised Thomism: Existential Personalism Viewed from Phenomenological Perspectives." *Proceedings of the American*

Catholic Philosophical Association 58 (1986): 38–49.

Wyles, J. "Vatican Prepares Attack on Sins of Capitalism." *Financial Times*, 9/10 March 1991, Sect. 2, 1.

Zablocki, J. "Les Conclusions polonaises de *Populorum Progressio*." *Wicz Polski* 12 (1969): 56–65.

———. "The Reception of Personalism in Poland." *Dialectics and Humanism* 5, no. 3 (1978): 160–166.

Zdybicka, Z. "Praktyczne aspekty dociekań przedstawionych w *Osoba i Czyn*" [The Practical Aspects of the Inquiries Presented in *The Acting Person*]. *Analecta Cracoviensia* 5/6 (1973/1974): 201–205.

Zięba, O.P., Z. "Two or Even Three Liberalisms: John Paul II and Contemporary Christianity." *Dialogue and Humanism* 4, no. 5 (1994): 89–99.

Zizola, G. "Les Revirements d'une encyclique." *L'Actualité religieuse dans le monde* 90 (1991): 10–11.

3. Doctoral Dissertations

Enright, V. "The Correlation of the Concepts of Existential Personalism and Interdependent Solidarity in *Sollicitudo Rei Socialis*." Catholic University of America, 1992.

Gooley, W. "Shared Visions: Human Nature and Human Work in *Rerum Novarum* and *Laborem Exercens*." Syracuse University, 1986.

Heaney, S. "The Concept of the Unity of the Person in the Thought of Karol Wojtyła." Marquette University, 1988.

Munera Velez, D. "Personalismo etico de participacion de Karol Wojtyła." Pontificia Universitas Gregoriana, 1985.

Piatek, J. "Persona e Amore nel pensiero filosofico del Cardinale Karol Wojtyła." Pontificia Universitas San Tommaso, 1976.

Pokerek, J. "La Normatività della cosciena morale nel personalismo di Karol Wojtyła." Pontificia Universitas Gregoriana, 1991.

Rostorowski, T. "Il Problema gnoseologico nell'opera *Persona et Atto* di Wojtyła." Pontificia Universitas Gregoriana, 1991.

Schuck, M. "The Context and Coherence of Roman Catholic Encyclical Social Teaching, 1740–1987." University of Chicago, 1991.

Wiseman, C. "Papal Social Thought and International Politics." University of Virginia, 1990.

Wittman, C. "The Relationship between Labor and Capital As Described in *Rerum Novarum, Quadragesimo Anno* and *Laborem Exercens*." University of Dayton, 1987.

Index

About the Author

Samuel Gregg is a moral theologian who has written and spoken extensively on questions of social and business ethics, civil society, issues of religion and political thought, as well as Catholic social teaching. He has an M.A. in political philosophy from the University of Melbourne, and a D.Phil. in moral theology from the University of Oxford.

Since completing his doctorate in 1998, he has been resident scholar at the Centre for Independent Studies in Sydney, Australia, and director of the Centre's Religion and the Free Society Program.